HARPER FORUM BOOKS

Martin E. Marty, General Editor

ON BEING RESPONSIBLE

Issues in Personal Ethics

HARPER FORUM BOOKS

Martin E. Marty, *General Editor*

Published:

IAN G. BARBOUR
SCIENCE AND RELIGION: New Perspectives on the Dialogue
A. ROY ECKARDT
THE THEOLOGIAN AT WORK: A Common Search for Understanding
JOHN MACQUARRIE
CONTEMPORARY RELIGIOUS THINKERS: From Idealist Metaphysicians to Existential Theologians
GIBSON WINTER
SOCIAL ETHICS: Issues in Ethics and Society
JAMES M. GUSTAFSON & JAMES T. LANEY
ON BEING RESPONSIBLE: Issues in Personal Ethics
EDWIN SCOTT GAUSTAD
RELIGIOUS ISSUES IN AMERICAN HISTORY
SAMUEL SANDMEL
OLD TESTAMENT ISSUES

Forthcoming: 1969

JOSEPH D. BETTIS
PHENOMENOLOGY OF RELIGION
WILLIAM DOUGLAS
THE HUMAN PERSONALITY: Religious and Non-Religious
 Views
WINTHROP HUDSON
RELIGION AND NATIONALITY: Concepts of American
 Identity and Mission
IAN RAMSEY
PHILOSOPHY OF RELIGION
OWEN C. THOMAS
ATTITUDES TOWARD OTHER RELIGIONS: Some Chris-
 tian Interpretations
FRANKLIN YOUNG
NEW TESTAMENT ISSUES

ON BEING
RESPONSIBLE

Issues in Personal Ethics

BY

James M. Gustafson

and

James T. Laney

HARPER & ROW, PUBLISHERS

NEW YORK, EVANSTON, AND LONDON

LIBRARY OF CONGRESS CATALOG CARD NUMBER: 68-17602

Published as a Harper Forum Book, 1968, by Harper & Row, Publishers, Incorporated, New York, Evanston, and London.

73 10 9 8 7 6

Harper Forum Books

Often dismissed with a shrug or accepted with thoughtless piety in the past, religion today belongs in the forum of study and discussion. In our society, this is particularly evident in both public and private colleges and universities. Scholars are exploring the claims of theology, the religious roots of culture, and the relation between beliefs and the various areas or disciplines of life. Students have not until now had a series of books which could serve as reliable resources for class or private study in a time when inquiry into religion is undertaken with new freedom and a sense of urgency. *Harper Forum Books* are intended for these purposes. Eminent scholars have selected and introduced the readings. Respectful of the spirit of religion as they are, they do not shun controversy. With these books a new generation can confront religion through exposure to significant minds in theology and related humanistic fields.

MARTIN E. MARTY, GENERAL EDITOR
The Divinity School
The University of Chicago

CONTENTS

I

ON BEING RESPONSIBLE

INTRODUCTION

"Mowing the lawn is Peter's responsibility."

"Students are responsible for getting their term papers in on time."

"It is the responsibility of the United States Congress to provide the means by which further rioting in the cities can be eliminated."

In each of these sentences the notion of responsibility is used. It is a term common in everyday speech, and refers to aspects of experience with which all of us are acquainted. These sentences indicate that we often use the word to suggest the obligations of others; the speaker is ascribing or recommending responsibility to others. But we use the term to refer to ourselves as well. "I accept the responsibility for having left the tea kettle on the hot burner." "I will assume responsibility for arranging the transportation to the picnic." "He refused to register for military service after many conversations we had. I suppose I'll have to accept some responsibility for his actions." In these sentences the reference is to one's own self, to the assumption of responsibility by the self for actions or events that have taken place or will take place.

In common-sense usage there is nothing about the notion of responsibility that is foreign to ordinary experience. Indeed, on the surface the word seems to *describe* situations in which persons are involved; it functions as a descriptive rather than as a normative term. The judgment of the responsibility of others, and the assumption of responsibility by ourselves, is very much a part of everyday life. We do not need to be told to be responsible; we accept our responsibility for many things that are said

or done during the course of an ordinary day. We live in relation to others, and part of the fabric of these relations is that of
responsibility. Others are responsible to us: professors appear
at the correct time and place to deliver lectures according to the
schedule that the registrar has fixed; our parents keep their
promises to provide the cost of tuition and other expenses for
our education; we and others drive our cars according to rules
established by civil law so that there is a degree of safety for
both drivers and pedestrians and an orderly flow of traffic.
Structures of mutual responsibility appear to be built into human
experience; they provide the framework within which orderly
interaction between persons and groups takes place. Such structures seem to be a fundamental requisite for the maintenance of
human life in communities. We are at least irked, and at times
thrown into chaos, when this fabric of mutual responsibility
begins to break down. We find it irritating when a professor
does not appear at the time and place set and agreed upon by all.
Our life is in danger when a reckless driver decides to violate
the rules of the road, when we cannot predict what he is going
to do in accordance with the expectations we all have of responsible ways to drive automobiles.

In some instances the order of responsibility is stipulated in
explicit forms: there are laws that all men are called upon to
obey; there are contractual agreements to pay our bills on time
that have the force of law; there are promises that we have
made to each other which make explicit what our obligations
are; there are covenants made to be faithful to each other "in
sickness and in health." In other instances we anticipate that
others will be where they are supposed to be, do what they are
supposed to do, say what they are supposed to say without the
formulation of these obligations in clear and explicit ways.
Husbands assume that their wives will have dinner ready in
the evening when they return home from work; wives assume
that their husbands will be home at the usual hour unless they
have informed them that they will not. Persons who have declared their love for each other assume that the other will not
normally be "playing the field." There are mutual expectations

which are part of the fabric of interrelations and interactions between persons and are not defined by signed agreements, over which no external authority has a power of sanction. Yet these are very much a part of ordinary experience, and if persons persist in violating this order of expectations we soon judge them to be untrustworthy and irresponsible.

We become accustomed to having others fulfill many of these expectations, so that neither we nor they make conscious decisions to meet certain responsibilities. A process of habituation takes place in experience that greatly facilitates our corporate existence. When we come to a red traffic light, we normally do not ask ourselves, "Should I stop, or should I drive through it?" Nor does the driver who has just seen a green signal normally have to ask about the cross traffic, "Are those drivers going to obey the lights or not?" We respond to the signals with customary reactions, and we assume that others will respond to signals in the appropriate way. Certain obligations become accepted by us and by others so that we need not be told, or even remind ourselves, that we are expected to behave in particular ways at particular times and places.

But not all the structures of mutual responsibility are as routinized and regularized as traffic patterns, and on not every occasion is habituated reaction available as the means of fulfilling obligations to others. There are many occasions that do not fall under a set of mutually accepted rules of behavior, and there are also times when we have to decide between opportunities and obligations that apparently conflict with each other. Decisions have to be made in full self-awareness; reflection has to take place to determine what our responsibility *really* is, to whom we are most responsible, and for what. It is not self-evident under all circumstances what we should or ought to do. This is also part of ordinary experience. When a term paper is due in the morning, and our best friend has a serious case of the blues and needs to talk, which responsibility has first claim upon us? Simply to ignore the needs of the friend would violate something that seems intrinsic to personal friendship itself. It would appear to place responsibility for the impersonal require-

ments of a professor who has set the date for his convenience
and that of the institution above our response to another person, above our caring for others. It would seem to say that our
first responsibility is to the rules and orders of institutions, or
even to ourselves, since violation of the rules of the institution
may cost us some personal penalty.

More seriously, when we face the possibility of being called
up for military service in a war the justice of which we have
come to question, there is no automatic determination of what
our responsible conduct ought to be. The authority and power
of the state, with its legitimacies, is one point of reference for
our decision-making. If this authority and power were not subject to conscientious reflection in the light of such concepts as
justice, the issues involved could be more easily settled in our
minds. But in the name of our personal integrity ("I cannot
violate my conscience by fighting in this particular war"), or in
the name of a "higher law" ("The laws of love and of justice
are not being honored in the action of the state, and I declare
that my responsibility to these laws supersedes my responsibility
to the state"), the obligation we have to the state is put under
serious question. Here the conscientious person is forced to
consider on what grounds he would exempt himself from his
obligations to the laws that indiscriminately govern all men in
his particular age group. He seeks reasons to support his claim
as an exception to the commonly assumed and legally established patterns of responsibility to the state.

Such experiences are also part of our common life. They are
simply examples of the many occasions we face in which the
choices we make have serious consequences for ourselves and for
other people. On occasions of hard decision we need not be told
by some teacher, counselor, or preacher that the choice involves
selections of loyalties, judgments about potential consequences,
and matters of personal integrity. As a result of our schooled
and internalized moral sensitivities we have an awareness of
conflicting obligations or responsibilities. Nor do we have to be
told that some rational discrimination between objects of responsibility is required to make a sound moral judgment. We

find ourselves sorting out what the consequences of one action will be as against the consequences of another, or what compromise with our sense of integrity is necessary in a given situation, and what the compensations might be that would legitimate such a compromise. For example, we have been trained to be aware that normally we ought to tell the truth, to give a factual account of what has occurred if we are asked to do so. Yet there are some occasions when telling the truth in this sense might create danger to others and to ourselves. Thus, if there is time for reflection, we probably engage in a rational sorting out of the issues. What is the cost of violating the normal practice of not lying? What is the cost of lying, and what compensations are there for violation of the rule? Moral reflection about different responsibilities is a normal part of human experience. It may be very unsophisticated and governed by "gut responses": I will do what I feel to be right on this occasion; my feelings are the proper guide to moral responsibility. It may be highly sophisticated and complex: I need to have accurate factual data about what the situation really is; I need to sort out clearly various opportunities and conflicting claims; I need to calculate the potential consequences of alternative courses of action.

One of the ways we sort out questions is to ask ourselves some relatively simple questions. To whom am I responsible? For what am I responsible? By raising these questions we make explicit some things that might have missed our attention. Responsibility is not a *thing,* a substance that is everywhere and always one and the same. It is a relationship between myself and others, or a relationship I have to certain situations. We might slip into saying, "George is a responsible man," and mean by this that he has a predisposition to take life seriously, to honor commitments, and to fulfill duties and opportunities. But there is not much moral particularity to this observation about predispositions. The moral particularity comes when we begin to ask: To whom is George committed? What purposes and values does he take seriously? What duties and opportunities is he predisposed to fulfill? Adolf Eichmann claimed to be a responsible man when he defended himself before the Israeli court where he was tried for his part in the murder of Jews in Europe during the Nazi barbarism. He claimed to be responsible *to* his Nazi superiors *for* the execution of the orders they gave him to fulfill. In one descriptive sense he was a "responsible man," but the almost universal abhorrence of the crimes of genocide points to a *normative* element that enters into *our* moral evaluation of Eichmann's moral judgments. A Christian might make his judgment in this way: Responsibility to God is of greater importance than responsibility to the state or to one's superiors in the state. If one is responsible to God as He is known in the tradition that began in Biblical times, one cannot accept the orders to participate in Jewish genocide as morally right. A secular humanist might make his judgment this way: responsibility to life and to mankind is of greater importance than any orders of the state or one's superiors. Thus, moral responsibility in this sense could only lead to disobedience to commands to participate in genocide.

The process of decision-making involves the recognition of those to whom we are responsible, and the sorting out of the things for which we are responsible. Normative judgments about our right conduct are governed in part by the ways in which we answer these questions, and by the choices we make between conflicting responsibilities *to* and *for*. Fortunately not all the choices we make have to do with mutually exclusive claims. I have responsibilities to myself to maintain my sense of moral identity and integrity; I have responsibilities to my neighbor to seek to meet his needs; I have responsibilities to God that I must acknowledge if I am a religious person. In many circumstances there is sufficient cohesion and harmony between these objects of responsibility so that choices are not crucial. Choices do become crucial when tension between these increases: between responsibility to God and humanity on the one hand, and the state on the other; between responsibility to parents and what they value on the one hand, and a strong sense of independence and integrity around different values on the other.

Choices also involve reflection about what I am responsible

for. If we assume a high degree of consistency between what God, parents, and personal integrity represent to us as objects of loyalty, it is still not necessarily clear what I am responsible for in my responsibility to them. Which neighbor's needs will I choose to meet? What action is most consistent with my moral integrity? What ways of action and of meeting the neighbor's needs are most effective to achieve my ends, and most consistent with my moral commitments? To choose to be responsible for one thing often excludes the possibility of being responsible for another; to choose to meet the needs of one neighbor often requires that the needs of another are not met. These observations point to the necessity to accept limitation, finitude, and contingency in the moral life. Surely the person who feels a sense of responsibility for the suffering and oppressed persons in the world, but who cannot accept some operational limits to his responsibility, is frustrated and morally paralyzed. Some doors have to be closed, some roads not traveled, some needs not met, some aspirations not achieved, since we are finite, limited beings who have to live under these conditions.

But this note of the necessity to particularize those things for which we are responsible needs to be heard together with another note, namely that of awareness of things for which one has responsibility that might not come readily to one's immediate attention. A person may have a great sense of responsibility for his family, and function with moral effectiveness in that limited community of mankind. But if this *for*-ness excludes an awareness of responsibility he has as a citizen and a Christian for the well-being of others in the world, he is, normatively speaking, suffering from acute moral myopia. Particular *for*-ness in responsibility needs to be surveyed and judged by a wider awareness of those for whom we are responsible. Sometimes needs beyond our immediate vision of responsibility to self and family require a suspension of those loyalties; sometimes our responsibility for the needs of the distant neighbor requires neglect of the near one.

There are occasions when responsibility for others does not and cannot take an active form. In interpersonal relations, most of us have experienced moments when others are seemingly not ready to have us help them even when we strongly desire to do so. Out of a sense of independence, or pride, or unreadiness, they seem to resist our openness to them. Under such circumstances our availability to them must become the form responsibility takes, and must await their request or readiness.

There are other occasions when our responsibility is partially a matter of bearing the cost of the consequences of decisions we have made in the past, consequences which are more destructive than we had anticipated. A national leader, for example, who orders men to war, is not directly responsible for the deaths of particular men on particular days, but nonetheless bears the burden of responsibility for deaths entailed in the execution of a policy he has deemed to be the best or right one. In interpersonal relationships this occurs as well. The person who breaks an engagement to be married might well believe he or she has done the right thing, but nonetheless bears the burden of the other's suffering at least for awhile.

So far we have seen that the notion of responsibility describes aspects of experience common to us all. In addition, we have also noted that there is a normative meaning associated with this concept, a meaning dependent upon our conscious acceptance of being responsible for certain things and to certain people. Thus there has been an implicit assumption in this discussion that to accept responsibility is a good thing, that responsibility is more than a *given* of experience it is an *ought* which persons need to be aware of. In a sense, this book is an exploration both of the various elements that make up the moral concept of responsibility and its expression in several selected areas of contemporary life. For instance, we are concerned not only with the way responsibility itself may be understood as a primary aspect of the moral life, but with how it may express itself in love, honesty, and citizenship. In Part I, however, we shall attempt to see how the term itself is understood by several influential thinkers.

Both H. Richard Niebuhr and Bernard Häring particularly stress the importance of the idea of "response" in responsibility.

The capacity to respond is central to this understanding of the moral life. Perhaps the notion of response can be distinguished from mere reaction. In the latter one's self-awareness and capacity to determine what one thinks, says, feels, and does, is not present to any significant degree, whereas in the former the "I," the self-aware center of existence, has that degree of independence and consciousness which makes the relationship more than a mechanical or habitual one. What one already is and is becoming can be altered or redirected as a result of the relationship within which one responds.

The notion of response may also contain the notion of action. Robert Johann, S.J., in a brief essay on responsibility, "The New Ideal," in *America* (August 1, 1964) makes the point as follows: "Action becomes primary. The meaning of a man's life is the difference his presence makes in the over-all process." One acts in response to others and to situations; one responds to the actions of others. Action involves the exertion of energy, the innovation of purposes into the events of which one is a part, the taking of risks (since one cannot fully control the consequences of his responses). Fundamental to the notion of action as part of responsibility is the conception of persons who have the capacity (freedom) to govern their responses to what occurs to them, and to give direction to the responses they in turn make.

Action and freedom imply further that response can be creative, and that our acceptance of moral responsibility in situations can be creative of new possibilities, new events, new relationships. Responsibility is not mere compliance with rigid sets of patterns in life on every occasion; in many situations one can and ought to respond creatively, altering the course of events, reforming the institutional patterns within which one lives, elevating a relationship to a different plane, transforming the modes and qualities of life of which one is a part. Part of our humanity is to be creatively involved in our responses to things around us, to seek to bring into being a good that does not now exist in actuality. Such freedom and creativity, however, are not boundless; they are set within patterns of human relationship.

They must come to grips with the realities of limitations set by finitude and by the resistance of others and of things to our efforts to bring in the new, and to exert changes in the course of events. They are also bounded by certain already existing commitments and loyalties.

Loyalty or fidelity is another aspect of responsibility. Among the readings in this section, Gabriel Marcel's stresses this particular point. For Marcel fidelity is not a static relationship, a mere external conformity with contracts or set agreements. It is a faithfulness and trustworthiness to others and to causes which at the same time is open to new shapes and forms of life, to new possibilities for human fulfillment. But within this openness there is the expectation of dependability, of reliability or trustworthiness. Responsible persons are those who can be trusted to fulfill duties creatively, exploiting the possibilities that are given to them; they are worthy of our trust. They can be expected to keep their commitments and fulfill their obligations unless there is a just cause, a higher obligation, that requires them to violate that trust.

In none of these aspects have we touched on the one that perhaps is the most obvious in common speech, namely, accountability. Niebuhr lists this, along with the capacity to respond, the interpretation of the situation in which we respond, and the solidarity with others that is the situation of life, as a main component of responsibility. As accountability, responsibility suggests its kinship with the more legal notion of liability. A judgment can be made upon one by himself or others as to the extent to which he shares credit or guilt for the effects of his actions. Everyday usage like the opening sentences of this Introduction suggests this to be the primary aspect of responsibility. Peter is accountable for whether the lawn does or does not get mowed. Further rioting in the cities will be laid partially at the door of the Congress if they do not provide funds to alleviate causes of oppression. Students have to pay a penalty if they do not get their term papers in on time. Each of these simple examples suggests a note of obligation: to be responsible is to accept obligations that one has by virtue of his commitments, his role in society, his power and authority. Whether one does or does not fulfill these obligations is a point on which we are judged by others and by ourselves.

Accountability and obligation have open and positive connotations as well as more restrictive ones. Men are to respond in a fitting way to the situations in which they are involved with others, to respond in a way that not only preserves the moral good that exists but develops new meanings and paths of life. The notion of fittingness in response is an old one; it can be found in Aristotle's *Nicomachean Ethics* as well as in modern pragmatic treatises. But what is fitting demands a larger context if it is to be helpful. Niebuhr suggests that we determine what action is most appropriate in the light of our interpretation of what is going on in a given situation. This interpretation is not read off lightly by one who accepts an obligation to be morally responsible. It involves not only an assessment of what is going on, in factual terms, but of what ought to go on, in normative terms. It considers the loyalties and values we affirm as well as those that others uphold. We seek to respond to situations in the light of moral ends and purposes, in the light of various commitments and obligations. Thus the "fitting" is not necessarily what first comes to mind or what one immediately feels like doing. In Christian ethics, one of the determinants of a fitting response is our understanding of what God requires and enables us to be and do as this is expressed in the beliefs of the church.

The notion of responsibility, then, charts a course between an ethics, on the one hand, of conformity to a law or an order that is given *a priori,* and an ethics that merely reacts in utter open-endedness to whatever is happening. The whipping boy of contemporary religious ethics is legalism—the most distorted form of ethics, consisting merely of conformity to law. Legalism can refer to two things: first, to a prescription of right conduct derived from some previous experience, or presumably from the rational discernment of the order of nature, which is applied without significant regard to the contingencies and particularities of the novel situation. Second, it can refer to the mind-set of a person, to his insistence on an authoritative and unambiguous determination of proper conduct, so that he can avoid the risk of making mistakes and incurring blame. This mind-set surrenders creativity, openness, and freedom for presumed moral certitude. It manifests what Catholic moralists nicely call "excessive scrupulosity," an attitude that cripples the movement of love and the development of the good among men. Legalism in both senses fosters a static morality, to use Bergson's term; it engenders an attitude of self-righteousness to a high degree; it is in the end uncreative and rigid.

At the other extreme from legalism is the stance of complete openness to whatever is happening, where one's response is determined by observing the situation bending to the pull of one's involvement in what happens to be going on. "Fitting" here might mean adjusting to the moral climate one is in or following the manner of life that flourishes in the community of which one is a part. It often means also responding to emotions and feelings aroused by the time, place, and closest neighbor. While this kind of response may be appropriate in terms of immediacy and feeling, upon reflection it may be considerably less fitting in a broader context. At that distance value conflicts, alternative courses of action, and multiple commitments to self and to others are seen to influence the understanding of "fitting" response. Moral reflection seeks to understand what is appropriate in relation both to the structures of life which support order and freedom and to the dynamics of life which allow new experiences and vitalities to emerge. It evaluates the drive toward self-realization within the limits imposed by our obligations to others. Reflection upon responsibility therefore moves between the inward look—where we examine ourselves—and the outward survey—where we attempt to appreciate the possibilities open to us within the limits of time and place in which we live. (The authors are not so much in disagreement with Joseph Fletcher's position, advanced in his *Situation Ethics,* as they are with what they believe to be a severe oversimplification of the moral life in his development of that position.)

Each reading in this section seeks to steer a course between legalism and absolute open-endedness, and each employs the idea of responsibility (or a related term like "deputyship" or "fidelity") as central to the interpretation of moral life.

For H. Richard Niebuhr, the notion of responsibility is one that can be contrasted with two traditional types of ethics, each of which has a long history in Western ethical thought. One is teleological ethics, the ethics of ends, for which Niebuhr uses the symbol man-the-maker. In this, one has a vision of the goal or pattern of life he seeks to achieve, in light of which he then proceeds much as a builder would to realize that purpose or plan. The other type is deontological ethics, the ethics of binding duty or obligation. Here Niebuhr uses the symbol of man-the-citizen (though man-the-law-obeyer might be more proper, since the idea of citizenship in our society also suggests a function in the formulation of the laws). In this view, certain rules define right conduct, and the moral life consists of the obligation to obey them. For the ethics of responsibility Niebuhr uses the symbol of man-the-answerer. Here man is in dialogue, "acting in response to action upon him." This involves a wider conception of the nature of moral experience, namely, man in a pattern of interaction with others, whose actions are themselves a response to the actions of still others in accord with an interpretation of those actions. Within this framework the aspects of responsibility listed above can be delineated. Man responds to the actions of others upon him. His response is governed by his interpretation of their actions, and that interpretation for Niebuhr ultimately includes understanding that the actions of others also convey God's own action upon us. He states: "Responsibility affirms: 'God is acting in all actions upon you. So respond to all actions upon you as to respond to his action'" (p. 126, *The Responsible Self*).

Apart from this, however, the selection from Niebuhr is written in a phenomenological tone. What he is saying about the nature of moral existence could be said by most men upon reflection. He does not have, in the chapter selected, an immediate theological witness to make, nor does he speak out of a confessional position. The passage from Bonhoeffer, on the other hand, is in marked contrast with this. He finds in the Biblical witness to Jesus Christ a pattern of responsibility, or in his term, deputyship. Jesus was, in an oft-quoted phrase from another of Bonhoeffer's writings, the "man for others." He was the responsible man *par excellence* in that his whole life was lived in service to others. This offers a clue to the meaning of responsibility in Bonhoeffer; it is a life of "complete surrender of one's own self to the other man." Responsibility is selflessness for the sake of others. This centrality of Jesus Christ is important. In one's response to others, one is to "correspond to reality," but that reality is itself understood in terms of Jesus Christ. What Christ is and means defines the reality to which men are to be conformed in their responses to others and to the world. Responses are concrete; they are in and to and for the world in its particularity. One is to be pertinent to the world, but in the light of the purposive relation of God to men. To live in this way requires that persons accept the burden both of their freedom and their potential guilt as they respond in conscience to the finite world in which they are called to deputyship. Thus Bonhoeffer offers a "structure of responsible life in terms of deputyship, correspondence with reality, acceptance of guilt, and freedom." One can think of this structure of responsible life in terms of particular areas of experience, occasions, and actions. But Bonhoeffer has a wider vision of the significance of this structure. In his view of vocation, man is to belong *wholly* to Christ. To be claimed by Christ embraces "work with things and relations with persons," it requires obedience in limited fields of possibilities which are never seen in isolation from the whole of reality. Indeed, "Vocation is responsibility and responsibility is a total response of the whole man to the whole of reality." Bonhoeffer commends a fundamental pattern of life that is disclosed and empowered by Jesus Christ, a pattern of life of deputyship, of "being for others."

Although Gabriel Marcel does not use the word responsibility explicitly, he speaks in a way congenial to what that notion has come to represent. Fidelity and obedience are to be seen in the context of a life of service. "Whom or what do you serve?" is a fruitful question to ask as one seeks to understand one's life.

For Marcel, obedience is only one way of serving and on the whole an immature way at that. It tends to degenerate into servility, itself much akin to legalism. Marcel recognizes that the idea of fidelity can be understood too rigidly; to be faithful to someone or something may be no more than not swerving from a predetermined path, in an unimaginative and constrained way. In the essay included here Marcel is particularly interested in the idea of faithfulness or responsibility to oneself, to maintaining one's integrity. Integrity could rest on a stubborn consistency and be little more than blind obedience. But in Marcel's essay it embodies openness and creativity. Because fidelity to oneself and to others at its best is creative, it transcends the limits of what can be specifically prescribed, while at the same time it recognizes the importance of one's commitments to others.

Like the passage from Niebuhr, the one from Marcel points toward wider theological considerations without using them as primary data on which to build an interpretation of responsible moral life. In contrast with these, Father Bernard Häring bases his concepts of response and responsibility upon Christian theology, upon the deposit of revelation given in the Bible. Häring's work needs to be seen in contrast to a legalistic morality that had often obtained both in the teaching of the church and in the attitudes of many Catholic people. His method is to distinguish from each other an ethic that springs from personal religious faith in a speaking and active God, and the view that derives external religious sanctions from a rationalistic form of natural law.

Protestants may find it difficult to appreciate the significance of this distinction unless they have been raised in a highly rule-bound authoritarian morality. The primary fact of the Christian moral life, in Häring's interpretation, is that man stands already in living fellowship with God who speaks to him and evokes his responses to Himself and to others in love. Häring is suggesting a dynamic morality of love for others in contrast to a morality that is preoccupied with self-perfection.

In doing this, however, Häring is careful not to leave the

ideas of commandment and law behind in favor of an unstructured ethic of intuitive love. Commandment is a religious concept and therefore is not necessarily alien to a Christian notion
of freedom. Concern for right order persists, but it is placed in
the context of a "spirit of loving fellowship." The more traditional elements are now seen within an interpretation of life as
dialogue, word and response in community. Man has the ability
to respond, and he is accountable for his free decision in his
own particular situation. His accountability, however, is not
simply before human authority (even the church), but before
God. The possibilities of such a life of responsibility are given
by God in His gracious love, and the pattern of it is found in
Christ himself as the New Testament bears witness to his life.
But the morality of imitation for Häring, as for Bonhoeffer, is
no mere external copying or conformity to an idealized picture
of man; it is, as he writes elsewhere, above all a life "in Christ."

Häring's interpretation rests on basic patterns of Biblical
thought—e.g., God and man in fellowship, and Christians being
in Christ—for both its vitality and the form of life of moral
responsibility would take. Within this religious context, then,
responsibility in particular relationships will be impelled and
governed by the originating love which engenders and redeems
life, the love of God. But there are also orders of created life
given in this love, orders that are violated at one's peril. The life
of responsible love, then, while free, is not utterly open-ended
and unstructured; it fulfills the purposes of God's love in His
creation of an ordered world.

These selections from four twentieth-century Christians reflect an awareness of the changing patterns of human life as
they have emerged in our time. Openness, dynamism, interaction, freedom, responsiveness, creativity—these ideas are prominent in their thinking. But at the same time they show an
appreciation for lines of continuity and direction, obligation,
accountability, and order in their understanding of the moral
life. From positions which have religious as well as empirical
foundations, these writers chart a course between legalism and
chaos.

H. Richard Niebuhr

THE MEANING OF RESPONSIBILITY*

I

The word *responsibility* and cognate terms are widely used in
our time when men speak about that phase of human existence
to which they customarily referred in the past with the aid of
such signs as *moral* and *good.* The *responsible citizen,* the *responsible society,* the *responsibilities of our office* and similar
phrases are often on our lips. This meaning of *responsibility* is
of relatively recent origin. There was a time when *responsible*
meant *correspondent* as in the statement "The mouth large but
not responsible to so large a body." But its use in sentences
such as "The great God has treated us as responsible beings,"
seems to have become common only in the nineteenth and twentieth centuries.[1] It is a relatively late-born child, therefore, in
the family of words in which duty, law, virtue, goodness, and
morality are its much older siblings. This history may mean
nothing more, of course, than that men have found a new sign
for a well-known phenomenon and an old idea; many writers,
indeed, so use it, as their definitions plainly show. But it is also
possible that the word gives us a new symbol with which to
grasp and understand not a really well-known phenomenon or
an old idea but the actuality of that human existence of which

* From H. RICHARD NIEBUHR, *The Responsible Self* (New York:
Harper & Row, 1963), Chapter I, "The Meaning of Responsibility," pp.
47-68. Copyright © 1963 by Florence M. Niebuhr. Reprinted by permission of Harper & Row, Publishers. H. Richard Niebuhr was Sterling
Professor of Theology and Christian Ethics at Yale Divinity School at
the time of his death in 1962.

other aspects came into view when we employed the older symbols of *the mores,* or of *the ethos,* or of *what is due,* or of *being virtuous,* that is, being manly. I believe that this is the case; the symbol of responsibility contains, as it were, hidden references, allusions, and similes which are in the depths of our mind as we grope for understanding of ourselves and toward definition of ourselves in action. But we are not concerned with the word nor with our subjective intentions as we use it. Our task rather is to try with the aid of this symbol to further the double purpose of ethics: to obey the ancient and perennial commandment, *"gnothi seauton,"* "Know thyself"; and to seek guidance for our activity as we decide, choose, commit ourselves, and otherwise bear the burden of our necessary human freedom.

In the history of man's long quest after knowledge of himself as agent—that is, as a being in charge of his conduct—he has used fruitfully several other symbols and concepts in apprehending the form of his practical life and in giving shape to it in action. The most common symbol has been that of the maker, the fashioner. What is man like in all his actions? The suggestion readily comes to him that he is like an artificer who constructs things according to an idea and for the sake of an end. Can we not apply to the active life as a whole the image we take from our technical working in which we construct wheels and arrows, clothes and houses and ships and books and societies? So not only common-sense thinking about ideals, and ends and means, but much sophisticated philosophy has construed human existence. Thus Aristotle begins his *Ethics*—the most influential book in the West in this field—with the statement: "Every art and every inquiry and similarly every action and pursuit, is thought to aim at some good."[2] Beyond all the arts of bridle-making and horse-riding and military strategy there must be then, he says, an art of arts, a master art, whose end is the actualization of the good man and the good society, whose material is human life itself. For the Greek philosopher and many who knowingly or unknowingly follow him, man is the being who makes himself—though he does not do so by himself—for the sake of a desired end. Two things in particular we say about ourselves: we act toward an end or are purposive; and, we act upon ourselves, we fashion ourselves, we give ourselves a form. Aristotle's great Christian disciple saw eye to eye with him. "Of the actions done by man," wrote Thomas Aquinas, "those alone are called properly *human,* which are proper to man as man. Now man differs from the irrational creatures in this, that he is master of his own acts. . . . But man is master of his own acts by reason and will: hence free-will is said to be *a function of will and reason.* Those actions, therefore, are properly called *human,* which proceed from a deliberate will. . . . Now it is clear that all the actions that proceed from any power are caused by that power acting in reference to its object. But the object of the will is some end in the shape of good. Therefore all human actions must be for an end."[3]

The image of man-the-maker who, acting for an end, gives shape to things is, of course, refined and criticized in the course of its long use, by idealists and utilitarians, hedonists and self-realizationists. But it remains a dominant image. And it has a wide range of applicability in life. Purposiveness and humanity do seem to go together. Everyone, even a determinist undertaking to demonstrate the truth of determinism, knows what it is to act with a purpose or a desired future state of affairs in mind, and knows also how important it is to inquire into the fitness of the steps taken moment by moment in his movement toward the desired goal. In most affairs of life we employ this practical ends-and-means reasoning and ask about our purposes. Education has its goals and so has religion; science is purposive though it defines its purpose only as knowledge of fact or as truth. Justice uses the idea when it asks about the culpability of the accused by raising the further question concerning his intentions and his ability to foresee consequences. Legislation thinks teleologically, that is, with respect to the telos—the goal—when it inquires into the desires of individual citizens and the various social groups, taking for granted that they all pursue some ends, whether these be power or prosperity or peace or pleasure; and when it raises the further question how manifold individual purposes can be organized into one common social purpose. Moral theories and moral exhortations to a large extent presuppose the future-directed, purposive character of human action and differ for the most part only—though seriously enough—in the ends they recommend or accept as given with human nature itself. The will to pleasure, the will to live, the will to power, the will to self-fulfillment, the will to love and be loved, the will to death and many another hormetic drive may be posited as most natural to man, whether as most compulsive or as setting before him the most attractive future state of affairs. When we are dealing with this human nature of ours, in ourselves and in others, as administrators of our private realms of body and mind or as directors of social enterprises—from families seeking happiness to international societies seeking peace—we cannot fail to ask: "At what long- or short-range state of affairs are we aiming, and what are the immediate steps that must be taken toward the attainment of the possible goal?" So the teleologist, in that double process of self-definition we call morals, interprets human life and seeks to direct it. The symbol of man-the-maker of many things and of himself also throws light not only on many enterprises but also on this strange affair of personal existence itself. The freedom of man appears in this context as the necessity of self-determination by final causes; his practical reason appears as his ability to distinguish between inclusive and exclusive, immediate and ultimate ends and to relate means to ends.

The men who have employed this image of man-the-maker in understanding and in shaping their conduct have, of course, by no means been unanimous in their choice of the ideals to be realized nor in their estimate of the potentialities of the material that is to be given the desired or desirable form. Whether the human end is to be achieved for the sake of delight or for further use toward another end, whether it is to be designed for the delight or the use of the self, or of the immediate society or of a universal community—these remain questions endlessly debated and endlessly submitted to individuals for personal decision. But the debates and decisions are carried on against the background of a common understanding of the nature of our personal existence. We are in all our working on selves—our own selves or our companions—technicians, artisans, crafts-men, artists.

Among many men and at many times another grand image of the general character of our life as agents prevails. It is the image of man-the-citizen, living under law. Those who conceive themselves and human beings in general with the aid of this great symbol point out the inadequacies and defects, as they see them, of that view of personal life which interprets it as *technē* or as art. In craftsmanship, they say, both the end and the means are relatively under our control. But neither is at our disposal when we deal with ourselves as persons or as communities.

Man-the-maker can reject material which does not fit his purposes. It is not so when the material is ourselves in our individual and in our social nature. Our body, our sensations, our impulses—these have been given us; whether to have them or not have them is not under our control. We are with respect to these things not as the artist is to his material but as the ruler of a city is to its citizens. He must take them for better or for worse. And so it is also with respect to the future. The favors or disfavors of fortune, as well as the "niggardly provisions of a step-motherly nature," put us at the mercy of alien powers so far as the completion of our lives as works of art is concerned. What use would it have been, had Socrates designed for himself that happy life which Aristotle described? This life we live amidst our fellow men and in the presence of nature's forces cannot be built over many generations like a cathedral. Who can plan his end? Who can by taking thought guarantee that his being, his character, his work, will endure even in the memory of those that come after? Neither the material then with which we work nor the future building is under our control when the work is directed toward ourselves. This life of ours is like poli-tics more than it is like art, and politics is the art of the possible. What is possible to us in the situation in which we find our-selves? That we should rule ourselves as being ruled, and not much more.

Many moral philosophers and theologians, otherwise disagreeing with each other, agree at least in this, that they understand the reality of our personal existence with the aid of the political image. It is indeed, as in the case of the technical symbol, more than an image for it is derived from our actual living. As a symbol it represents the use of a *special* experience for the interpretation of *all* experience, of a part for the whole. We come to self-awareness if not to self-existence in the midst of *mores,* of commandments and rules, *Thou shalts* and *Thou shalt nots,* of directions and permissions. Whether we begin with primitive man with his sense of *themis,* the law of the community projected outward into the total environment, or with the modern child with father and mother images, with repressions and permissions, this life of ours, we say, must take account of morality, of the rule of the mores, of the ethos, of the laws and the law, of heteronomy and autonomy, of self-directedness and other-directedness, of approvals and disapprovals, of social, legal, and religious sanctions. This is what our total life is like, and hence arise the questions we must answer: "To what law shall I consent, against what law rebel? By what law or system of laws shall I govern myself and others? How shall I administer the domain of which I am the ruler or in which I participate in rule?"

As in the case of the symbol of the maker, the symbol of the citizen has a wide range of applicability in common life and has been found useful by many a special theorist. In intellectual action, for instance, man not only directs his thoughts and investigations toward the realization of a system of true knowledge that will be useful to other ends or give delight in itself, but carries on his work of observation, conceptualization, comparison, and relation under laws of logic or of scientific method. It is important for him, if he is a person and not only a reasoning animal, that he govern his inquiries by adherence to such rules or laws. Again, what man does in the political realm is not only or perhaps even primarily to seek the ends of order, peace, prosperity, and welfare but to do all that he does under the rule of justice. If we are to associate the two symbols with each other, as indeed we often do, we must say that justice itself is an end, though when we do this peculiar difficulties arise. The image has applicability to all our existence in society. We come into being under the rules of family, neighborhood, and nation, subject to the regulation of our action by others. Against these rules we can and do rebel, yet find it necessary—morally necessary, that is—to consent to some laws and to give ourselves rules, or to administer our lives in accordance with some discipline.

Again, as in the case of the maker image, those who employ the citizen symbol for the understanding and regulation of self-conduct, have various domains in view. For some the republic that is to be governed is mostly that of the multifarious self, a being which is a multiplicity seeking unity or a unity diversifying itself into many roles. It is a congeries of many hungers and urges, of fears and angers and loves that is contained somehow within one body and one mind, which are two, yet united. The multiplicity of the body is matched by an at least equal variety of mental content. How to achieve that unity of the self, that organization of manifoldness we call personality, is a challenging question for the administrative self. It is not done in fact without external rule and regulation. How this self-government is in fact achieved is one of the problems of much psychology and the concern of moralists. Or the republic in view is a human community of selves in which the manifoldness is that of many persons with many desires and subject to many regulations issuing from each other. The communal life then is considered as both consenting to law and as law-giving. Or again, the community we have in mind may be universal society, and the quest may be after those laws of nature or that will of the universal God which the person is asked to accept not only with consent but actively, as legislating citizen in a universal domain.

The effort so to conceive the self in its agency as legislative, obedient, and administrative has had a long history. Its use has raised many theoretical and practical problems, but it has also been very fruitful. The symbol of man the law-maker and law-abider may be a primordial or only a cultural symbol; but in any case it has been helpful in enabling us to understand large areas of our existence and to find guidance in the making of complex decisions.

II

In the history of theoretical ethics, but also in practical decisions, the use of these two great symbols for the understanding of our personal existence as self-acting beings has led to many disputes as well as to many efforts at compromise and adjustment. Those who consistently think of man-as-maker subordinate the giving of laws to the work of construction. For them the right is to be defined by reference to the good; rules are utilitarian in character; they are means to ends. All laws must justify themselves by the contribution they make to the attainment of a desired or desirable end. Those, however, who think of man's existence primarily with the aid of the citizen image seek equally to subordinate the good to the right; only right life is good and right life is no future ideal but always a present demand. Federalist schools, as they have been called by C. D. Broad, tend to say that we cannot apprehend our existence with the aid of one image but must employ both. They leave us as a rule with a double theory, of which the two parts remain essentially unharmonized. The conflict of theories is but an expansion of the practical one which takes place in the personal and social life as we try to answer the questions: "What shall *I* do?" or "What shall *we* do?" We find ourselves moving there from the debate about the various ideals according to which we might shape our personal and social existence to the debate about what is required or demanded and by whom it is required. Or the movement may be from debate about the law to be obeyed to the question: "What laws can be justified in view of the ideal before us?" Practical debate on the achievement of desegregation, for example, moves between the insistence that the law of the country must be obeyed and the young Negroes' demand that the ideal state of affairs be realized.

What these debates suggest to us is that helpful as the fundamental images are which we employ in understanding and directing ourselves, they remain images and hypotheses, not truthful copies of reality, and that something of the real lies beyond the borders of the image; something more and something different needs to be thought and done in our quest for truth about ourselves and in our quest for true existence.

In this situation the rise of the new symbolism of responsibility is important. It represents an alternative or an additional way of conceiving and defining this existence of ours that is the material of our own actions. What is implicit in the idea of responsibility is the image of man-the-answerer, man engaged in dialogue, man acting in response to action upon him. As in the case of maker and of citizen, man-the-answerer offers us a synecdochic analogy. In trying to understand ourselves in our wholeness we use the image of a part of our activity; only now we think of all our actions as having the pattern of what we do when we answer another who addresses us. To be engaged in dialogue, to answer questions addressed to us, to defend ourselves against attacks, to reply to injunctions, to meet challenges —this is common experience. And now we try to think of all our actions as having this character of being responses, answers, to actions upon us. The faculty psychology of the past which saw in the self three or more facient powers, and the associationist psychology which understood the mind to operate under laws of association, have been replaced by a psychology of interaction which has made familiar to us the idea that we act in reaction to stimuli. Biology and sociology as well as psychology have taught us to regard ourselves as beings in the midst of a field of natural and social forces, acted upon and reacting, attracted and repelling. We try also to understand history less by asking about the ideals toward which societies and their leaders directed their efforts or about the laws they were obeying and more by inquiring into the challenges in their natural and social environment to which the societies were responding. It will not do to say that the older images of the maker and the citizen have lost their meaning in these biological, psychological, sociological, and historical analyses, but when we compare a modern psychology, a modern study of society, a modern history, with older examples of similar studies the difference thrusts itself upon one. The pattern of thought now is interactional, however much other great images must continue to be used to describe how we perceive and conceive, form associations, and carry on political, economic, educational, religious, and other enterprises.

The use of this image in the field of ethics is not yet considerable. When the word, responsibility, is used of the self as agent, as doer, it is usually translated with the aid of the older images as meaning direction toward goals or as ability to be moved by respect for law.[4] Yet the understanding of ourselves as responsive beings, who in all our actions answer to action upon us in accordance with our interpretation of such action, is a fruitful conception, which brings into view aspects of our self-defining conduct that are obscured when the older images are exclusively employed.

The understanding of ourselves with the aid of this image has been prefigured, as it were, by certain observations made by moralists of an older time. Aristotle may have had something of the sort in mind (something of the idea of what we would call a fitting response) when he described what he meant by the *mean* which constitutes virtue. He said that to feel fear, confidence, appetite, anger, and pity "at the right time, with reference to the right objects, toward the right people, with the right motive and in the right way, is what is intermediate and best. . . ."[5] Stoic ethics is usually interpreted as either primarily teleological or as primarily concerned with law; but it receives much of its peculiar character from the way in which it deals with the ethics of suffering, that is, with the responses which are to be made to the actions upon them that men must endure. The Stoic's main question is: "How may one react to events not with passion— that is, as one who is passive or who is subject to raw emotions called forth by events—but with reason?" And this reason for him is not first of all the law-giving power which rules the emotions, nor yet the purposive movement of the mind seeking to realize ideals. It is rather the interpretative power which understands the rationale in the action to which the self is subject and so enables it to respond rationally and freely rather than under the sway of passion. In Spinoza this idea of response guided by rational interpretation of events and beings to which the self reacts plays a major role. To be sure, he is an idealist after a fashion, who asks how he may "discover and acquire the faculty of enjoying throughout eternity continual supreme happiness."[6] But he quickly notes that this end is not attainable except through that correction of the understanding which will permit men to substitute for the unclear and self-centered, emotion-arousing interpretations of what happens to them, a clear, distinct interpretation of all events as intelligible, rational events in the determined whole. The freedom of man from his passions, and from the tyranny of events over him exercised via the passions, is freedom gained through correct interpretation with the consequent changing of responses by the self to the events that go on within it and happen to it. Other intimations of the idea of response are to be found in naturalistic ethics and Marxism.

Outside the realm of philosophic theory practical life has made this approach to the solution of the problem of our action almost inevitable in two particular situations, in social emergencies and in personal suffering. It has often been remarked that the great decisions which give a society its specific character are functions of emergency situations in which a community has had to meet a challenge. Doubtless ideals, hopes and drives toward a desirable future play their part in such decisions; inherited laws are also important in them. Yet the decision on which the future depends and whence the new law issues is a decision made in response to action upon the society, and this action is guided by interpretation of what is going on. The emergence of modern America out of the Civil War when measures were adopted in response to challenges that the founding fathers had not foreseen; the welfare-state decisions of the New Deal era in reaction to depression and the entrance of the nation into the sphere of international politics in reaction to foreign wars despite all desire for isolation—such events give evidence in the social sphere of the extent to which active, practical self-definition issues from response to challenge rather than from the pursuit of an ideal or from adherence to some ultimate laws. In the case of individuals we are no less aware of the way in which opportunity on the one hand, limiting events on the other, form the matrix in which the self defines itself by the nature of its responses.

Perhaps this becomes especially evident in the case of suffering, a subject to which academic ethical theory, even theological ethics, usually pays little attention. Yet everyone with any experience of life is aware of the extent to which the characters of people he has known have been given their particular forms by the sufferings through which they have passed. But it is not simply what has happened to them that has defined them; their responses to what has happened to them have been of even greater importance, and these responses have been shaped by their interpretations of what they suffered. It may be possible to deal with the ethics of suffering by means of the general hypothesis of life's purposiveness; however when we do so there is much that we must leave out of consideration. For it is part of the meaning of suffering that it is that which cuts athwart our purposive movements. It represents the denial from beyond ourselves of our movement toward self-realization or toward the actualization of our potentialities. Because suffering is the exhibition of the presence in our existence of that which is not under our control, or of the intrusion into our self-legislating existence of an activity operating under another law than ours, it cannot be brought adequately within the spheres of teleological and deontological ethics, the ethics of man-the-maker, or man-the-citizen. Yet it is in the response to suffering that many and perhaps all men, individually and in their groups, define themselves, take on character, develop their ethos. And their responses are functions of their interpretation of what is happening to them as well as of the action upon them. It is unnecessary to multiply illustrations from history and experience of the actuality and relevance of the approach to man's self-conduct that begins with neither purposes nor laws but with responses; that begins with the question, not about the self as it is in itself, but as it is in its response-relations to what is given with it and to it. This question is already implied, for example, in the primordial action of parental guidance: "What is the fitting thing? What is going on in the life of the child?"

In summary of the foregoing argument we may say that purposiveness seeks to answer the question: "What is my goal, ideal, or telos?" Deontology tries to answer the moral query by asking, first of all: "What is the law and what is the first law of my life?" Responsibility, however, proceeds in every moment of decision and choice to inquire: "What is going on?" If we use value terms then the differences among the three approaches may be indicated by the terms, the *good*, the *right,* and the *fitting;* for teleology is concerned always with the highest good to which it subordinates the right; consistent deontology is concerned with the right, no matter what may happen to our goods; but for the ethics of responsibility the *fitting* action, the one that fits into a total interaction as response and as anticipation of further response, is alone conducive to the good and alone is right.

The idea of responsibility, if it is to be made useful for the understanding of our self-action, needs to be brought into mind more clearly than has been done by these preliminary references to its uses in past theory and in common experience. Our definition should not only be as clear as we can make it; it should, if possible, be framed without the use of symbols referring to the other great ideas with which men have tried to understand their acts and agency. Only so will it be possible for us to develop a relatively precise instrument for self-understanding and also come to an understanding of the instrument's possibilities and limitations.

The first element in the theory of responsibility is the idea of *response*. All action, we now say, including what we rather indeterminately call moral action, is response to action upon us. We do not, however, call it the action of a self or moral action unless it is response to *interpreted* action upon us. All actions that go on within the sphere of our bodies, from heartbeats to knee jerks, are doubtless also reactions, but they do not fall within the domain of self-actions if they are not accompanied and infused, as it were, with interpretation. Whatever else we may need to say about ourselves in defining ourselves, we shall need, apparently, always to say that we are characterized by awareness and that this awareness is more or less that of an intelligence which identifies, compares, analyzes, and relates events so that they come to us not as brute actions, but as understood and as having meaning. Hence though our eyelids may react to the light with pure reflex, the self responds to it as *light,* as something interpreted, understood, related. But, more complexly, we interpret the things that force themselves upon us as parts of wholes, as related and as symbolic of larger meanings. And these large patterns of interpretation we employ seem to determine—though in no mechanical way—our responses to action upon us. We cannot understand international events, nor can we act upon each other as nations, without constantly interpreting the meaning of each other's actions. Russia and the United States confront each other not as those who are reflexively reacting to the manufacture of bombs and missiles, the granting of loans, and the making of speeches; but rather as two communities that are interpreting each other's actions and doing so with the aid of ideas about what is in the other's mind. So Americans try to understand Russia's immediate actions as expressions of the Communist or the Russian mind, which is the hidden part of the overt action, and we make our responses to the alien action in accordance with our interpretation of it as symbolic of a larger, an historic whole. The process of interpretation and response can be followed in all the public encounters of groups with each other. When we think of the relations of managers and employees we do not simply ask about the ends each group is consciously pursuing nor about the self-legislated laws they are obeying but about the way they are responding to each other's actions in accordance with their interpretations. Thus actions of labor unions may be understood better when we inquire less about what ends they are seeking and more about what ends they believe the managers to be seeking in all managerial actions. One must not deny the element of purposiveness in labor and in management, yet in their reactions to each other it is the interpretation each side has of the other's goals that may be more important than its definition of its own ends. Similarly in all the interactions of large groups with each other, law and duty seem to have a larger place in the interpretation of the other's conduct to which response is being made than they have in the immediate guidance of the agent's response. We use the idea of law less as a guide to our own conduct than as a way of predicting what the one will do to whom we are reacting or who will react to us. When lawyers try to discover under what law the judge will make his decisions, they are doing something akin to what we do in all our group relations; as Catholics or Protestants, also, we act less with an eye to our own law than to the other's action under his law, as we understand that law.

The point so illustrated by reference to groups applies to us as individuals. We respond as we interpret the meaning of actions upon us. The child's character may be formed less, the psychologists lead us to believe, by the injunctions and commandments of parents than by the child's interpretation of the attitudes such commandments are taken to express. The inferiority and superiority feelings, the aggressions, guilt feelings, and fears with which men encounter each other, and which do not easily yield to the commandment of neighbor-love, are dependent on their interpretations of each other's attitudes and valuations. We live as responsive beings not only in the social but also in the natural world where we interpret the natural events that affect us—heat and cold, storm and fair weather, earthquake and tidal wave, health and sickness, animal and plant— as living-giving and death-dealing. We respond to these events in accordance with our interpretation. Such interpretation, it need scarcely be added, is not simply an affair of our conscious, and rational, mind but also of the deep memories that are buried within us, of feelings and intuitions that are only partly under our immediate control.

This, then, is the second element in responsibility, that it is not only responsive action but responsive in accordance with our *interpretation* of the question to which answer is being given. In our responsibility we attempt to answer the question:

"What shall I do?" by raising as the prior question: "What is going on?" or "What is being done to me?" rather than "What is my end?" or "What is my ultimate law?" A third element is *accountability*—a word that is frequently defined by recourse to legal thinking but that has a more definite meaning, when we understand it as referring to part of the response pattern of our self-conduct. Our actions are responsible not only insofar as they are reactions to interpreted actions upon us but also insofar as they are made in anticipation of answers to our answers. An agent's action is like a statement in a dialogue. Such a statement not only seeks to meet, as it were, or to fit into, the previous statement to which it is an answer, but is made in anticipation of reply. It looks forward as well as backward; it anticipates objections, confirmations, and corrections. It is made as part of a total conversation that leads forward and is to have meaning as a whole. Thus a political action, in this sense, is responsible not only when it is responsive to a prior deed but when it is so made that the agent anticipates the reactions to his action. So considered, no action taken as an atomic unit is responsible. Responsibility lies in the agent who stays with his action, who accepts the consequences in the form of reactions and looks forward in a present deed to the continued interaction. From this point of view we may try to illuminate the question much debated in modern times of the extent to which a person is to be held socially accountable for his acts. In terms of responsibility the question is simply this: "To whom and in what way ought a society through its courts and other agencies respond?" If a homicide has taken place, is the only one to whom there is to be reaction the killer himself, or is there to be response also to the society in which he acted as a reactor? Further, is the reaction to the individual criminal agent to be reaction guided by purely legal thinking, which interprets him solely as an unobedient and perhaps a self-legislating being, or is it to be informed by a larger interpretation of his conduct— one which takes into account other dimensions of his existence as a self? Is the criminal to be dealt with as a self who can anticipate reactions to his actions and so be acted upon as a potentially responsive person, or is the social reaction to him to be confined to his antisocial physical body only and he be regarded as a being that cannot learn to respond with interpretation and anticipation? Is education, psychiatry, or only incarceration the fitting response?

The third element in responsibility—the anticipation of reaction to our reaction—has brought us within view of what at least for the present seems to be its fourth and final significant component, namely *social solidarity*. Our action is responsible, it appears, when it is response to action upon us in a continuing discourse or interaction among beings forming a continuing society. A series of responses to disconnected actions guided by disconnected interpretations would scarcely be the action of a self but only of a series of states of mind somehow connected with the same body—though the sameness of the body would be apparent only to an external point of view. Personal responsibility implies the continuity of a self with a relatively consistent scheme of interpretations of what it is reacting to. By the same token it implies continuity in the community of agents to which response is being made. There could be no responsible self in an interaction in which the reaction to one's response comes from a source wholly different from that whence the original action issued. This theme we shall need to develop more fully in the second lecture.

The idea or pattern of responsibility, then, may summarily and abstractly be defined as the idea of an agent's action as response to an action upon him in accordance with his interpretation of the latter action and with his expectation of response to his response; and all of this is in a continuing community of agents.

The idea of the moral life as the responsible life in this sense not only has affinities with much modern thinking but it also offers us, I believe, a key—not *the* key—to the understanding of that Biblical ethos which represents the historic norm of the Christian life. In the past many efforts have been made to understand the ethos of the Old and New Testaments with the aid of the teleological theory and its image of man-the-maker. Thus the thinking of the lawgivers and prophets, of Jesus Christ and the apostles, has been set before us in the terms of a great idealism. Sometimes the ideal has been described as that of the vision of God, sometimes as perfection, sometimes as eternal happiness, sometimes as a harmony of all beings, or at least of all men, in a kingdom of God. Each of these interpretations has been buttressed by collections of proof texts, and doubtless much that is valid about the Bible and about the Christian life which continues the Scriptural ethos has been said within the limits of this interpretation. But much that is in Scriptures has been omitted by the interpreters who followed this method, and much material of another sort—the eschatological, for instance—has had to be rather violently wrenched out of its context or laid aside as irrelevant in order to make the Scriptures speak in this fashion about the self. At all times, moreover, but particularly among the German interpreters in whom the Kantian symbolism holds sway, the deontological interpretation of man the obedient legislator has been used not only as the key to Biblical interpretation but for the definition of the true Christian life. For Barth and Bultmann alike in our times, not to speak of most interpreters of the Old Testament, the ethics of the Bible, and Christian ethics, too, is the ethics of obedience. How to interpret Christian freedom and what to make of eschatology within this framework has taxed the ingenuity of the interpreters severely. Bultmann has transformed eschatology into existentialism in order to maintain an ethics of radical obedience; Barth has had to transform the law into a form of the gospel and the commandment into permission in order to reconcile the peculiarity of gospel ethos with deontological thinking. There is doubtless much about law, commandment, and obedience in the Scriptures. But the use of this pattern of interpretation does violence to what we find there.

If now we approach the Scriptures with the idea of responsibility we shall find, I think, that the particular character of this ethics can be more fully if not wholly adequately interpreted. At the critical junctures in the history of Israel and of the early Christian community the decisive question men raised was not

"What is the goal?" nor yet "What is the law?" but "What is happening?" and then "What is the fitting response to what is happening?" When an Isaiah counsels his people, he does not remind them of the law they are required to obey nor yet of the goal toward which they are directed but calls to their attention the intentions of God present in hiddenness in the actions of Israel's enemies. The question he and his peers raise in every critical moment is about the interpretation of what is going on, whether what is happening be, immediately considered, a drought or the invasion of a foreign army, or the fall of a great empire. Israel is the people that is to see and understand the action of God in everything that happens and to make a fitting reply. So it is in the New Testament also. The God to whom Jesus points is not the commander who gives laws but the doer of small and of mighty deeds, the creator of sparrows and clother of lilies, the ultimate giver of blindness and of sight, the ruler whose rule is hidden in the manifold activities of plural agencies but is yet in a way visible to those who know how to interpret the signs of the times.

It will not do to say that the analysis of all our moral life in general and of Biblical ethics in particular by means of the idea of responsibility offers us an absolutely new way of understanding man's ethical life or of constructing a system of Christian ethics. Actuality always extends beyond the patterns of ideas into which we want to force it. But the approach to our moral existence as selves, and to our existence as Christians in particular, with the aid of this idea makes some aspects of our life as agents intelligible in a way that the teleology and deontology of traditional thought cannot do.

Some special aspects of life in responsibility are to occupy us in the succeeding lectures. In none of them shall I take the deontological stance, saying, "We *ought* to be responsible"; nor yet the ideal, saying, "the *goal* is responsibility"; but I shall simply ask that we consider our life of response to action upon us with the question in mind, "To whom or what am I responsible and in what community of interaction am I myself?"

NOTES

[1] *Oxford English Dictionary.*
[2] *The Works of Aristotle,* W. D. Ross, ed. (Oxford: Clarendon Press, 1925), Vol. IX, *Ethica Nicomachea,* Bk. I, 1.
[3] *Summa Theologica,* Prima Secundae, Q. I., Resp. Translation above by J. Rickaby, S.J., *Aquinas Ethicus* (London: Burns & Oates, 1896), Vol. I.
[4] Cf. W. Fales, *Wisdom and Responsibility* (Princeton, N.J.: Princeton University Press, 1946). "There is much evidence that man is . . . determined by final ends which are not an object of his contemplation although they account for his personality and constitute his will. The pressure which the final ends exert upon man is felt as responsibility" (pp. 4 f.). Fales tries to account for the *feeling* of responsibility but never analyzes the feeling itself. Cf. pp. 56-58, 67, 71, 144.
[5] *Op. cit.,* Bk. II, 6.
[6] *Tractatus de intellectus emendatione,* I, 1. (The English translations of this treatise that I have consulted do not carry over the paragraph divisions by numerals that stand in the Latin text. However, the sentence quoted above occurs at the virtual beginning of the essay.—ED.)

Dietrich Bonhoeffer

THE STRUCTURE OF
RESPONSIBLE LIFE*

The structure of responsible life is conditioned by two factors: life is bound to man and to God and a man's own life is free. It is the fact that life is bound to man and to God which sets life in the freedom of a man's own life. Without this bond and without this freedom there is no responsibility. Only when it has become selfless in this obligation does a life stand in the freedom of a man's truly own life and action. The obligation assumes the form of deputyship and of correspondence with reality; freedom displays itself in the self-examination of life and of action and in the venture of a concrete decision. This gives us the arrangement for our discussion of the structure of responsible life.

DEPUTYSHIP

The fact that responsibility is fundamentally a matter of deputyship is demonstrated most clearly in those circumstances in which a man is directly obliged to act in the place of other men, for example as a father, as a statesman or as a teacher. The father acts for the children, working for them, caring for them, interceding, fighting and suffering for them. Thus in a real sense he is their deputy. He is not an isolated individual, but he

* From DIETRICH BONHOEFFER, *Ethics*, Eberhard Bethge, ed., Neville Horton Smith, trans. (New York: The Macmillan Co., 1965, paperback), pp. 224-62. Used by permission. Bonhoeffer is the German theologian martyred by the Nazis in 1945.

39

combines in himself the selves of a number of human beings. Any attempt to live as though he were alone is a denial of the actual fact of his responsibility. He cannot evade the responsibility which is laid on him with his paternity. This reality shatters the fiction that the subject, the performer, of all ethical conduct is the isolated individual. Not the individual in isolation but the responsible man is the subject, the agent, with whom ethical reflection must concern itself. This principle is not affected by the extent of the responsibility assumed, whether it be for a single human being, for a community or for whole groups of communities. No man can altogether escape responsibility, and this means that no man can avoid deputyship. Even the solitary lives as a deputy, and indeed quite especially so, for his life is lived in deputyship for man as man, for mankind as a whole. And, in fact, the concept of responsibility for oneself possesses a meaning only in so far as it refers to the responsibility which I bear with respect to myself as a man, that is to say, because I am a man. Responsibility for oneself is in truth responsibility with respect to the man, and that means responsibility with respect to mankind. The fact that Jesus lived without the special responsibility of a marriage, of a family or of a profession, does not by any means set Him outside the field of responsibility; on the contrary, it makes all the clearer His responsibility and His deputyship for all men. Here we come already to the underlying basis of everything that has been said so far. Jesus, life, our life, lived in deputyship for us as the incarnate Son of God, and that is why through Him all human life is in essence a life of deputyship. Jesus was not the individual, desiring to achieve a perfection of his own, but He lived only as the one who has taken up into Himself and who bears within Himself the selves of all men. All His living, His action and His dying was deputyship. In Him there is fulfilled what the living, the action and the suffering of men ought to be. In this real deputyship which constitutes His human existence He is the responsible person *par excellence*. Because He is life all life is determined by Him to be deputyship. Whether or not life resists, it is now always deputyship, for life or for death, just as the father is always a father, for good or for evil.

Deputyship, and therefore also responsibility, lies only in the complete surrender of one's own life to the other man. Only the selfless man lives responsibly, and this means that only the selfless man *lives*. Wherever the divine "yes" and "no" become one in man, there is responsible living. Selflessness in responsibility is so complete that here we may find the fulfillment of Goethe's saying about the man of action being always without conscience. The life of deputyship is open to two abuses; one may set up one's own ego as an absolute, or one may set up the other man as an absolute. In the first case the relation of responsibility leads to forcible exploitation and tyranny; this springs from a failure to recognize that only the selfless man can act responsibly. In the second case what is made absolute is the welfare of the other man, the man towards whom I am responsible, and all other responsibilities are neglected. From this there arises arbitrary action which makes mock of the responsibility to God who in Jesus Christ is the God of all men. In both cases there is a denial of the origin, the essence and the goal of responsible life in Jesus Christ, and responsibility itself is set up as a self-made abstract idol.

Responsibility, as life and action in deputyship, is essentially a relation of man to man. Christ became man, and He thereby bore responsibility and deputyship for men. There is also a responsibility for things, conditions and values, but only in conjunction with the strict observance of the original, essential and purposive determination of all things, conditions, and values through Christ (John 1:3), the incarnate God. Through Christ the world of things and of values is once more directed towards mankind as it was in the Creation. It is only within these limits that there is a legitimate sense in speaking, as is often done, about responsibility for a thing or for a cause. Beyond these limits it is dangerous, for it serves to reverse the whole order of life, making things the masters of men. There is a devotion to the cause of truth, goodness, justice and beauty which would be profaned if one were to ask what is the moral of it, and which indeed itself makes it abundantly clear that the highest values must be subservient to man. But there is also a deification of all these values which has no connexion at all with responsibility; it springs from a demoniacal possession which destroys the man in sacrificing him to the idol. "Responsibility for a thing" does not mean its utilization for man and consequently the abuse of its essential nature, but it means the essential directing of it towards man. Thus that narrow pragmatism is entirely excluded which, in Schiller's words, "makes a milch-cow of the goddess" when that which has value in itself is in a direct and short-sighted manner subordinated to human utility. The world of things attains to its full liberty and depth only when it is grasped in its original, essential and purposive relevance to the world of persons; for, as St. Paul expresses it, the earnest expectation of the creature waits for the manifestation of the glory of the children of God; and indeed the creature itself shall be delivered from the bondage of corruption (which also consists in its own false self-deification) into the glorious liberty of the children of God (Rom. 8:19-21).

CORRESPONDENCE WITH REALITY

The responsible man is dependent on the man who is concretely his neighbor in his concrete possibility. His conduct is not established in advance, once and for all, that is to say, as a matter of principle, but it arises with the given situation. He has no principle at his disposal which possesses absolute validity and which he has to put into effect fanatically, overcoming all the resistance which is offered to it by reality, but he sees in the given situation what is necessary and what is "right" for him to grasp and to do. For the responsible man the given situation is not simply the material on which he is to impress his idea or his programme by force, but this situation is itself drawn in into the action and shares in giving form to the deed. It is not an "absolute good" that is to be realized; but on the contrary it is part of the self-direction of the responsible agent that he prefers what is relatively better to what is relatively worse and that he perceives that the "absolute good" may sometimes be the very worst. The responsible man does not have to impose upon reality a law which is alien to it, but his action is in the true sense "in accordance with reality."

This concept of correspondence to reality certainly needs to be defined more exactly. It would be a complete and a dangerous misunderstanding if it were to be taken in the sense of that "servile conviction in the face of the fact" that Nietzsche speaks of, a conviction which yields to every powerful pressure, which on principle justifies success, and which on every occasion chooses what is opportune as "corresponding to reality." "Correspondence with reality" in this sense would be the contrary of responsibility; it would be irresponsibility. But the true meaning of correspondence with reality lies neither in this servility towards the factual nor yet in a principle of opposition to the factual, a principle of revolt against the factual in the name of some higher reality. Both extremes alike are very far removed from the essence of the matter. In action which is genuinely in accordance with reality there is an indissoluble link between the acknowledgement and the contradiction of the factual. The reason for this is that reality is first and last not lifeless; but it is the real man, the incarnate God. It is from the real man, whose name is Jesus Christ, that all factual reality derives its ultimate foundation and its ultimate annulment, its justification and its ultimate contradiction, its ultimate affirmation and its ultimate negation. To attempt to understand reality without the real man[1] is to live in an abstraction to which the responsible man must never fall victim; it is to fail to make contact with reality in life; it is to vacillate endlessly between the extremes of servility and revolt in relation to the factual. God became man; He accepted man in the body and thereby reconciled the world of man with God. The affirmation of man and of his reality took place upon the foundation of the acceptance, and not the acceptance upon the foundation of the affirmation. It was not because man and his reality were worthy of the divine affirmation that God accepted them and that God became man, but it was because man and his reality were worthy of divine being that God accepted man and affirmed him by Himself becoming man in the body and thereby taking upon Himself and suffering the curse of the divine "no" to the human character. It is from this action of God, from the real man, from Jesus Christ, that reality now receives its "yes" and its "no," its right and its limitations. Affirmation and contradictions are now conjoined in the concrete action of him who has recognized the real man. Neither the affirmation nor the contradiction now comes from a world which is alien to reality, from a systematic opportunism or idealism; but they come from the reality of the reconciliation of the world with God which has taken place in Jesus Christ. In Jesus Christ, the real man, the whole of reality is taken up and comprised together; in Him it has its origin, its essence and its goal. For that reason it is only in Him, and with Him as the point of departure, that there can be an action which is in accordance with reality. The origin of action which accords with reality is not the pseudo-Lutheran Christ who exists solely for the purpose of sanctioning the facts as they are, nor the Christ of radical enthusiasm whose function is to bless every revolution, but it is the incarnate God Jesus who has accepted man and who has loved, condemned and reconciled man and with him the world. Our conclusion from this must be that action which is in accordance with Christ is action which is in accordance with reality. This propostion is not an ideal demand, but it is an assertion which springs from the knowledge of reality itself. Jesus Christ does not confront reality as one who is alien to it, but it is He who alone has borne and experienced the essence of the real in His own body, who has spoken from the standpoint of reality as no man on earth can do, who alone has fallen victim to no ideology, but who is the truly real one, who has borne within Himself and fulfilled the essence of history, and in whom the law of the life of history is embodied. He is the real one, the origin, essence and goal of all that is real, and for that reason He is Himself the Lord and the Law of the real. Consequently the word of Jesus Christ is the interpretation of His existence, and it is therefore the interpretation of that reality in which history attains to its fulfillment. The words of Jesus are the divine commandment for responsible action in history in so far as this history is the reality of history as it is fulfilled in Christ, the responsibility for man as it is fulfilled in Christ alone. They are not intended to serve the ends of an abstract ethic; for an abstract ethic they are entirely incomprehensible and they lead to conflicts which can never be resolved, but they take effect in the reality of history, for it is from there that they originate. Any attempt to detach them from this origin distorts them into a feeble ideology and robs them of the power, which they possess in their attachment to their origin, of witnessing to reality.

Action which is in accordance with Christ is in accordance with reality because it allows the world to be the world; it reckons with the world as the world; and yet it never forgets that in Jesus Christ the world is loved, condemned and reconciled by God. This does not mean that a "secular principle" and a "Christian principle" are set up in opposition to one another. On the contrary, any such attempt to achieve some sort of commensurability between Christ and the world at least in the form of a general principle, any such attempt to provide a theoretical basis for Christian action in the world, leads, in the form of secularism or the theory of the autonomy of the various domains of life, or else in the form of enthusiasm, to the ruin and destruction of the world which in Christ is reconciled with God; it leads to those eternal conflicts which constitute the underlying material of all tragedy and which precisely in this destroy the totally untragic unity of Christian life and action. When a secular and a Christian principle are opposed, the ultimate reality is taken to be the law, or more exactly a multiplicity of irreconcilably contradictory laws. It is the essence of Greek tragedy that a man's downfall is brought about by the conflict of incompatible laws. Creon and Antigone, Jason and Medea, Agamemnon and Clytemnestra, all are subject to the claim of these eternal laws which cannot be reconciled in one and the same life; obedience is rendered to the one law at the price of guilt in respect of the other law. The meaning of all genuine tragedies is not that one man is right and the other wrong, but that both incur guilt towards life itself; the structure of their life is an incurring of guilt in respect of the laws of the gods. This is the most profound experience of classical antiquity. Especially since the Renaissance it has exercised a decisive influence over western thought; in the early periods of the

Church and in the Middle Ages there were no tragedies, but in modern times it has only very rarely been perceived that this tragic experience has been overcome by the message of Christ. Even the modern Protestant ethic invokes the pathos of tragedy in its representation of the irreconcilable conflict of the Christian in the world, and claims that in this it is expressing an ultimate reality. All this unconsciously lies entirely under the spell of the heritage of antiquity; it is not Luther, but it is Aeschylus, Sophocles and Euripides who have invested human life with this tragic aspect. The seriousness of Luther is quite different from the seriousness of the classical tragedians. For the Bible and for Luther what ultimately requires to be considered in earnest is not the disunion of the gods in the form of their laws, but it is the unity of God and the reconciliation of the world with God in Jesus Christ; it is not the inescapability of guilt, but it is the simplicity of the life which follows from the reconciliation; it is not fate, but the gospel as the ultimate reality of life; it is not the cruel triumph of the gods over falling man, but it is the election of man to be man as the child of God in the world which is reconciled through grace.

To contrast a secular and a Christian principle as the ultimate reality is to fall back from Christian reality into the reality of antiquity, but it is equally wrong to regard the Christian and the secular as in principle forming a unity. The reconciliation which is accomplished in Christ between God and the world consists simply and solely in the person of Jesus Christ; it consists in Him as the one who acts in the responsibility of deputyship, as the God who for love of man has become man. From Him alone there proceeds human action which is not worn away and wasted in conflicts of principle but which springs from the accomplishment of the reconciliation of the world with God, an action which soberly and simply performs what is in accordance with reality, an action of responsibility in deputyship. It is now no longer established in advance what is "Christian" and what is "secular"; both of these are recognized, with their special qualities and with their unity, only in the concrete responsibility of action which springs from the reconciliation that has been effected in Jesus Christ.

We have just said that for action which corresponds with reality the world remains the world, but in the light of our whole discussion so far it is clear that this cannot now mean that the world is in principle isolated or that it is declared to be autonomous. If the world remains the world, that must be because all reality is founded upon Jesus Christ Himself. The world remains the world because it is the world which is loved, condemned and reconciled in Christ. No man has the mission to overleap the world and to make it into the kingdom of God. Nor, on the other hand, does this give support to that pious indolence which abandons the wicked world to its fate and seeks only to rescue its own virtue. Man is appointed to the concrete and therefore limited responsibility which knows the world as being created, loved, condemned and reconciled by God and which acts within the world in accordance with this knowledge. The "world" is thus the sphere of concrete responsibility which is given to us in and through Jesus Christ. It is not some general concept from which it is possible to derive a self-contained system. A man's attitude to the world does not correspond with reality if he sees in the world a good or an evil which is good or evil in itself, or if he sees in it a principle which is compounded of both good and evil and if he acts in accordance with this view; his attitude accords with reality only if he lives and acts in limited responsibility and thereby allows the world ever anew to disclose its essential character to him.

Action which is in accordance with reality is limited by our creatureliness. We do not ourselves create the conditions of our action, but we find ourselves placed in these conditions from the outset. Our action is limited by definite boundaries in the forward but never in the backward direction, and these boundaries cannot be overstepped. Our responsibility is not infinite; it is limited, even though within these limits it embraces the whole of reality. It is concerned not only with the good will but also with the good outcome of the action, not only with the motive but also with the object; it seeks to attain knowledge of the given totality of the real in its origin, its essence and its goal; it

discerns it as subject to the divine "yes" and "no." Since we are
not concerned with the realization of an unrestricted principle,
it is necessary in the given situation to observe, to weigh up, to
assess and to decide, always within the limitations of human
knowledge in general. One must risk looking into the immediate
future; one must devote earnest thought to the consequences
of one's action; and one must endeavour to examine one's own
motives and one's own heart. One's task is not to turn the world
upside-down, but to do what is necessary at the given place and
with a due consideration of reality. At the same time one must
ask what are the actual possibilities; it is not always feasible to
take the final step at once. Responsible action must not try to be
blind. And all this must be so because in Christ God became
man, because He said "yes" to mankind, and because it is only
we ourselves, as men and in human restriction of judgment and
of knowledge in relation to God and to our neighbour, who
possess the right and the obligation to live and to act. But
because it was *God* who became man, it follows that responsible action, in the consciousness of the human character of its
decision, can never itself anticipate the judgment as to whether
it is in conformity with its origin, its essence and its goal, but
this judgment must be left entirely to God. All ideological
action carries its own justification within itself from the outset
in its guiding principle, but responsible action does not lay
claim to knowledge of its own ultimate righteousness. When
the deed is performed with a responsible weighing up of all the
personal and objective circumstances and in the awareness that
God has become *man* and that it is *God* who has become man,
then this deed is delivered up solely to God at the moment of its
performance. Ultimate ignorance of one's own good and evil,
and with it a complete reliance upon grace, is an essential property of responsible historical action. The man who acts ideolog-
ically sees himself justified in his idea; the responsible man
commits his action into the hands of God and lives by God's
grace and favour.

A further consequence of this limitedness of responsible life
and action is that it takes into account the responsibility of the
other man who confronts it. Responsibility differs from violence

and exploitation precisely in the fact that it recognizes the other man as a responsible agent and indeed that it enables him to become conscious of his responsibility. The responsibility of the father or of the statesman is limited by the responsibility of the child and of the citizen, and indeed the responsibility of the father and of the statesman consists precisely in rendering conscious and in strengthening the responsibility of those who are committed to their care. There can, therefore, never be an absolute responsibility, a responsibility which is not essentially limited by the responsibility of the other man.

We have now seen that the limit of responsible action lies in the fact that the deed ends in the grace and judgment of God and is bounded by the responsibility of our neighbours, and at the same time it becomes evident that it is precisely this limit which makes the action a responsible one. God and our neighbour, as they confront us in Jesus Christ, are not only the limit, but, as we have already perceived, they are also the origin of responsible action. Irresponsible action may be defined precisely by saying that it disregards this limit, God and our neighbour. Responsible action derives its unity, and ultimately also its certainty, from the fact that it is limited in this way by God and by our neighbour. It is precisely because it is not its own master, because it is not unlimited and arrogant but creaturely and humble, that it can be sustained by an ultimate joy and confidence and that it can know that it is secure in its origin, its essence and its goal, in Christ.

THE WORLD OF THINGS—PERTINENCE—STATECRAFT

On the basis of our knowledge that responsibility is always a relation between persons which has its foundation in the responsibility of Jesus Christ for men, on the basis of our knowledge that the origin, essence and goal of all reality is the real, that is to say, God in Jesus Christ, we are now enabled and obliged to say something also about the relation of the responsible man to the domain of things. We will call this relation pertinence. That has two implications.

The first is that that attitude to things is pertinent which keeps steadily in view their original, essential and purposive relation to God and to men. This relation does not corrupt them in their character as things, but it purifies this character, it does not extinguish the ardour of devotion to a cause, but it refines and intensifies it. The greater the purity of the service to a cause or to a thing, and the more completely this service is free from personal subsidiary aims, the more thoroughly the thing itself will recover its original relation to God and to man, and the more completely it will set man free from himself. The thing for the sake of which the ultimate personal sacrifice is made must serve man precisely in this. If, for example, an attempt is made to render a science useful to men in an illegitimately direct manner for demagogic, pedagogic or moralistic purposes, then it is not only the man but also the science which is ruined. If, on the other hand, in this science man exclusively and unreservedly serves the cause of truth, then in the selfless surrender of all his own wishes he finds himself, and the thing for the sake of which he has rendered this selfless service must in the end serve him. Thus it is essential to the pertinence of the action, to the correspondence of the action with the thing, that one should never overlook this relation of the thing or the cause to the person. It is true that we know this relation only in a thoroughly imperfect form. Either the thing makes itself independent of the person or the person makes himself independent of the thing, or else the two stand side by side completely unrelated. What is needful is the restoration of the original relation on the basis of the responsibility which has its foundation in Jesus Christ.

The second implication is that from its origin there is inherent in every thing its own law of being, no matter whether this thing is a natural object or a product of the human mind, and no matter whether it is a material or an ideal entity. We take the word "thing" in this sense as meaning any datum in which there is inherent an essential law of this kind, no matter whether or to what extent it is a neutral or rather a personal entity. This definition will include the axioms of mathematics and of logic as well as the state or the family, a factory or a commercial company; in every case it is necessary to discover the particular inherent law by virtue of which this entity exists. The more intense the connexion between the thing and the existence of man, the more difficult it becomes to define the law of its being. The laws of logical thought are more easily defined than, for example, the law of the state; and again it is easier to detect the law of a joint-stock company than the law of an organic growth, of the family or of a people. The correspondence of responsible action with reality also involves the detection and pursuit of these laws. The law appears in the first place as a formal technique which requires to be mastered; but the more closely the particular thing with which we are concerned is connected with human existence, the clearer it will become that the law of its being does not consist entirely in a formal technique, but rather that this law renders all technical treatment questionable. The problem of a technique of statecraft is the best example of this, while a technique of radio manufacture is relatively unproblematic. There can be no doubt that statecraft, political science, also has its technical side; there is technique of administration and a technique of diplomacy; in its widest sense this technical side of statecraft includes all positive legislation, all positive treaties and agreements, and even all those rules and conventions of internal and international political coexistence which are not legally defined but which are sanctioned by history. Finally, it even includes all the generally accepted moral principles of the life of the state. No statesman can disregard any one of these laws and conventions with impunity. Arrogant disdain for them or violation of them denotes a failure to appreciate reality which sooner or later has to be paid for. Pertinent action will conform with these laws and conventions; its observance of them will not be merely hypocritical, but it will regard them as an essential element in all order; it will acknowledge and turn to advantage the wisdom of these conventions which has been achieved through the experience of many generations.[2] Precisely at this point pertinent action will be incontrovertibly compelled to recognize that the essential law of the state comprises something more than these rules and conventions of statecraft. Indeed, precisely, because the state is indissolubly bound up with human existence, its essential law extends ultimately far beyond the range of anything that can be expressed in terms of rules. And it is precisely at this point that the full depth of responsible action is achieved.

In the course of historical life there comes a point where the exact observance of the formal law of a state, of a commercial undertaking, of a family, or for that matter of a scientific discovery, suddenly finds itself in violent conflict with the ineluctable necessities of the lives of men; at this point responsible and pertinent action leaves behind it the domain of principle and convention, the domain of the normal and regular, and is confronted by the extraordinary situation of ultimate necessities, a situation which no law can control. It was for this situation that Machiavelli in his political theory coined the term *necessità*. In the field of politics this means that the technique of statecraft has now been supplanted by the necessity of state. There can be no doubt that such necessities exist; to deny their existence is to abandon the attempt to act in accordance with reality. But it is certain that these necessities are a primary fact of life itself and cannot, therefore, be governed by any law or themselves constitute a law. They appeal directly to the free responsibility of the agent, a responsibility which is bound by no law. They create a situation which is extraordinary; they are by nature peripheral and abnormal events. They no longer leave a multiplicity of courses open to human reason but they confront it with the question of the *ultima ratio*. In the political field this *ultima ratio* is war, but it can also be deception and the breaking of treaties for the sake of one's own vital needs. In the economic field it is the destruction of human livelihoods in the interest of the necessities of business. The *ultima ratio* lies beyond the laws of reason, it is irrational action. The true order is completely reversed if the *ultima ratio* itself is converted into a rational law, if the peripheral case is treated as the normal, and if *necessità* is made a technique. Baldwin was right when he said that there was only one greater evil than violence and that this was violence as a principle, as a law and standard. He did not mean by this the extraordinary and abnormal necessity of the use of violence as the *ultima ratio;* if he had meant that he would have been a mere enthusiast and not a statesman; above all he did not wish to see the extraordinary and peripheral case confused with the normal case, with the law. He wished to preserve the relative order which is secured through the pertinent observance of law and convention, when to abandon this order for the sake of a peripheral event would mean chaos.

The extraordinary necessity appeals to the freedom of the men who are responsible. There is now no law behind which the responsible man can seek cover, and there is, therefore, also no law which can compel the responsible man to take any particular decision in the face of such necessities. In this situation there can only be a complete renunciation of every law, together with the knowledge that here one must make one's decision as a free venture, together also with the open admission that here the law is being infringed and violated and that necessity obeys no commandment. Precisely in this breaking of the law the validity of the law is acknowledged, and in this renunciation of all law, and in this alone, one's own decision and deed are entrusted unreservedly to the divine governance of history.

There can be no theoretical answer to the question whether in historical action the ultimate goal is the eternal law or free responsibility in the face of all law but before God. Great nations are opposed in this in an insurmountable and ultimate antinomy. The greatness of British statesmen, and I am thinking here, for example, of Gladstone, is that they acknowledge the law as the ultimate authority; and the greatness of German statesmen—I am thinking now of Bismarck—is that they come before God in free responsibility. In this neither can claim to be superior to the other. The ultimate question remains open and must be kept open, for in either case man becomes guilty and in either case he can live only by the grace of God and by forgiveness. Each of these men, the one who is bound by the law and the one who acts in free responsibility, must hear and bow before the accusation of the other. Neither can be the judge of the other. It is always for God to judge.

THE ACCEPTANCE OF GUILT

From what has just been said it emerges that the structure of responsible action includes both readiness to accept guilt and freedom.

When we once more turn our attention to the origin of all responsibility it becomes clear to us what we are to understand by acceptance and guilt. Jesus is not concerned with the proclamation and realization of new ethical ideals; He is not concerned with Himself being good (Matt. 19:17); He is concerned solely with love for the real man, and for that reason He is able to enter into the fellowship of the guilt of men and to take the burden of their guilt upon Himself. Jesus does not desire to be regarded as the only perfect one at the expense of men; He does not desire to look down on mankind as the only guiltless one while mankind goes to its ruin under the weight of its guilt; He does not wish that some idea of a new man should triumph amid the wreckage of a humanity whose guilt has destroyed it. He does not wish to acquit Himself of the guilt under which men die. A love which left man alone in his guilt would not be love for the real man. As one who acts responsibly in the historical existence of men Jesus becomes guilty. It must be emphasized that it is solely His love which makes Him incur guilt. From His selfless love, from His freedom from sin, Jesus enters into the guilt of men and takes this guilt upon Himself. Freedom from sin and the question of guilt are inseparable in Him. It is as the one who is without sin that Jesus takes upon Himself the guilt of His brothers, and it is under the burden of this guilt that He shows Himself to be without sin. In this Jesus Christ, who is guilty without sin, lies the origin of every action of responsible deputyship. If it is responsible action, if it is action which is concerned solely and entirely with the other man, if it arises from selfless love for the real man who is our brother, then, precisely because this is so, it cannot wish to shun the fellowship of human guilt. Jesus took upon Himself the guilt of all men, and for that reason every man who acts responsibly becomes guilty. If any man tries to escape guilt in responsibility

he detaches himself from the ultimate reality of human existence, and what is more he cuts himself off from the redeeming
mystery of Christ's bearing guilt without sin and he has no share
in the divine justification which lies upon this event. He sets his
own personal innocence above his responsibility before men,
and he is blind to the more irredeemable guilt which he incurs
precisely in this; he is blind also to the fact that real innocence
shows itself precisely in a man's entering into the fellowship of
guilt for the sake of other men. Through Jesus Christ it becomes
an essential part of responsible action that the man who is
without sin loves selflessly and for that reason incurs guilt.

CONSCIENCE

There is a reply to all this which undeniably commands respect. It comes from the high authority of conscience; for conscience is unwilling to sacrifice its integrity to any other value,
and it therefore refuses to incur guilt for the sake of another
man. Responsibility for our neighbor is cut short by the inviolable call of conscience. A responsibility which would oblige
a man to act against his conscience would carry within it its
own condemnation. In what respects is this true and in what
respects is it false?

It is true that it can never be advisable to act against one's
own conscience. All Christian ethics is agreed in this. But what
does that mean? Conscience comes from a depth which lies
beyond a man's own will and his own reason and it makes itself
heard as the call of human existence to unity with itself. Conscience comes as an indictment of the loss of this unity and as a
warning against the loss of one's self. Primarily it is directed not
towards a particular kind of doing but towards a particular
mode of being. It protests against a doing which imperils the
unity of this being with itself.

So long as conscience can be formally defined in these terms
it is extremely inadvisable to act against its authority; disregard
for the call of conscience will necessarily entail the destruction
of one's own being, not even a purposeful surrender of it; it

will bring about the decline and collapse of a human existence. Action against one's own conscience runs parallel with suicidal action against one's own life, and it is not by chance that the two often go together. Responsible action which did violence to conscience in this formal sense would indeed be reprehensible.

But that is not by any means the end of the question. The call of conscience arises from the imperilling of a man's unity with himself, and it is therefore now necessary to ask what constitutes this unity. The first constituent is the man's own ego in its claim to be "like God," *sicut deus,* in the knowledge of good and evil. The call of conscience in natural man is the attempt on the part of the ego to justify itself in its knowledge of good and evil before God, before men and before itself, and to secure its own continuance in this self-justification. Finding no firm support in its own contingent individuality the ego traces its own derivation back to a universal law of good and seeks to achieve unity with itself in conformity with this law. Thus the call of conscience has its origin and its goal in the autonomy of a man's own ego. A man's purpose in obeying this call is on each occasion anew that he should himself once more realize this autonomy which has its origin beyond his own will and knowledge "in Adam." Thus in his conscience he continues to be bound by a law of his own finding, a law which may assume different concrete forms but which he can transgress only at the price of losing his own self.

We can now understand that the great change takes place at the moment when the unity of human existence ceases to consist in its autonomy and is found, through the miracle of faith, beyond the man's own ego and its law, in Jesus Christ. The form of this change in the point of unity has an exact analogy in the secular sphere. When the national socialist says "My conscience is Adolf Hitler" that, too, is an attempt to find a foundation for the unity of his own ego somewhere beyond himself. The consequence of this is the surrender of one's autonomy for the sake of an unconditional heteronomy, and this in turn is possible only if the other man, the man to whom I look for the unity of my life, fulfills the function of a redeemer for me. This, then, provides an extremely direct and significant parallel to the Christian truth, and at the same time an extremely direct and significant contrast with it.

When Christ, true God and true man, has become the point of unity of my existence, conscience will indeed still formally be the call of my actual being to unity with myself, but this unity cannot now be realized by means of a return to the autonomy which I derive from the law; it must be realized in fellowship with Jesus Christ. Natural conscience, no matter how strict and rigorous it may be, is now seen to be the most ungodly self-justification, and it is overcome by the conscience which is set free in Jesus Christ and which summons me to unity with myself in Jesus Christ. Jesus Christ has become my conscience. This means that I can now find unity with myself only in the surrender of my ego to God and to men. The origin and the goal of my conscience is not a law but it is the living God and the living man as he confronts me in Jesus Christ. For the sake of God and of men Jesus became a breaker of the law. He broke the law of the Sabbath in order to keep it holy in love for God and for men. He forsook His parents in order to dwell in the house of His Father and thereby to purify His obedience towards His parents. He sat at table with sinners and outcasts; and for the love of men He came to be forsaken by God in His last hour. As the one who loved without sin, He became guilty; He wished to share in the fellowship of human guilt; He rejected the devil's accusation which was intended to divert Him from this course. Thus it is Jesus Christ who sets conscience free for the service of God and of our neighbour; He sets conscience free even and especially when man enters into the fellowship of human guilt. The conscience which has been set free from the law will not be afraid to enter into the guilt of another man for the other man's sake, and indeed precisely in doing this it will show itself in its purity. The conscience which has been set free is not timid like the conscience which is bound by the law, but it stands wide open for our neighbour and for his concrete distress. And so conscience joins with the responsibility which has its foundation in Christ in bearing guilt for the sake of our neighbour. Human action is poisoned in a way which differs from essential original sin, yet as responsible action, in contrast to any self-righteously high-principled action, it nevertheless indirectly has a part in the action of Jesus Christ. For responsible action, therefore, there is a kind of relative freedom from sin, and this shows itself precisely in the responsible acceptance of the guilt of others.

From the principle of truthfulness Kant draws the grotesque conclusion that I must even return an honest "yes" to the enquiry of the murderer who breaks into my house and asks whether my friend whom he is pursuing has taken refuge there; in such a case of self-righteousness of conscience has become outrageous presumption and blocks the path of responsible action. Responsibility is the total and realistic response of man to the claim of God and of our neighbour; but this example shows in its true light how the response of a conscience which is bound by principles is only a partial one. If I refuse to incur guilt against the principle of truthfulness for the sake of my friend, if I refuse to tell a robust lie for the sake of my friend (for it is only the self-righteously law-abiding conscience which will pretend that, in fact, no lie is involved), if, in other words, I refuse to bear guilt for charity's sake, then my action is in contradiction to my responsibility which has its foundation in reality. Here again it is precisely in the responsible acceptance of guilt that a conscience which is bound solely to Christ will best prove its innocence.

It is astonishing how close Goethe came to these ideas with a purely profane knowledge of reality. In the dialogue in which Pylades tries to persuade Iphigenia to overcome the inner law and to act responsibly we read:

Pylades
An over-strict demand is secret pride.
Iphigenia
The spotless heart alone is satisfied.[3]
Pylades
Here in the temple you no doubt were so;
And yet life teaches us to be less strict
With others and ourselves; you too will learn.

This human kind is intricately wrought
With knots and ties so manifold that none
Within himself or with the rest can keep
Himself quite disentangled and quite pure.
We are not competent to judge ourselves;
Man's first and foremost duty is to go
Forward and think about his future course:
For he can seldom know what he has done,
And what he now is doing even less . . .
One sees that you have rarely suffered loss;
For if that were not so you would not now
Refuse this one false word to escape this evil.

Iphigenia

Would my heart like a man's could be resolved
And then be deaf to any other voice!

However greatly responsibility and the conscience which is set free in Christ may desire to be united, they nevertheless continue to confront one another in a relation of irreducible tension. Conscience imposes two kinds of limit upon that bearing of guilt which from time to time becomes necessary in responsible action.

In the first place, the conscience which is set free in Christ is still essentially the summons to unity with myself. The acceptance of a responsibility must not destroy this unity. The surrender of the ego in selfless service must never be confused with the destruction and annihilation of this ego; for then indeed this ego would no longer be capable of assuming responsibility. The extent of the guilt which may be accepted in the pursuit of responsible action is on each occasion concretely limited by the requirement of the man's unity with himself, that is to say, by his carrying power. There are responsibilities which I cannot carry without breaking down under their weight; it may be a declaration of war, the violation of a political treaty, a revolution or merely the discharge of a single employee who thereby loses the means of supporting his family; or it may be simply a piece of advice in connexion with some personal decisions in life. Certainly the strength to bear responsible decisions can and should grow; certainly any failure to fulfill a responsibility is in itself a responsible decision; and yet in the concrete instance the summons of conscience to unity with oneself in Jesus Christ remains irresistible, and it is this which explains the infinite multiplicity of responsible decisions.

Secondly, even when it is set free in Jesus Christ conscience still confronts responsible action with the law, through obedience to which man is preserved in that unity with himself which has its foundation in Jesus Christ. Disregard for this law can give rise only to irresponsibility. This is the law of love for God and for our neighbor as it is explained in the decalogue, in the sermon on the mount and in the apostolic parenesis. It has been correctly observed that in the contents of its law natural conscience is in strikingly close agreement with that of the conscience which has been set free in Christ. This is due to the fact that it is upon conscience that the continuance of life itself depends; conscience, therefore, contains fundamental features of the law of life, even though these features may be distorted in detail and perverted in principle. The liberated conscience is still what it was as the natural conscience, namely the warner against transgression of the law of life. But the law is no longer the last thing; there is still Jesus Christ; for that reason, in the contest between conscience and concrete responsibility, the free decision must be given for Christ. This does not mean an everlasting conflict, but the winning of ultimate unity; for indeed the foundation, the essence and the goal of concrete responsibility is the same Jesus Christ who is the Lord of conscience. Thus responsibility is bound by conscience, but conscience is set free by responsibility. It is now clear that it is the same thing if we say that the responsible man becomes guilty without sin or if we say that only the man with a free conscience can bear responsibility.

When a man takes guilt upon himself in responsibility, and no responsible man can avoid this, he imputes this guilt to himself and to no one else; he answers for it; he accepts responsibility for it. He does not do this in the insolent presumptuousness of his own power, but he does it in the knowledge that this liberty is forced upon him and that in this liberty he is dependent on grace. Before other men the man of free responsibility is justified by necessity; before himself he is acquitted by his conscience; but before God he hopes only for mercy.

FREEDOM

We must therefore conclude our analysis of the structure of responsible action by speaking of freedom.

Responsibility and freedom are corresponding concepts. Factually, though not chronologically, responsibility presupposes freedom and freedom can consist only in responsibility. Responsibility is the freedom of men which is given only in the obligation to God and to our neighbour.

The responsible man acts in the freedom of his own self, without the support of men, circumstances or principles, but with a due consideration for the given human and general conditions and for the relevant questions of principle. The proof of his freedom is the fact that nothing can answer for him, nothing can exonerate him, except his own deed and his own self. It is he himself who must observe, judge, weigh up, decide and act. It is man himself who must examine the motives, the prospects, the value and the purpose of his action. But neither the purity of the motivation, nor the opportune circumstances, nor the value, nor the significant purpose of an intended undertaking can become the governing law of his action, a law to which he can withdraw, to which he can appeal as an authority, and by which he can be exculpated and acquitted.[4] For in that case he would indeed no longer be truly free. The action of the responsible man is performed in the obligation which alone gives freedom and which gives entire freedom, the obligation to God and to our neighbour as they confront us in Jesus Christ. At the same time it is performed wholly within the domain of relativity, wholly in the twilight which the historical situation spreads over good and evil; it is performed in the midst of the innumerable perspectives in which every given phenomenon appears. It has not to decide simply between right and wrong and between good and evil, but between right and right and between wrong and wrong. As Aeschylus said, "right strives with right." Precisely in this respect responsible action is a free venture; it is not justified by any law; it is performed without any claim to a valid self-justification, and therefore also without any claim to an ultimate valid knowledge of good and evil. Good, as what is responsible, is performed in ignorance of good and in the surrender to God of the deed which has become necessary and which is nevertheless, or for that very reason, free; for it is God who sees the heart, who weighs up the deed, and who directs the course of history.

With this there is disclosed to us a deep secret of history in general. The man who acts in the freedom of his own most personal responsibility is precisely the man who sees his action finally committed to the guidance of God. The free deed knows itself in the end as the deed of God; the decision knows itself as guidance; the free venture knows itself as divine necessity. It is in the free abandonment of knowledge of his own good that a man performs the good of God. It is only from this last point of view that one can speak of good in historical action. We shall have to take up these considerations again later at the point at which we have left off.

Before that we still have to give some space to a crucial question which makes an essential contribution to the clarification of our problem. What is the relationship between free responsibility and obedience? It must seem at first sight as though everything we have said about free responsibility is applicable in practice only when a man finds himself in what we call a "responsible position" in life, in other words when he has to take independent decisions on the very largest scale. What connexion can there be between responsibility and the monotonous daily work of the labourer, the factory worker, the clerk, the private soldier, the apprentice or the schoolboy? It is a different matter already with the owner-farmer, the industrial contractor, the politician or statesman, the general, the master craftsman, the teacher and the judge. But in their lives, too, how much there is of technique and duty and how little of really free decision! And so it seems that everything that we have said about responsibility can in the end apply only to a very small group of men, and even to these only in a few moments of their lives; and consequently it seems as though for the great majority of men one must speak not of responsibility but of obedience and duty. This implies one ethic for the great and the strong, for the rulers, and another for the small and the weak, the subordinates; on the one hand responsibility and on the other obedience, on the one hand freedom and on the other subservience. And indeed there can be no doubt that in our modern social order, and especially in the German one, the life of the individual is so exactly defined and regulated, and is at the same time assured of such complete security, that it is granted to only very few men to breathe the free air of the wide open spaces of great decisions and to experience the hazard of responsible action which is entirely their own. In consequence of the compulsory regulation of life in activity, our lives have come to be relatively free from ethical dangers; the individual who from his childhood on has had to take his assigned place in accordance with this principle is ethically emasculated; he has been robbed of the creative moral power, freedom. In this we see a deep-seated fault in the essential development of our modern social order, a fault which can be countered only with a clear exposition of the fundamental concept of responsibility. As things stand, the large-scale experimental material for the problem of responsibility must be sought for among the great political leaders, industrialists and generals; for indeed those few others who venture to act on their own free responsibility in the midst of the pressure of everyday life are crushed by the machinery of the social order, by the general routine.

Yet it would be an error if we were to continue to look at the problem from this point of view. There is, in fact, no single life which cannot experience the situation of responsibility; every life can experience this situation in its most characteristic form, that is to say, in the encounter with other people. Even when free responsibility is more or less excluded from a man's vocational and public life, he nevertheless always stands in a responsible relation to other men; these relations extend from his family to his workmates. The fulfillment of genuine responsibility at this point affords the only sound possibility of extending the sphere of responsibility once more into vocational and public life. Where man meets man—and this includes the encounters of professional life—there arises genuine responsibility, and these responsible relationships cannot be supplanted by any general regulation or routine. That holds true, then, not only for the relation between married people, or for parents and children, but also for the master and the apprentice, the teacher and his pupil, the judge and the accused.

But we can go one step further than this. Responsibility does not only stand side by side with relationships of obedience; it has its place also within these relationships. The apprentice has a duty of obedience towards his master, but at the same time he has also a free responsibility for his work, for his achievement and, therefore, also for his master. It is the same with the schoolboy and the student, and indeed also with the employee in any kind of industrial undertaking and with the soldier in war. Obedience and responsibility are interlinked in such a way that one cannot say that responsibility begins only where obedience leaves off, but rather that obedience is rendered in responsibility. There will always be a relation of obedience and dependence, all that matters is that these should not, as they already largely do today, leave no room for responsibilities. To know himself to be responsible is more difficult for the man who is socially dependent than for the man who is socially free, but a relationship of dependence does not in any case in itself exclude free responsibility. The master and the servant, while preserving the relationship of obedience, can and should answer for each other in free responsibility.

The ultimate reason for this lies in that relation of men to God which is realized in Jesus Christ. Jesus stands before God as the one who is both obedient and free. As the obedient one He does His Father's will in blind compliance with the law which is commanded Him, and as the free one He acquiesces in God's will out of His own most personal knowledge, with open eyes and a joyous heart; He recreates this will, as it were, out of

Himself. Obedience without freedom is slavery; freedom without obedience is arbitrary self-will. Obedience restrains freedom; and freedom ennobles obedience. Obedience binds the creature to the Creator and freedom enables the creature to stand before the Creator as one who is made in His image. Obedience shows man that he must allow himself to be told what is good and what God requires of him (Micah 6:8); and liberty enables him to do good himself. Obedience knows what is good and does it, and freedom dares to act, and abandons to God the judgment of good and evil. Obedience follows blindly and freedom has open eyes. Obedience acts without questioning and freedom asks what is the purpose. Obedience has its hands tied and freedom is creative. In obedience man adheres to the decalogue and in freedom man creates new decalogues (Luther).

In responsibility both obedience and freedom are realized. Responsibility implies tension between obedience and freedom. There would be no more responsibility if either were made independent of the other. Responsible action is subject to obligation, and yet it is creative. To make obedience independent of freedom leads only to the Kantian ethic of duty, and to make freedom independent of obedience leads only to the ethic of irresponsible genius. Both the man of duty and the genius carry their justification within themselves. The man of responsibility stands between obligation and freedom; he must dare to act under obligation and in freedom; yet he finds his justification neither in his obligation nor in his freedom but solely in Him who has put him in this (humanly impossible) situation and who requires this deed of him. The responsible man delivers up himself and his deed to God.

We have tried to define the structure of responsible life in terms of deputyship, correspondence with reality, acceptance of guilt, and freedom. Now the demand for more concrete formulation brings us to the question whether it is possible to advance a more exact definition of the place, the *locus*, at which responsible life is realized. Does responsibility set me in an unlimited field of activity? Or does it confine me strictly within the limits which are implied in my daily concrete tasks? What does not lie within the scope of my responsibility? Is there any purpose in regarding myself as responsible for everything that takes place in the world? Or can I stand by and watch these great events as an unconcerned spectator so long as my own tiny domain is in order? Am I to wear myself out in impotent zeal against all the wrong and all the misery that is in the world? Or am I entitled, in self-satisfied security, to let the wicked world run its course, so long as I cannot myself do anything to change it and so long as I have done my own work? What is the place and what are the limits of my responsibility?

The Place of Responsibility

VOCATION

In having recourse to this concept which has come to be of almost unique significance for the history of ethics, namely, the concept of the calling, we must from the outset bear clearly in mind the following four points. First of all, we are not thinking here of the secularized concept of the calling which Max Weber defines as a "limited field of accomplishments." Secondly, we are not thinking of that pseudo-Lutheran view for which the concept of vocation simply provides the justification and sanctification of secular institutions. Thirdly, even Luther's own conception of vocation cannot unreservedly be identified with the New Testament conception, just as in his translation of Rom. 3:28 he very boldly ascribes to the New Testament concept (I Cor. 7:20) a fullness of meaning which is indeed essentially justified but which goes beyond the normal linguistic usage. We shall therefore base ourselves on the biblical text as we find it. Fourthly, even though the terms "vocation" and "responsibility" in our current language are not identical with the New Testament concepts, they nevertheless correspond so remarkably happily that there is especially good reason for employing them.

In the encounter with Jesus Christ man hears the call of God and in it the calling to life in the fellowship of Jesus Christ. Divine grace comes upon man and lays claim to him. It is not man who seeks out grace in its own place—God dwelleth in the light which no man can approach unto (I Tim.: 6:16), but it is grace which seeks and finds man in *his* place—the Word was made flesh (John 1:14)—and which precisely in this place lays claim to him. This is a place which in every instance and in every respect is laden with sin and guilt, no matter whether it be a royal throne, the parlour of a respectable citizen or a miserable hovel. It is a place which is of this world. This visitation of man by grace occurred in the incarnation of Jesus Christ, and it occurs in the word of Jesus Christ which is brought by the Holy Ghost. The call comes to man as a Gentile or as a Jew, free man or slave, man or woman, married or single. At the precise place where he is he is to hear the call and to allow it to lay claim to him. This does not mean that servitude or marriage or celibacy in itself is thereby justified; but the man who has been called can in any of these places belong to God. It is only through the call which I have heard in Christ, the call of the grace which lays claim to me, that, as a slave or as a free man, married or celibate, I can live justified before God. From the standpoint of Christ this life is now my calling; from my own standpoint it is my responsibility.

This will have excluded two disastrous misunderstandings, the secular Protestant one and the monastic one. It is not in the loyal discharge of the earthly obligations of his calling as a citizen, a worker and a father that a man fulfils the responsibility which is imposed on him, but it is in hearing the call of Jesus Christ. This call does indeed summon him to earthly duties, but that is never the whole of the call, for it lies always beyond these duties, before them and behind them. The calling, in the New Testament sense, is never a sanctioning of worldly institutions as such; its "yes" to them always includes at the same time an extremely emphatic "no," an extremely sharp protest against the world. Luther's return from the monastery to the world, to the "calling," is, in the true New Testament sense, the fiercest attack and assault to be launched against the world since primitive Christianity. Now a man takes up his position against the world *in* the world; the calling is the place at which the call of Christ is answered, the place at which a man lives responsibly. Thus the task which is appointed for me in my calling is a limited one, but at the same time the responsibility to the call of Jesus Christ breaks through all limits.

The misunderstanding on the part of medieval monasticism does not lie in its recognition of the fact that the call of Jesus Christ involves man in a struggle against the world but in its attempt to find a place which is not the world and at which this call can, therefore, be answered more fitly. In this vain endeavour to escape from the world no serious consideration is given either to the "no" of God, which is addressed to the whole world, including the monastery or to God's "yes," in which He reconciles the world with Himself. Consequently, even in its "no" to the world, God's call is taken less seriously in the monastic undertaking than in the secular calling as Luther (though not indeed pseudo-Lutheranism) understood it. It is entirely in line with Luther if we say that in a certain concrete instance the answer to the call of Jesus Christ may even consist in leaving a particular earthly calling in which one can no longer live responsibly. This thought is unacceptable only to pseudo-Lutheranism, with its belief in the sanctity of vocational duties and of earthly institutions as such, and with its belief that the world is everywhere good. Monasticism is right in so far as it is a protest against the misrepresentation of the New Testament idea of vocation. Luther, in his return to the world, was concerned solely for the total responsibility to the call of Christ. In this respect the monastic solution is doubly wrong. It restricts the compass of ultimately responsible life to the walls of the monastery, and it can only interpret as worthless compromise the life in which a man endeavours to unite in concrete responsibility to the call of Jesus Christ the "yes" and the "no" to life in the world which are implicit in that call. In answer to this failure to appreciate the responsibility of men, Luther invested his responsibility with a significance which is limited and yet at the same time has its foundations in the limitless. While doing this he rewarded the fulfilment of the earthly calling in responsibility to the call of Jesus Christ with the free and joyful conscience which springs from fellowship with Jesus Christ. The good and free conscience, therefore, does not come from the fulfillment of earthly vocational duty as such, for here conscience continues to be wounded by the unresolved conflict between a plurality of duties, so that the best that can be hoped for is the compromise of a divided conscience. It is only when the concrete vocation is fulfilled in responsibility towards the call of Jesus Christ, it is only upon the foundation of the knowledge of the incarnation of Jesus Christ, that conscience can be free in concrete action. The call of Christ alone, when it is responsibly obeyed in the calling, prevails over the compromise and over the conscience which this compromise has rendered insecure.

It follows from this that on the one side the centre of my responsibility is determined by the call of Jesus Christ which is addressed to me.

Our enquiry as to the place and the limit of responsibility has led us to the concept of the calling. The answer is properly applicable only when the calling is understood simultaneously in all its dimensions. The calling is the call of Jesus Christ to belong wholly to Him; it is the laying claim to me by Christ at the place at which this call has found me; it embraces work with things and relations with persons; it demands a "limited field of accomplishments," yet never as a value in itself, but in responsibility towards Jesus Christ. Through this relation to Christ the "limited field of accomplishments" is freed from its isolation. Its boundary is broken through not only from above, that is to say by Christ, but also in an outward direction. If, for example, I am a physician, then in the concrete instance I serve not only my patients but also medical science and with it science and the knowledge of truth in general. Although in practice I perform this service at my concrete position, for example at the bedside of a patient, yet I am consciously aware of my responsibility for the whole, and it is only in this that I fulfill my calling.

Furthermore, it may happen that I, as a physician, am obliged to recognize and fulfill my concrete responsibility no longer by the sick-bed but, for example, in taking public action against some measure which constitutes a threat to medical science or to human life or to science as such. Vocation is responsibility and responsibility is a total response of the whole man to the whole of reality; for this very reason there can be no petty and pedantic restricting of one's interests to one's professional duties in the narrowest sense. Any such restriction would be irresponsibility. The essential character of free responsibility makes it impossible to establish laws defining when and to what extent such a departure from the "limited field of accomplishments" forms part of a man's calling and of his responsibility towards men. Such a departure can be undertaken only after a serious weighing up of the vocational duty which is directly given, of the dangers of interference in the responsibility of others, and finally of the totality of the question which is involved; when this is done I shall be guided in the one direction or the other by a free responsibility towards the call of Jesus Christ. There is a wrong and a right restriction and there is a wrong and a right extension of responsibility: there is an enthusiastic breaking-down of all limits, and there is a legalistic setting-up of limits. It is difficult, or even impossible, to judge from outside whether in a particular concrete instance an action is responsible or whether it is enthusiastic or legalistic; there are, however, criteria for self-examination, though even these cannot afford complete certainty about one's own ego. The following are among such criteria. Neither the limitation nor the extension of my responsibility must be based on a principle; the only possible basis for them is the concrete call of Jesus. If I know myself to be by character inclined towards reforming zeal, towards knowing better and towards fanaticism and unrestraint, then I shall be in danger of extending my responsibility in an arbitrary fashion and confusing my natural impulses with the call of Jesus. If I know myself to be prudent, cautious, diffident and law-abiding, then I shall have to guard against representing the restriction of my responsibility to a narrow field as the call of Jesus Christ. And finally, it is never in thinking of myself, but it is always in thinking of the call of Christ, that I shall be set free for genuine responsibility.

Nietzsche, without knowing it, was speaking in the spirit of the New Testament when he attacked the legalistic and philistine misinterpretation of the commandment which bids us love our neighbour. He wrote: "You are assiduous in your attentions to your neighbour and you find beautiful words to describe your assiduity. But I tell you that your love for your neighbour is a worthless love for yourselves and then you try to make a virtue of it; but I see through your 'unselfishness'. . . . Do I advise you to love your neighbour? I advise you rather to shun your neighbour and to love whoever is furthest from you!" Beyond the neighbour who is committed to us by the call of Jesus there stands also for Jesus the one who is furthest from us, namely, Jesus Christ Himself, God Himself. If beyond this neighbour a man does not know this one who is furthest from him as this neighbour, then he does not serve his neighbour but himself; he takes refuge from the free open space of responsibility in the comforting confinement of the fulfillment of duty. This means that the commandment of love for our neighbour also does not imply a law which restricts our responsibility solely to our neighbour in terms of space, to the man whom I encounter socially, professionally or in my family. My neighbour may well be one who is extremely remote from me, and one who is extremely remote from me may well be my neighbour. By a terrible miscarriage of justice in the United States in 1831 nine young Negroes, whose guilt could not be proved, were sentenced to death for the rape of a white girl of doubtful reputation. There arose a storm of indignation which found expression in open letters from some of the most authoritative public figures in Europe. A Christian who was perturbed by this affair asked a prominent cleric in Germany whether he, too, ought not to raise his voice in the matter, and on the grounds of the "Lutheran" idea of vocation, that is to say, on the grounds of the limitation of his responsibility, the clergyman refused. In the event the protests which came in from all parts of the world led to a revision of the judgment. Here perhaps it is from the point of view of the call of Jesus Christ that we may understand the saying of Nietzsche: "My brothers, I do not counsel you to love your neighbour; I counsel you to love him who is furthest from you." We do not say this in order to pass judgment in the particular case to which we have just referred. We say it in order to keep open the boundary.

No one can fail to hear the Bible's admonitions to do what is waiting to be done (Eccl.: 9:10), to be exact in small obligations before undertaking greater duties (I Tim.: 3:5), and to refrain from interfering in the functions of others (I Pet.: 4:15). Yet all these admonitions are contingent on the call of Christ, and they do not, therefore, imply any law which sets limits to the free responsibility towards this call. In the course of the struggle of the churches in Germany it happened often enough that a minister refused to intervene publicly and responsibly in cases of distress and persecution of various kinds precisely because his own flock were not yet themselves affected; he did not do this from cowardice or from lack of enterprise but solely because he considered such an intervention to be unlawful overstepping of the calling which had been given to him, namely, his vocation to assist his flock in their distress and in their temptations. If subsequently his own flock came to be involved, then there often ensued an act of thoroughly authoritative and free responsibility. This again is not said in order to anticipate judgment but in order to preserve the openness of the commandment of brotherly love in the face of any false limitation and in order to safeguard the concept of vocation in the liberty with which the gospel invests it.

But is not all responsible action in one's calling confined within inviolable limits by the law of God as it is revealed in the ten commandments as well as by the divine mandates of marriage, labour and government? Would not any overstepping of these limits constitute an infringement of the manifest will of God? Here there arises once again in its most acute form the problem of law and liberty. This problem now threatens to implant a contradiction in the will of God itself. Certainly there can be no responsible action which does not devote extremely serious consideration to the limit which is given through God's law, and yet it is precisely responsible action which will not separate this law from its Giver. It is only as the Redeemer in Jesus Christ that responsible action will be able to recognize the God who holds the world in order by His law; it will recognize Jesus Christ as the ultimate reality towards which it is responsible, and it is precisely by Him that it will be set free from the law for the responsible deed. For the sake of God and of our neighbour, and that means for the sake of Christ, there is a freedom from the keeping holy of the Sabbath, from the honouring of our parents, and indeed from the whole of the divine law, a freedom which breaks from the whole of the divine law, a freedom which breaks this law, but only in order to give effect to it anew. The suspension of the law can only serve the true fulfillment of it. In war, for example, there is killing, lying and expropriation solely in order that the authority of life, truth and property may be restored. A breach of the law must be recognized in all its gravity. "Blessed art thou if thou knowest what thou doest; but if thou knowest it not, then art thou accursed and a transgressor of the law" (Luke 6:4 in Codex D). Whether an action arises from responsibility or from cynicism is shown only by whether or not the objective guilt of the violation of the law is recognized and acknowledged, and by whether or not, precisely in this violation, the law is hallowed. It is in this way that the will of God is hallowed in the deed which arises from freedom. But since this is a deed which arises from freedom, man is not torn asunder in deadly conflict, but in certainty and in unity with himself he can dare to hallow the law truly even by breaking it.

NOTES

[1] In the first picture of his Dance of Death, which represents the Creation, Hans Holbein personifies the sun, the moon and the wind. In this way he gives expression in a naïve form to the fact that reality consists ultimately in the personal. In this respect there is an element of truth in primitive animism.

[2] Pertinent action is not by any means necessarily dependent on specialist training, as was all too long supposed in Germany. In England pertinent action on a large scale is entrusted not to the specialist but to the amateur. Sociologically speaking, pertinent action will be most effectively ensured by a sound balance of specialism and dilettantism. *Translator's note: sachgemäss* ("pertinent") may bear various meanings within the range "expedient-appropriate-realistic."

[3] (More exactly: . . . has enjoyment of itself.) The introduction of the characteristic concept of "enjoyment" is also to be noted here.

[4] This makes it unnecessary to raise the fallacious question of determinism and indeterminism, in which the essence of mental decision is incorrectly substituted for the law of causality.

Gabriel Marcel

OBEDIENCE AND FIDELITY*

To Bertrand D'ASTORG

It seems to me impossible to consider the spiritual decadence
which has been going on for more than half a century in our
own country, among others, without being led to emphasize the
increasingly flagrant disrepute in which the value of fidelity has
been held. It is therefore indispensable for anyone who wants to
start upon the immense work of moral reconstruction which is
necessary, to strive to re-establish this same value in the place
which rightly belongs to it—that is to say in the very centre of
human life, of life no longer degraded, alienated or prostituted,
but lived in all the fullness of its true significance. As a matter
of fact the code of ethics which is beginning to take shape in
many places—above all, of course, in youth movements—is
necessarily based on fidelity.

But there is no doubt that if we want to avoid dangerous
simplifications and fatal confusions we must analyse the closely
connected notions of obedience and fidelity as thoroughly as
possible; otherwise an abuse is likely to be made of them by
those who find it useful to exploit for their own ends a good
will, degenerating little by little into a systematic docility and
finally into a passivity of belief and intention.

I think it would be well to point out first of all the essential
difference which separates obedience and fidelity: a difference

* From GABRIEL MARCEL, *Homo Viator,* Emma Crawford, trans.
(Chicago: Henry Regnery Co., 1951), pp. 125-34. Used by permission
of Editions Montaigne, 13, Quai de Conti, Paris (VIV), France.
Marcel is a contemporary French Catholic existentialist.

which in fact tends to become obliterated by the somewhat vague use ordinarily made of the verb to serve.

Let us begin by noticing that the very meaning of the word serve is ambiguous, and that we must not forget the difference of spiritual level between *servir* (to serve) and *servir à* (to be useful). If I come across a tool or machine of which I do not know the purpose, I ask: "For what does that serve?" In this context it is only a question of instruments used by beings endowed with a will, people working for the realisation of definite ends. There would, on the other hand, be something rather shocking about asking a human being, "For what do you serve?" This is precisely because it would be treating him as though he were a thing. Let us notice at this point that to represent the human being as an instrument inevitably leads at last to extreme consequences, such as the pure and simple doing away with old people and incurables: they no longer "serve any useful purpose," hence they are only fit for the rubbish heap: why should we take the trouble to keep up and feed machines which are past use?

There would, on the other hand, be nothing in any way shocking, at any rate if a certain degree of intimacy had been reached, if we asked the same human being, "Whom or what do you serve?" And if he took exception to such a question he would actually prove, by that very fact, that the deeper meaning of life had escaped him. It is clear, indeed, that all life is a service. This does not of course mean that it has to be devoted to some particular individual, but only that it is its essential nature to be *consecrated to* God, or some high purpose such as knowledge or art, etc., or even to some deliberately chosen social end. To serve in this second sense is to put oneself at the service of. Moreover here the accent should be put on the word "oneself," the reflective pronoun. To live in the full sense of the word is not to exist or subsist, to limit oneself to existing or subsisting, but it is to make oneself over, to give oneself.

It is unhappily too clear that these two meanings, of such distinctly different orders, have tended to become confused for minds more and more misinformed, or deformed. A crazy idea has taken possession of an increasing number of misguided individuals, the idea according to which to serve has something humiliating about it for him who serves. The person, considering himself more and more as a centre of claims and demands, such as "I, for my part . . .," has thus hypnotised himself not only about his rights and prerogatives, but further about the feelings of envy inspired by the advantages with which others seem to him to be unduly favoured. "Why him? Why not me?" Resentment has without a doubt been constantly at work beneath a levelling process whose roots a detestable set of psychologists have too long omitted to expose. This has brought innumerable minds to reject the notion of any hierarchy whatever and to rebel against the idea of having to serve anyone at all. It is only just to add that those among the leaders or rulers who have allowed the sense of their responsibility to waste away in the depth of their being, have helped to an extent it is impossible to exaggerate to prepare the way for this crisis in the idea of service. What however is certain is that this anarchism, not violent but ill-tempered and full of sneering hatred, has terribly impoverished souls, and, even on the biological plane itself, has paved the way for France's devitalisation. The general lowering of the human tone, above all of course since 1918, probably constitutes the most outstanding fact of our recent history, the one perhaps which best explains our disaster. We must re-learn how to serve, but this does not simply mean we must re-learn how to obey, for to obey is only one way of serving. There are others.

Here a very simple remark will help to direct us. It is often said of a child that he is, or he is not, obedient. It would clearly be unfitting or even absurd to judge an adult in the same way. Why is this so? It is because the child has not the experience or the powers of reasoning which would enable him to decide for himself what has to be done, so that it behooves him to obey his parents, his teachers, in short all those who are qualified to make decisions about his daily existence. It follows that obedience is a virtue in the child, it is the mark not only of a way of behaviour but of an inner disposition which corresponds with his condition as a child. It is obviously different for the adult, if we consider his existence as a whole. An adult who was obedient in his whole manner of living, in all his acts, no matter whether they were connected with sexual or civic matters, would be unworthy of the name of man. One could consider him only as a being degraded to a state most adequately to be described as infantile. But it is no less clear that in certain special departments of his existence, the adult finds that he also has to obey. Only here, to obey does not mean to be obedient, it is the act by which he has to reply to the act of the chief, which is that of commanding. The function of the chief is to command, the function of the subordinate is to execute orders, that is to say to obey. I have said it is a function, hence the duty of obedience does not fundamentally and necessarily involve the being of him who obeys. This obligation only affects the definite actions which he is required to carry out, or from which he is required to abstain, whatever his personal feelings or his judgment may actually be. There could be no sense in claiming that on the level of feelings or judgment he is obliged to approve of the orders he has received. All that we can say is that he must not allow himself to show these feelings or this judgment, otherwise the obedience will be no more than a pretence, a sham obedience. We are not actually concerned at the moment with knowing whether the way the orders are given in any particular case is wise or not, or whether the prescribed action is good or not, neither are we wondering whether there are not some circumstances in which the refusal to obey would be justified. That is quite another problem which is quite outside the framework of these reflections. Here the question is solely to decide what the limits are within which the expression "to owe obedience" makes sense.

I should then be inclined to believe that obedience as such is given to the chief as chief, that is to say to the function. It is not given to the chief as a man, in so far as he is one man rather than another. Where the human quality of the chief is introduced it is a question of fidelity. Moreover, it goes without saying that in concrete experience—for instance, in a fighting unit—

obedience and fidelity are very difficult to distinguish from each other; no doubt it is even highly desirable that this distinction should not reach the level of consciousness. None the less, from the point of view of reflection it is well to formulate it as clearly as possible. We might add that obedience bears with it a certain statute, whether explicit or not, defining the sphere in which it can be claimed. The more the frontiers of this zone of application tend to become obliterated, the more obedience is liable to be debased and to become confused with a general servility of which the degrading character ought not only to be recognized but proclaimed.

Fidelity presents problems of quite another order, which in the last analysis only the highest philosophy is capable not only of resolving, but of stating with exactitude.

In saying that obedience can and should be required (under certain conditions) and that fidelity on the other hand should be deserved, we are preparing to discuss the originality of this virtue so discredited at the present time or so generally misunderstood.

Let us observe to begin with that when we use the words *to be faithful to,* it is possible that we mean simply *to conform to* (a programme, for instance, or an intention), or negatively, *not to swerve from* (an allotted path). We only find here an impoverished meaning, obtained by diluting a far richer experience which we must try to grasp in its palpitating life.

Immediately the question arises: in the last analysis to what, or more exactly to whom, am I to be faithful? Must we not grant to idealism that the other person, as such, must always remain unknown to me and that consequently I cannot foresee what he will be: how under such conditions could I bind myself directly to him? Would it not be better on that account to recognise that the only true fidelity is fidelity to myself, and that it is by such fidelity alone that I can give proof of what is incorrectly regarded as fidelity to another? In other words, I may make it a point of honour to perform certain actions which are to the advantage of another person, but in the last analysis my only real obligation is to myself.

Let us, however, notice that we are starting from a postulate here. We take it as a matter of course that fidelity to oneself is not only justifiable but that it is clearly discernible and that we know exactly of what it consists. Is this really so? In the first place, what is this self to whom I undertake to be faithful?

To take the case of the artist—a case to which it is always useful to refer because it presents us with a strictly identifiable datum, his work: in what sense or under what conditions can the artist be said to be faithful to himself? Supposing that he conscientiously sets to work to imitate himself, that he strives to reproduce certain processes which enabled him to obtain the "effects" to which he owed his first successes. Should we say that he is faithful to himself? Certainly not, because really, in so far as he labours to reproduce these same "effects," he ceases to be himself. Instead of an artist, he becomes a manufacturer. He loses his identity among the patented productions which he sets out to deliver to his customers in as large quantities as possible. Notice in passing, that if in the actual act of creation, the artist tends to become merged in his work and to identify himself with it temporarily, he is none the less bound to detach himself from it in some sort when it is accomplished. This does not in any way mean that he disowns it; between him and it there will always be a sensual bond, a bond of affection and pain. Nevertheless, he will only continue to be himself on condition that he breaks free from it to some extent. From this privileged case, then, it appears that to be faithful to myself is to respond to a particular inner call which enjoins me not to be hypnotised by what I have done, but on the contrary, to get clear of it, that is to say to go on living and thus find renewal. There is no doubt that outsiders are inclined to express surprise and to take exception to this renewal. The artist had been catalogued as a painter of still-life, why does he now paint seascapes or portraits? And why has he changed his style which it was so gratifying to recognise at the first glance? What treason! All this comes to the same as saying that in such a case fidelity is difficult to appreciate from outside. Only the artist himself can know whether he has responded to the inner call or whether on the contrary he has remained deaf to it. Even he can only know this to a certain degree; for here it is not just a question of good intentions or a good will. It is only by an always imperfect comparison between the accomplished work and the indistinct consciousness of the work to be accomplished that he can decide whether he has been faithful or not.

In spite of appearances, the question is not very different for man in general. If I admit without discussion that to be faithful to myself means to be faithful to certain principles which I have adopted once and for all, I am in danger of introducing into my life as foreign, and we can even say as destructive, an element as the artist who copies himself does. If I were absolutely sincere I should have to compel myself to examine these principles at frequent intervals, and to ask myself periodically whether they still correspond to what I think and believe. How is it possible not to mistrust the natural laziness which prompts me to place these principles above all possible discussion? In this way I spare myself the always disagreeable test of a revision of my opinions. It may quite well happen that these principles or these opinions end by covering up and stifling my own special reality; in that case, how am I to be faithful to myself? I am no longer there, I do not exist any more. I have really been replaced by a machine. Moreover, the action of social life helps to further this substitution of the automatic for the personal. I am known, I am classified as professing such and such an opinion, and thus I am sure of having my special place on the social chess-board. In upsetting the accepted judgment of myself, however, I should be regarded as inconsistent, people would no longer take me seriously. Now I like people to attach importance to what I say, I want my opinions to have weight. Thus society, with which a whole section of myself is in league, tends to deter me from proceeding with this inner revision, though I should consider myself bound to proceed with it if I did not contrive to lose contact with myself. Moreover, it goes without saying that the spirit of contradiction, which sometimes impels me to defy other people's opinion and to disconcert them deliberately, is no better than this mediocre conformity.

So, then, everything obliges us to recognise that fidelity to oneself is both difficult to achieve and to discern. In order to be faithful to oneself it is first of all necessary to remain alive, and that is precisely what it is not so easy to do. The causes within and without us which militate in favour of sclerosis and devitalisation are innumerable. But these words are not perfectly adequate; it would be better to say that I tend to become increasingly profane in relation to a certain mystery of my *self* to which access is more and more strictly forbidden me. I should add that this unquestionably comes about in so far as the child that I used to be, and that I should have remained were I a poet, dies a little more each day. This profane self is a deserter, having adopted the point of view of "the outsider." For such a self fidelity tends to be reduced to a stubbornly maintained agreement between myself and certain expressions, ideas, ways of living, to which I have fixed the label *mine*. But this agreement is only maintained at the expense of a certain intimacy, now broken and lost.

If, however, we make an honest enquiry, experience will force us to the paradoxical conclusion that the more I am able to preserve this intimacy with myself, the more I shall be capable of making real contact with my neighbour, and by neighbour I do not mean one of those depersonalised others whose jeers and censure I fear, but the particular human being I met at a definite time in my life and who, even though I may never see him again, has come for good into the personal universe which, as it were, wraps me round—my spiritual atmosphere, which, perhaps I shall take with me in death. But, inversely, the more I become a profane outsider to myself, the more I condemn myself to nothing but the falsehood and mockery, beloved of comic authors, in my relations with others.

It is therefore well to remember that contrary to what might have been expected, my self-presence (*présence à moi-même*) is not a fact which we can take for granted. The truth is rather that it is liable to be eclipsed and must constantly be reconquered. You may ask what this presence is, and what is the self to which it is so difficult to remain faithful. The reply would have to be that it is the particle of creation which is in me, the gift which from all eternity has been granted to me of participating in the universal drama, of working, for instance, to humanise the earth, or on the contrary to make it more uninhabitable. But when all is said and done, such definitions are bound to be fallacious; whoever has loved knows well that what he loved in the other cannot be reduced to describable qualities—and in exactly the same way the mystery of what I am in myself is the very thing about me which is only revealed in love.

There is then no valid reason for thinking that fidelity to oneself should be more intelligible than fidelity to another and should clearly come first. It seems much rather that the opposite is true. I am undoubtedly less immediately present to myself than is the person to whom I have given my word. "Yet," you may say, "does not my fidelity to another person inevitably come down to the fidelity which I have vowed to a particular idea I have formed of him, and is not this idea simply myself once more?" We must reply that such an opinion has been arrived at *a priori,* and that experience distinctly disproves it. Does it not happen every day that one being remains faithful to another, although he has been forced to admit that he had formed an idealised representation of him? Should we say in this case that it is because of his pride that he determines to be faithful in spite of everything, so that no one can say that circumstances have been too much for him? Such an interpretation, although it may be right in certain cases, does not account for genuine fidelity. Is it not true that the most faithful hearts are generally the most humble? Fidelity cannot be separated from the idea of an oath; this means that it implies the consciousness of something sacred. I give you an undertaking not to forsake you, and I regard this undertaking as increasingly sacred in proportion to the freedom with which I give it, added to your own lack of power to use against me should I break it. I know, moreover, that from the very fact that I have thus bound myself absolutely, the means will be surely given me to keep faith; for although this oath in its origin and essence is my act, or to go deeper, *because* it is my act, it has become the most unyielding obstacle there could possibly be to everything in me which tends towards weakening or dissolution.

I have not, however, the right to bind myself thus except in very rare cases, on the basis of an intuition by which it is given me to recognise that I ought and I wish to place myself at your disposal, not only without lowering myself in my own eyes, but, on the contrary, honouring and as it were exalting myself by this very act. Fidelity then and the oath which seals it cannot be coined, they cannot be vulgarised. Perhaps it should further be said that in fact fidelity can never be unconditional, except when it is Faith, but we must add, however, that it aspires to unconditionality. It is as though my oath were accompanied by this prayer: "May heaven grant that I shall not be led into temptation, that is to say that no event shall cause me to think myself authorised to deny my promise on the pretext that the implicit conditions on which it rests have been changed in a way I could not foresee when I made it." I cannot perhaps go beyond this prayer without presuming too much on my own strength: but still it must be really sincere, and I must maintain within myself the will to fight against this temptation if ever it assails me.

It is true in a general way to say that the quality of a being can be recognised and proved by the fidelity of which he is capable. Yet we might well add that there are probably indiscernible fidelities, and that not one of us is authorised to assert that another person is entirely unfaithful. Moreover, fidelity cannot be humanly exacted, any more than love or life. I cannot force another to reply to me, I cannot even force him in reason to hear me, and it will always be possible for me to think that if he does not reply it is because he has not heard me. In such a domain prescriptions cannot go beyond the *as if* (*comme si*), and only deal with behaviour. I charge you to behave towards me as though you had sworn fidelity to me. But it is impossible not to recognise the fragility of such a fiction. It is because fidelity is creative that, like liberty itself, it infinitely transcends the limits of what can be prescribed. Creative when it is genuine, it is so fundamentally and in every way, for it possesses the mysterious power of renewing not only the person who practices it, but the recipient, however unworthy he may have been of it to start with. It is as though it had a chance—it is certain that there is nothing final here—to make him at long last pervious to the spirit which animates the inwardly consecrated soul. It is in this way that fidelity reveals its true nature, which is to be an evidence, a testimony. It is in this way, too, that a code of ethics centred on fidelity is irresistibly led to become attached to what is more than human, to a desire for the unconditional which is the requirement and the very mark of the Absolute in us.

LE PEUCH*
March, 1942

* The locale in France where Marcel wrote this essay.

Bernard Häring

ESSENTIAL CONCEPTS OF
MORAL THEOLOGY*

I. Morality of Responsibility

Religion truly lived must have as essential characteristic the element of response. Response, responsibility, dialogue belong to religion essentially. We have religion only if man conceives of the Holy as a Power which advances toward him and to whom he can turn in dialogue. Religion and morality are not simply synonymous. Some elements of morality may well survive after religion has lost its vitality. Within the religious-ethical we can distinguish two grand types: the first springs from religion which animates it essentially; the second is given form and sanction by religion which is rather accessory and superimposed from without.

If religion essentially has the character of response and responsibility, it must follow that an ethic is truly religious only to the extent that it bears the mark of response. The pure type of religious ethic is of the nature of response, in which moral conduct is understood as response to the summons of a person who is holy, who is absolute. The prototype of the non-religious ethic is monologue rather than dialogue, and all moral tasks, norms, laws have their center and meaning in the human person

---

* From Bernard Häring, C.SS.R., *The Law of Christ*, Edwin G. Kaiser, C.P.P.S., trans. (Westminster, Md.: Newman Press, 1963), Vol. I, pp. 35-53. Used by permission. Father Häring is a contemporary German Catholic theologian.

and its perfection. Systems of religious ethics which in any way are centered in man himself are at best systems in which religion is superimposed. By setting up this standard of relation to religion, we can acquire a true insight into the type of the religious-ethic systems which prevail. Accordingly, we shall undertake the task of measuring and judging the essential nature of every religious ethic by the standard of the essential religious form which affects it.

i. RELIGION AS COMMUNITY OF PERSON IN WORD AND RESPONSE

For the Christian, religion is infinitely more than any sentiment. It is more than any need or experience, even more than "saving one's soul," striving for "happiness." It is fellowship with the living God. The reality of religion is not reached merely through concern for one's soul nor through profound self-absorption of the devout. Not even the glory and majesty of God give us religion. We come to the heart of religion only at the point of encounter between the word of God and the response of man. God and man in fellowship, in community, *Deus et anima* (God and the soul) in the trenchant phrase of Augustine, this is the essence of religion.

Religion is supported by two immovable pillars: God, the infinite personal God, and the finite created person, which is man. Religion also comprises two essential themes: God in the glory of His love and man in the favor of God's grace. True community of persons is possible only if two persons commune seriously, in deadly earnest. God takes man seriously, He speaks to man. This makes religion possible. The tremendous earnestness of God regarding man even to the point of sacrificing His only-begotten Son for him on the cross—this constitutes the superabundant treasure, the ineffable mystery of the true religion. In turn, man must take God seriously, God all-holy— this is the first demand of religion upon man.

Religion lies between two poles, man and God—an infinite distance between them. Where this essential diversity, this infinite distance between man and God is lost sight of and with it the transcendent holiness of God is made to disappear from our view, the essence of religion is lost, for where there is no encounter with the "Holy" there is no true religion. But religion ceases to exist also as soon as either of the two poles, even though it be the human one, is no longer taken seriously. For with this earnestness personal fellowship stands or falls.

As soon as the soul really encounters God, it reflects the splendor of His holiness. It has worth before God, a value which indeed is intimately entwined with this fellowship with God. The soul exults before the majesty of the all-holy God, not only adoration, but also in astonishment at the glance of divine love resting upon it. God is the soul's salvation. All the great dogmas of creation, Incarnation, and Redemption have as their theme, besides the glory of God, the salvation of the soul. When we chant and pray: *"Qui propter nos homines et propter nostram salutem descendit de coelis"* ("Who for us men and for our salvation descended from heaven"), we sing the jubilant hymn of our participation in the loving glory of God. God reveals His glory to us in the condescension of His love, his *agape,* and His holiness in the work of our salvation.

Deus et anima, God and the soul, the terrifying and beautifying mystery of the I-Thou communion between God and the soul is also the mystery of the Word of God. In the Word, the Logos, through the Word, and in the image of the Word we are created. In Christ the Word-made-man God comes to us and we to Him. (Man's likeness to God is the significant key word of moral theology!)

God speaks to us in words comprehensible to us. From the truth that our objective I-Thou intimacy with God flows from the Person, who is the Word of God, all the words which God directs to us, whether in the natural or supernatural revelation, assume an ineffable splendor and earnestness. Every word of God that is addressed to us comes from His will to establish the bond of fellowship and ultimately from the divine mystery of the Trinity. Every answer on our part affects our bond of unity with Him and the formation of the divine image in us.

2. FUNDAMENTAL ROLE OF PRAYER

All of this sheds a light on the fundamental role of prayer as an essential manifestation of religion. To pray is nothing less than to harken reverently to the Word of God and to attempt, however falteringly, to respond to it. Religion thrives on prayer because *religio* (bond with God) cannot exist without the Word of God and our power to respond. In the Second Person of the Trinity, the Word of the Father, religion has its source, and in the Word and our response it is exercised. The more deeply the religious man enters into the Word of God addressed to him and the more his life bears the stamp of response to God's Word, the more is his religion (*religio*), the bond with God, perfected and the divine likeness manifested within him.

Man is only then fully religious when the fellowship of his word with God has penetrated to that depth in which he regards his own person and his own salvation only from the standpoint of the loving will of God. And the concern for one's own salvation is no longer anything but the response, inspired by the breath of divine love, to the gracious offer of God's favor and beatitude. It follows, therefore, that Christian personalism does not culminate in the cult of one's own personality, but rather in the relation—the word-and-response relation between God all-holy and the soul called to salvation. Christian personalism is altogether different from any form of religion centering in the I. Ever open and receptive to the word of love, true personalism exists only in man's fellowship with God.

We can realize the true meaning of human personality only in the light of man's likeness to God. The more intimate the bond between man and God, the word-response relation, so much the more is the personality enriched and perfected as "image and likeness of God," who imparts in word and in love the glory of the intimate life of the Trinity. Religion as community with God is also the foundation of the human community, the genuine fellowship of persons. True community of men rests on word and love, and perfects itself in the dialogue of love. The capacity for word and love, which centers in the very heart of the

Thou, is fulfilled in us, however, only in so far as we are caught
up by the word and love of God and give to God our response
and love in return. Fellowship with God in word and love develops and fulfills our individual personality (the image of God
in us) and at the same time reveals our essentially social nature.
Therefore religious living, if it develops its own sound dynamic,
places us necessarily in the human community—the word-love
fellowship with our fellow men.

The expression "God and the soul," *Deus et anima,* must not
be construed in an individualistic sense. It is a monstrous error
on the part of Kierkegaard and many others with him to maintain that the religious life looses the bonds of community and
places the individual naked and alone before God! To be
pierced by the word of the divine love obviously means to be
liberated from the masses, from the namelessness and ano-
nymity of the flux of life. For in truth God calls us personally,
each by his own name. In His presence we find ourselves, but
we also find our neighbour and the way to fellowship and community. To come to God we must renounce chatter with men.
But in accepting the word of God directed to us we find the way
opened to the word-love relation with our neighbor. The Father
created all things in the Word (Jn 1:3). We enjoy community
with the Father in Christ the Incarnate Word. To be in Christ
means necessarily to be bound up with all those who have fellowship in Christ, who are called by Christ. Hence it belongs to
the essence of religious living that it place us in the community
with our neighbor because it is a life in Christ, the Incarnate
Word of God.

II. Morality as Fellowship:
Challenge and Responsibility

Our moral life must be nourished entirely and utterly on the
religious relation to God. Religion must not be looked upon as a
mere external aid and sanction to morality, but as its very spirit.

Only if it is imbued with religion, centered in the religious, can morality be correctly judged. The more fully it conforms to the basic laws of the religious, the more it is animated by the essential spirit of the religious, the more sound and wholesome will it be. In the following pages therefore we shall examine the most significant of the central moral concepts and key terms in the light of this criterion.

I. MORALITY OF SELF-PERFECTION AND RELIGIOUS ETHICS

Although the only rational basis and foundation for true morality is religion, there have been moral efforts and there are moral systems not primarily centered in religion or at least not based on the divine fellowship. What characterizes all these systems?—We immediately discard all "scientific" systems of ethics and all pragmatic methods of shaping human conduct which sacrifice the human person to the collective or to any other impersonal end, for they cannot form any serious basis of morality at all. They rather destroy morality. We can take up for serious consideration only the systems which recognize the value of the human person. They all agree in making it the duty of man to perfect himself. For Aristotle, for the Stoic, for Kant and Schleiermacher (to mention only a few), man himself and his own greatness form the foundation of ethics and constitute its goal.

Even though in many instances the existence of a personal God is not formally denied, nevertheless the human person and moral life are not centered in Him. To a degree these systems preserve the earnestness of morality, since they place man in a comprehensive framework of meaning, value, and law to which he must conform. But the ultimate in meaning and goal is always man and his own development and perfection: "The truly noble man never forgets his dignity. He never loses it in things which are inferior to him." The value of all values for him is his own soul, the preservation and development of the worth of his own person. Center of all these ethical systems is man himself. His moral obligation is self-perfection.

If religion exerts influence upon a previously accepted ethical attitude of this kind, the soul is raised to a higher realm of values. Once we have entered into the sphere of the religious, we no longer speak of mere self-perfection, but of salvation of our soul. No matter how extreme the difference between the Indian religious concept of self-purification and the Stoical ethic of self-perfection, the Hindu and all kindred religious orientations are basically nothing more than a projection of the anthropocentric ethic of self-perfection into the sphere of religion.

It is a simple fact that man must think in terms of "person." If God is not thought of as a person or at least if no fellowship is sought with Him, it must inevitably follow that the human person alone can occupy the center of attention. And this is true even when man seeks salvation in the escape from the personal, as in Indian pantheism. Whether the Indian seeks Nirvana as a positive beatitude of a soul which survives after death, or whether he seeks its extinction, the motivation and central meaning of all his asceticism and virtue is man, his own salvation.

Obviously, salvation of soul in the Christian sense is something altogether different. It is not a blessed solitude of existence nor a blissful absorption into an impersonal essence, but loving community with the living God. For this very reason even the Aristotelian or Stoic concepts of self-perfection cannot consistently remain projected into an essentially Christian morality. This means that concern for one's salvation may not be centered in self-perfection. The Christian religion as personal fellowship with God cannot tolerate man as center and focal point of ethics.

Viewed in the perspective of religion, the human person can be understood only from the standpoint of personal community and fellowship with God. Nevertheless, as a matter of fact, at least at the beginning of the religious life things are usually different. Particularly the man who at first directed his moral efforts predominantly toward his own perfection is all too readily inclined, once he turns to religion, to seize on it as a means to perfect himself and save his own soul. Instead of viewing religion in the proper perspective as first of all a loving community with God and seeking this in fellowship, he sees in it and seeks in it the furtherance and assurance of his own salvation, which flows from such fellowship. If one continues in this attitude, consciously or unconsciously, he closes to himself the surest and deepest approach to God. He disregards the keystone of religion, the holiness of God, which can never be a means to anything, only the end. He loses the sense of loving communion which leads us to eternal bliss only if we seek it first and above all else.

Some may object: it is evident that God's glory and loving homage to Him are central in our religious relation to God, but our moral effort is simply directed to man and his salvation! In reply we stress that the effort is indeed concerned with man. This we cannot deny. But must not this very concern for man ultimately be also a concern about God, about obedience to Him, abiding in His love, the coming of His kingdom?

The greatest hazard to genuine religious life arises from making man its center, from viewing all divine worship and all communion with God primarily from the standpoint of the profit it brings to man. But even in the strictly religious activity where such hazard is avoided, there still lurks the danger of a fatal dichotomy between worship and the moral life. Prayer and sacrifice on the one hand have their center and meaning in the divine fellowship, and the moral life is more or less independent —something parallel to or alongside of it—with its ultimate goal man and his salvation. Inevitably the religious and moral life will be estranged and divorced or the man-centered moral orientation will lead to anthropocentric orientation of religion.

The efforts of non-religious man to perfect himself, we must note, are not worthless. They have, in fact, a positive value, at least as long as religion is not dismissed as meaningless. And this positive value can be coordinated with the religious orientation, but not without being reformed, Christianized. In some manner it must be removed from its previous non-religious moorings. To be truly embodied in the realm of the sacred, it must be placed in the service of holiness.

Ultimately morality and religion must have the same center: community and fellowship with God. This is true both for the scientific presentation of the Christian moral doctrine and for popular instruction and preaching. But unfortunately both the one and the other were too often, especially after the days of the Enlightenment, a continuation of Aristotle (self-perfection) rather than of the Gospel (the sovereignty of God).

We cite only one example chosen from among many: Anthony Koch, a highly esteemed moralist of the Tuebingen school, makes the following significant remark in his moral theology: "Whereas dogmatic theology concerns itself with the nature of God and His external works, with Christ and His Redemptive work, moral teaching has man for its object in as much as it shows him the way prescribed by God to reach his eternal goal."[1] "The aim of moral life is consequently the eternal perfection and the beatitude flowing from it."[2] "According to Catholic moral theology happiness is the goal of all moral endeavor."[3] It is true that this view is poles apart from that of Aristotle, for the simple reason that the Christian cannot attain happiness through his own unaided efforts, but depends for it entirely on God and community of life with God. But precisely because this is presented as something merely accessory or even in a measure extrinsic, or we might say as an afterthought, as though the living friendship with God was only an essential means for the full attainment of the moral purpose—it is evident that the concept of self-perfection or external happiness and salvation cannot be the sound and appropriate foundation for a religious moral system.

Instead of having as its foundation the dialogue between God and man, this system is on the level of the monologue—man to himself and within himself—scheme of morality. Or it is at best, when measured by the standard of the essence of true religion, imperfect dialogue. Dialogue between man and God, word and response, is not basic and essential in this system, but accessory and secondary, something super-added to the monolithic morality centering in man.

2. COMMANDMENT, LAW, AND ETHICS OF RESPONSE

Commandment and law are and always must be central ideas in the Christian moral teaching. The sermon or instruction on the commandments must be God-centered and at the same time dialogical; this is to say, essentially based on the dialogue between man and God, on the word and response, for the simple reason that *commandment* is an entirely religious concept. God Himself prefaced the promulgation of the commandments on Sinai with the twofold theme of religion: His sovereign majesty and His revelation of love: "I am the Lord thy God, who brought thee out of the land of Egypt, out of the house of bondage" (Ex 20:2). The commandments of God are words of the divine Love addressed to us, expressed in the great command of love. And true fulfillment of the command is the obedient response of love, obedient love.

As the ethic of commandment, so the ethic of law in its very concept is religious, founded on the response of man to God. It is true that the concept of natural law as the expression of the order of creation is directly borrowed from the moral philosophy of the Stoics. But Christian ethics, above all in the thought of Augustine, purged it of all impersonal and fatalistic elements. For Augustine, law is the expression of the all-holy essence and will of God. It is engraved in every human heart by God Himself as appeal and invitation, altogether personal and addressed to every man. Nevertheless, the explanation and enunciation of Catholic moral doctrine in sermon and instruction did not altogether escape the influence of the Nominalistic interpretation of commandment nor of the rationalistic-Kantian concept of law. We must conclude that, since the commandment in the Nominalistic doctrine is not based on the all-holy nature or essence of God, but only on the sovereign will of God, all inquiry into its intrinsic foundation and beauty is devoid of meaning. In fact, such inquiry would bear the obvious and dangerous implication that the less evident the intrinsic value of the commandment, the more meritorious and praiseworthy it would be to obey it.

We do not at all deny that particular instances of this type of obedience can be fruitful, provided of course that the superior's authority and intent are evident. An example is the Biblical instance of the obedience of Abraham! But what if we were to make a rule of the exception? The result would be incalculable loss in the sphere of value, which ultimately would be discerned exclusively in the light of obedience. And eventually even this very virtue of obedience itself would be lost, since it would no longer enter into the sphere of all values and influence them. Such obedience places man in the presence of God, surely, but not in the full fellowship of the word and of love. For such fellowship is granted only when the summons of the divine word is accepted lovingly with all its wealth of meaning by man and lovingly answered. But it would be really hazardous, constituting an extreme danger to true morality, if a Nominalistic conception of law would lead us to exact blind obedience to mere men without concern for the right order of things to which all commandments and commands must conform.

A conception of this kind demanding obedience to commandment is sometimes found linked with the subjectivistic ethic of self-perfection (though not correctly nor legitimately). Sometimes unreflecting and implicit obedience is extolled as the best and safest means of perfecting one's self. It does not appear too disturbing that in the process objective right and good may be lost through the act of blind obedience: "How happy the obedience which assures our salvation of soul and absolves us from all responsibility!" But what of the Kingdom of God in all this? It is quite clear that such a development of the doctrine of obedience to authority is not imbued with the spirit of loving fellowship. It is not based on the word of God with the loving response, not on the loving community with God and fellow-man.

It is characteristic of our present day moral teaching that, by contrast with the "ethic of law," it shows a marked preference for the subjective correctness of interior disposition rather than the pure and simple objective observance of the commandment, but—we make the point—do we not often forget that subjective correctness consists precisely in the endeavor to do with all devotion that which is right and good in itself? Ethic of right disposition and inner spirit must be wedded to the ethic of commandment. In this way both preserve their true and genuine dialogue. On the one hand, an ethic of disposition which is not truly genuine because it labors under the spell of a subjective ideal of self-perfection will poison morality more completely than any system which combines self-perfection with obedience of the kind just described. Still, such obedience, since it is not pervaded with the sense and beauty of what is prescribed, cannot bear the stamp of personal responsibility or at least is little affected by it.

The Kantian-rationalistic way of thinking robs the morality of law of its dialogical mould in another way. Under the spell of the universal validity of the law, the man of the Kantian cast of mind overlooks the force of law as affecting the individual in each instance. He views law as an abstract absolute which dominates the whole order of creation. He ignores the particular powers and endowments of each individual and the circumstances of each each situation, although God manifests His will through these just as truly as He does through universal law. The law in its most universal form is presented as the sole and adequate expression of the divine will. But in reality the laws of reason are only abstractions which are totally incapable of reflecting the richness of the concrete individual. Even the positive divine laws, for the greatest part, embody only the minimum requirements. Their very prohibitive and negative formulation is ample evidence of this point. As far as they have reference to the call to virtue in each individual, they are only the first step to right understanding which is the exclusion of error and misconceptions. A moral system content with a morality of law which is exclusively abstract and universal leads to impoverishment of morality, implicit legal minimalism, and moral sterility.

Under the influence of Kantian theory, conscience descends to the level of logical function. Just as the moral life is confined to observance of universal law, so conscience is reduced to a

mere syllogistic application of universal to the particular instance. No one denies, of course, that the individual instance
reflects the universal norm and is bound by it. But it is surely
deplorable if the concrete particular realities and possibilities
for good are scorned. The deeper and richer the moral life of a
man, the more he is brought to a realization and appreciation of
concrete individual and personal values with the obligation they
impose. He learns that the talent given us by God may not be
buried nor hidden. It must be used.

In genuine personal religious morality, man is not confronted
by universal law (though, of course, it exists). But God calls
man personally, as he is able to perceive from the special gifts
and endowments and from the circumstances of the particular
situation in which he lives. Obviously knowledge of the universal law must preserve him from seeing his own self-interest in
the law. But vital morality demands more than mere acquaint-
ance with the norms of law; it demands the fine delicacy of
tactful conscience, the sense for the particular and special,
which goes beyond mere knowledge of law. This is prudence.

Law in the Kantian concept intervenes as an impersonal
power between God and the human conscience. Indeed it is
unfortunate that there is a melancholy reality within us which
corresponds to this rationalistic ethic of law. Deep down within
fallen man is a radical tendency to conceive of himself and his
existence, not in relation to God, not after the manner of dialogue with God, but entirely in relation to self, after the manner
of monologue. To be redeemed means to live in intimacy with
God, to know and love the will of God our Father. But for the
"unredeemed," God is a "stranger." And God's law is alien,
dead!

In fact, God finally becomes so much a stranger to him that
he no longer sees God, but only the law. There remains only the
"alien," impersonal law. In this fashion the law of the "alien"
God is transformed into an impersonal principle. Enslaved by
the dead law, which he himself brought to its death, the unredeemed seeks his salvation in this, he endeavors to adopt as his
own law this alien law which still, though remotely, refers to

God. He seeks to make his own law, a law indeed which looks only to man.

True personalism and authentic moral of law are in living dialogue with God. The "personalism" of fallen man and his law do not transcend the "monologue" of the I itself. In consequence, the law no longer leads to the living God of religion, but comes between God and the soul. An ethic of law in the "Kantian" sense will inevitably increase this peril lurking in original sin.

3. MORALITY OF RESPONSIBILITY

The foregoing should be sufficient evidence that in our work the terms *salvation of soul, commandment* and *law* do not suffer any loss of meaning. Such terms and their concepts will retain their full value. However, none of them is the focal center of Catholic moral teaching. To our mind the term *responsibility* understood in its religious sense is the more apt; even from the mere standpoint of etymology the word designates the personal-essential characteristic of religion. It apparently is the most apposite to express the personal relation between God and man —which is the I and Thou relation—of word and response— specifically God's word calling and inviting man and the human decision in response of acceptance. The word also refers directly to man's likeness to God. Hence responsibility means that in a community between man and God, man responds to God's word with the responsibility of his personal decision and action. But we must make a point of the distinction between the purely religious and the religious-moral relation between man and God. This is necessary to preserve the distinctive character of morality as responsibility.

a. RELIGIOUS LIFE AS RESPONSE TO THE WORD OF GOD

Religion consists of word and response. In the eternal Word, God draws nigh to us. In Christ the Incarnate Word we enter into community with God. Only in the light of the word and response relation with God in such fellowship can we under-

stand the three divine virtues. For they are surely more than a
turning to God Himself. Essentially they are also a drawing
nigh to His Word given to us, to all the words of truth, of the
promises, of love. Since in this world God does not reveal Himself to us through vision, face to face, but "only" in His Word,
so it is that only progressively do we develop in our response to
His Word, through growth in Christ, the Word, and thereby in
fellowship with God.

The virtue of religion is our response to the majesty of God,
our Creator and Father revealing Himself to us in the word (Jn
1), to the glory of Redemption which envelops us in Christ, in
the Church, in the sacraments. This virtue is differentiated from
the theological virtues in that it includes external acts. But it is
focused on these divine virtues because by its very existence it
must turn to God. It looks to the moral virtues because it is
responsible for something of our true pattern of life. In fact,
that which is most essential in the fabric of our living depends
on the virtue of religion, namely, whether the worship of God is
accorded its rightful place in our private and public life. Is the
divine cult afforded the time and place for its correct formation
and manifestation so that all visible creation is directed to the
glory of God?

b. Moral Life as Responsibility

The other moral virtues are more sharply differentiated from
the theological virtues than is the virtue of religion. They do not
essentially and necessarily,[4] and never immediately or directly,
look to God, respond to God. They have to do with the fulfillment of created order, with created persons, goods, and values.
Since they are directly concerned with created order, they are
not in the full religious sense of the word response and responsibility. Response assumes that there is a person to whom response is made. The character of dialogue, response and responsibility to God, comes only when they penetrate through
created order to God.

The believer detects in the order of creation the message of
the Lord and Creator; the child of God hears in all things the

word of His Father. He is sustained by the inner vital bond of the three divine virtues with the inner word and response. In community and fellowship with God through this word and response of the divine virtues, his responsibility to God is expressed in religious response to God. From this it is evident that the term *respons*-ibility is best suited to express the interpenetration and formation of the moral through the religious, and also the distinction of the two.

To bring this distinction into clearer relief, we must stress the following points: the moral order is concerned with the fulfillment of the order of creation. It is response to God, the correct response precisely to the extent that man takes his terrestrial tasks seriously, and earnestly accepts created values.

The very core of moral decision is the spirit of obedience to God. It is saying yes to God's will. But this decision is essentially more than a simple or lighthearted saying yes or no to God. It proceeds much further in a personal effort to discover the proper response which should be made to God. It is the hazard and venture of response itself, or, shall we say, it is daring to answer God. The moral decision requires humble and docile attention to the will of God our Creator and Father from the very beginning, but often it is completed by faltering or bold hazard of choice among a multitude of possibilities that lie open before us. In this manner man bears the responsibility for his free decision in his own particular situation. His response is his responsibility.

One cannot evade this responsibility toward God through recourse to human authority. One is accountable for his obedience as well as for his disobedience, though in a different manner. No one has the right to shoulder the responsibility of outright refusal of the assistance which God offers through authority, through community, through prudent counselors in seeking to discover the divine will. But even the seeking of counsel and the actual obedience to authority can never serve as excuse for shirking personal responsibility. These cannot be viewed as exemption from responsibility, but only as the exhausting of all available possibilities in preparation for the decision for which one is altogether accountable. Naturally one is particularly responsible for non-obedience to lawful authority. One must carefully probe his own motives to assure himself that he is truly disinterested and unselfish in any such decision. Moreover, one must carefully weigh the consequences of the decision in so far as they concern and affect the community. Refusal to obey can never be justified without a clear perception of all that is involved in the case. Particularly important in obedience to human authority is this very bearing on community and the responsibility to society. This should always be a matter of serious reflection, most particularly when there is justification for non-compliance.

Every moral act involves accountability before God and responsible cultivation of a value which has an appeal for some individual. But it is much more. The moral act is always in greater or less measure weighted with responsibility toward our neighbor and toward the natural and supernatural community in which we live and upon which our individual moral decisions and our whole religious-moral life react. The mystery of the Mystical Body of Christ makes us fully conscious of this truth. To be in fellowship with God through the Word, to be in Christ the Incarnate Word, implies that we are immediately united with all the other members of the Body of Christ and act in immediate communion with them.

In every moral decision and, above all, when his moral integrity is endangered, man senses that his response to God involves his very existence, his salvation. Moral conduct can never be freed from the bond of obligation. In the moral act the person must be answerable to himself. The final judgment will be the eventual revelation in the presence of God of this very responsibility of the individual to himself. This aspect of responsibility, of course, belongs to the actual religious act in the same way. In fact, in the religious act man is more immediately aware that his salvation depends on giving the right response to the Word of God all-holy. Both areas belong to moral theology. It has as its object the religious life and activity as well as the whole sphere of religious moral responsibility.

4. RESPONSIBILITY AND PERSONAL SALVATION

Even though we refuse to see in self-perfection and salvation of soul the central concept of Christian morality, but place it rather in the idea of "responsibility," nevertheless we should not forget that under a certain aspect our personal salvation occupies the first place in our responsibility. It takes precedence absolutely over all the impersonal values for which we are accountable, though not over the Kingdom of God as a whole and the salvation of our neighbor. However, we are more responsible for our own salvation than for that of others. Responsibility of each individual for himself exceeds in a measure his co-responsibility for his neighbour, because he has immediate free control of his own will alone. Responsibility and freedom of will, however, are in close interdependence. So we are most accountable for what is most subject to our own voluntary acts. Hence we may and must take direct and immediate care of the salvation of our own souls. And a great number of acts may be subordinated and directed to this goal, for example, discipline of will and ascetic exercises.

Our occupation with all the passing things of this life may be viewed at least partially under this aspect (even though it is not the supreme aspect). But it would be an error to subordinate our co-responsibility for our neighbor and the Kingdom of God to ourselves and to the care for our own personal worth and value. Because the former are not intrinsically inferior in value to our own personal salvation, it follows that our moral endeavor ought not to subordinate, but rather coordinate them and hold them equal to our salvation in striving for eternal happiness (cf. the first section in volume three). However, it must never be overlooked that the common center of all values is God, the love of communion with Him, responsibility before Him.

In the hierarchy of values in the Christian moral teaching, as just outlined, the thought of our own salvation and personal sanctification may not appear so prominently as in the popular instruction and preaching on the moral life. However, the urgency of our own salvation is merely increased by being viewed in relation to the more central idea of morality. Finally, one very important point should not be lost sight of. The formation of the moral-religious takes place by slow degrees and continuous growth. The great masters of the spiritual life attribute this progress precisely to the progressive subordination of self, with the I viewed more and more in the light of its proper position in the whole scale of values. From the very outset the spiritual director must have a clear view of the absolute hierarchy of values. But he must also take into consideration the actual spiritual condition of the soul he directs: what is its present degree of perfection? What forces and motives are available in each concrete instance for the most effective promotion of spiritual advancement?

The moral sermon or moral directive intended for beginners, or even for those estranged from God, which neglects the prudent appeal to man's craving for happiness and his legitimate concern for his own salvation, may well prove a tragic failure! Desire for happiness and morality are not identical—we hope that we have made the point clear—but they do belong to each other. Desire for happiness is the grand ally of the moral *ought;* often no other appeal can be heard in the desolation and abyss of sin into which the soul has been plunged. Or should we say it is the last faint echo of God's call to obedience and love?

In the moral sermon as well as in our personal moral effort we must keep the entire goal in mind from the very beginning: our total conversion to God. But in each instance we must present the motives which are calculated to prove the most effective in the concrete circumstances. The clarion call to "save your soul" may not be perverted into an invitation to egotistic and egocentric moral-religious effort. It must be the true call to response and responsibility in God's sight. The call to salvation must be an appeal to the entire breadth and depth of the soul's moral endeavor. But it must be clearly understood that the immediate legitimate interest in self, the unrest of the soul far from God, is like a tiny crevice through which the heavenly light can penetrate to the soul imprisoned in sin.

Finally, it is scarcely possible for us pilgrims in this earthly sojourn to attain a degree of perfection in love in which the innate desire for happiness need not be called upon to assist our progress as the ally of our love.[5] The unrest in our souls is not yet love of God but rather the mainspring which tautens the powers of the soul for the movement of love. God Himself sets this force at work by drawing the soul to divine love through a holy fear and hope. Happiness and self-perfection constitute a moral goal, but not the sole and ultimate one. Legitimate interest in one's own salvation is like the lever of Archimedes. It can raise the soul from the false basis of self to the true and lofty level of hope whence it can turn to God. But from the very outset it must be clearly realized that we are concerned with an important aim indeed, though not with the final goal. The fulcrum is only the means of reaching the higher level! The alarm is only to alert one to the danger and should not be confused with the actual message it calls to our attention.

III. Responsibility and Imitation of Christ

The object and purpose of moral theology is not involved in the philosophical analysis of "responsibility" nor in the explanation of the term. And it is equally certain that it is not the function of the moral sermon or instruction to offer such an analysis. Their purpose is to present the rich and vital content of the history of salvation and our loving fellowship with God in Christ. The word *responsibility* merely reflects something essential in all this. All the requirements arising from the foregoing considerations on responsibility are abundantly fulfilled in a moral teaching which has our community with Christ as center, in a moral teaching on the Kingdom of Christ and on the imitation of Christ. In a moral teaching based on the imitation of Christ, the essential characteristics of religion as fellowship with God in Christ. The word *responsibility* merely reflects something essential in all this. All the requirements arising from the

foregoing considerations on responsibility are abundantly fulfilled in a moral teaching which has our community with Christ
as center, in a moral teaching on the Kingdom of Christ and on
the imitation of Christ. In a moral teaching based on the imitation of Christ, the essential characteristics of religion as fellowship with God, and morality as responsibility before God, are
entirely in the foreground.

The foundation for the imitation of Christ is the incorpora-
tion of the disciple in Christ through grace. Imitation of Christ
in our lives is accomplished through activity of love and obedience in objective union with Christ. Imitation binds us to the
word of Christ: in His grace, in the gift of love, Christ binds
us to Himself. In love we unite ourselves with His Person, the
Incarnate Word. Our obedience unites us with Him through the
following of His example eloquently inviting us to imitate Him.
In obeying Him, we make of every word flowing from His
sacred lips a bond of union with Him. For the true disciple
receives the word of Christ, actively fulfilling it in his life on his
own responsibility and in his own individuality, according to his
own unique possession of particular gifts and endowments be-
stowed on him with all self-accountability in the sight of God.

To be in Christ means to be incorporated into His Kingdom.
To be a member in the Kingdom of Christ (in the Body of
Christ) demands of us the responsibility of active participation.
We in our own person, with all our individual powers, must
assert ourselves for the Kingdom of Christ, for our neighbor.
Imitation of Christ bears with it the concept and notion of
responsibility. We cannot speak of the imitation of Christ with-
out implying responsibility for every soul redeemed by Christ,
without proclaiming responsibility for service in the Kingdom of
Christ.

Neither the natural ideal of personal perfection nor the
supernatural ideal of personal salvation is simply central for the
disciple of Christ, but they are best attained through following
the Master. It is true that the disciple does not see in the imitation a mere means to save his soul. Yet when seen in the light of
our Saviour's love, salvation becomes a matter of tremendous

importance. The disciple who at first looked to the promises of the Master rather than to His immense love learns in following Christ to see his own soul in a new light, to love his soul in a new way, namely, in the love for the Master. Now our love for ourselves rests in the love of the Master for us and in our love for Him. Salvation of souls now appears in the splendor of God's loving glory and the beauty of His kingdom.

Christian moral teaching, it is evident, is not anthropocentric. It does not center in man. Nor is it theocentric in a sense alien to man and foreign to his world. It centers in grace-endowed fellowship of man with God, in the dialogue of word and response, in "responsibility." Only if it is centered in Christ does our moral life possess the worth of response made to God, for Christ is the Word in whom the Father seeks and calls us. Our loving obedience in the imitation of Christ is the echo, the image, the participation in the triune, eternal life of God, in the Word and the response of love.

It is possible for us to follow Christ, to imitate Him, because He is the "Word" in whom our likeness to God rests and through whom it has been wonderfully restored by the Redemption. In the fulfillment of the imitation, our likeness to God becomes manifest. And just as all discussion about an image refers back to the original or prototype which has been copied, so too must moral theology direct the Christian life in all points to the Word or Logos, the divine pattern in whom and through whom man made to the divine image lives and to whom he can respond.

NOTES

[1] A. Koch, *Lehrbuch der Moraltheologie* (3 ed.; Freiburg, 1910), 3.
[2] *Ibid.*, 11.
[3] *Ibid.*, 8.
[4] The term as used here is phenomenological and is not intended to be understood in a metaphysical sense of essence or in a metaphysical sense of exigence.
[5] Saint Bernard, *Liber de diligendo Deo,* Cap. XV. PL 182, 998.

"Imprimis ergo diligit seipsum homo propter se. . . . Cumque videt per se non subsistere posse, Deum quasi sibi necessarium incipit per fidem inquirere et diligere. Diligit itaque in secundo gradu Deum, sed propter se, non propter ipsum. . . . Gustato quam suavis est Dominus transit ad tertium gradum, ut diligat Deum non jam propter se, sed propter ipsum. Sane in hoc gradu statur: et nescio, si a quoquam hominum quartus in hac vita perfecte apprehenditur, ut se scilicet diligat homo tantum propter Deum." But for Saint Bernard it is essential to "caritas" as a divine virtue at least to strive for this fourth degree of love. (Freely translated the words of Saint Bernard are as follows: "Therefore in the first place man loves himself for his own sake. . . . However, when he finds that he cannot subsist of himself alone, he begins to search for God as necessary for himself. He begins to inquire through faith and to love. Thereby he loves God in the second degree, but for himself, not for God's own sake. But once having tasted how sweet God is he passes on to the third degree of love, so that he loves God no longer on account of himself, but for God's own sake. In this degree of love he remains, and I doubt if any one can be found in this life who has attained the fourth degree of love, so that he loves himself only on account of God.")

II

ON BEING RESPONSIBLE IN SPEECH

INTRODUCTION

Should we always tell the truth? No doubt all of us were brought up with clear instructions to do so. Yet many of us may also recall occasions when we told a "white lie" or held back information that was requested, occasions which resulted in punishment by parents or teachers. Even at an early age we began to notice a difference between lying to save ourselves and a reluctance to implicate others. While telling the truth might be right, we already knew that tattling was also wrong. Some colleges have established their disciplinary system on the obligation each student assumes to tell the truth. Such honesty not only includes the promise not to cheat, oneself, but the obligation to report others who have cheated. Under such systems students are called upon to police each other, and the "honor" system requires them to be both judge and accuser. Some students feel that being responsible in speech may not always accord so simply with the "truth" as such systems would assume.

Professional life provides many instances in which the question of truthtelling becomes at least as complex as it is in student life. Professors write references for their students: are they obliged to tell all the pertinent facts that they know? If they do, they may well put the student at a disadvantage for getting into graduate school or for obtaining a position in education, industry or government. If they do not, the student may be unable to meet the expectations aroused by the recommendation. Not only does the student in question suffer, but the future value of faculty judgment is compromised.

Are physicians obligated to tell all that they know about the prognosis of an illness to the patient? To his family? To whom

111

does such information rightly belong? Joseph Fletcher, in *Morals and Medicine,* 1954, argues that the information belongs to the patient and that he has a right to know what the prognosis is. Further, if he discovers that information is being withheld, or wrong information is being given him, the relationship of personal trust between patient and doctor is jeopardized. From the physician's point of view there might be several reasons for not giving the prognosis to the patient. He might judge that the knowledge would have a debilitating psychological effect, which in turn could have ramifications for the patient's health. In instances where the basis for making the prognosis is not scientifically certain, he might wish to withhold information because of the tentative character of his judgment. What does telling the truth mean in such situations? Is it simply a one-to-one correlation between the words used and the actual matter at hand as one perceives them? Or is there involved in truthtelling a relationship with others that has greater value than this "maximum verbal veracity," which sets the issue of responsible speech in a wider interpersonal context?

There are instances in which simple truthtelling may not only disrupt relations with others, but endanger their lives as well. According to international agreements, prisoners-of-war are required to give only their names, ranks, and serial numbers to their enemy captors. But through brainwashing and torture efforts are made to get prisoners to disclose all that they know. Certainly the prisoner is under no moral obligation to inform the enemy of positions, strength of weapons, and planned movements just because he is asked for them. Most persons would agree that there is a moral obligation to withhold such information, and would even agree that suicide, as the ultimate way of resisting such pressure, can be an honorable course.

There are also quite different experiences. People may be told only what those who have access to information think they have a right to know. When they discover that they have purposely been misinformed about situations over a long period of time, a "credibility gap" arises. In national life this can become a major problem. During the "Bay-of-Pigs" operation in 1961, when the American CIA developed plans for an invasion of Cuba, there were a number of newspaper accounts indicating that some such build-up was in progress, not only in the United States, but in Central America as well. Yet there were official denials of invasion intentions. The failure of that invasion and the complications involved in both its planning and its execution, became the first serious crisis in President John F. Kennedy's administration. There was indignation because official spokesmen lied to the public; there was further indignation because the qualms of the administration led to a weakening of the will to pursue the task undertaken. Were the official denials morally justified? The argument goes on.

The Vietnam war has introduced the term "credibility gap" into the American vocabulary. Those who assert its existence point to the many occasions when the public has been assured by officials that good progress was being made in the war, that American involvement would not increase but would diminish, that a resolution of the conflict was in sight. When none of these things occur, disbelief begins to spread about the trustworthiness of what is being said by government officials about the war. One can respond in various ways. One can say that the government knows best and that its officials are entitled to make serious mistakes, to withhold information from the public, and to misinform the public in order to pursue the course of official policies. Or one can become cynical and take everything officially stated "with a grain of salt" just as one learns to discount the official reports of enemy casualties. (Recall the claims made by the Arab states of the destruction of the Israeli Air Force during the early hours of the Arab-Israel war in June, 1967, only to have that "destroyed" air force itself retaliate in devastating attacks on the Arabs.) Or a pervasive mood of doubt can spread not only in the minds of individual citizens but across a nation. If official reports time and time again prove to be wrong by a vast margin of error, whom is one to believe? When are officials to be believed, and when not? If one cannot believe what is said about a war, can one believe what is said about other things by the same people? Distrust begins to replace confidence, and regardless of what excuses or justifications are given for past misstatements, the expectations of honesty have been shattered. The effects of this on a society can be as serious as the effects on a friendship when one person discovers that the other is making a practice of lying. Stability and confidence in human relationships depend heavily on the reliability of the words of people.

Genuine veracity may also entail an appreciation of the meaning our words convey, a meaning not always expressed by a strict adherence to local usage. For example, on a recent trip to England a man at a London station information desk was asked if a certain train went to Durham. He was assured that it did. But as the train sped through Durham on to Newcastle he realized that though the train did indeed go there, it did not stop there. Was this simply a difference in usage of words? Or did the agent know that the import of the question had been evaded?

The readings in this section were selected to provide an understanding of some of the different points of view regarding the responsible use of words. The reader will find it instructive to reflect upon the issues of truthtelling in the light of the readings in Part I. Is one always under an obligation to obey the rule, "You should tell the truth," and to interpret that rule as strict correspondence between what one says and what one knows to be the case, regardless of the consequences? This would appear to be an extreme instance of what H. Richard Niebuhr describes as the ethics of man-the-citizen, of a deontological or rule ethic. Immanuel Kant's famous essay, "On the Supposed Right to Lie from Altruistic Motives," points toward this position, and in part provides the provocation of the materials included in this section from Bonhoeffer and Paul Lehmann. If one is not obligated to obey the rule to "tell the truth" at all costs, does one have the right to decide what he will say with reference to certain "good" ends? If so, truth becomes relative to its utility in achieving a particular end. Man-the-maker would be the model at work. A salesman would have a right to "lie" about his product in order to make a sale. A patient's family physician would have the right to tell him he is going to recover fully even when he knows that are no grounds for such hopes, in order to "keep up his spirit." A prisoner-of-war would have the right to lie about his unit, its arms, and its movements to his interrogators in order to protect them. A government would have the right to misinform the people about what is really going on in a war in order to keep up their morale and to gain support for its policies.

Again, responsible speech may be framed in light of one's particular relationship at a particular time. In such a case, words are relative to what is "fitting" in the moment. Man becomes the answerer, the responder. What is fitting, however, as we noted in the Introduction to Part I, is relative to the values one holds. If one considers openness between persons the most important, one will avoid words that would impair it. Or if one were seeking to establish a relationship, the choice of words would be in accord with what would engender and nourish such a relation. The readings from Bonhoeffer and Lehmann point in this direction, though with important differences between them.

One might propose that we are obligated to tell the truth in the more rigorous and literal fashion except in those instances in which there is a serious justification for the violation of the rule. It is taken as a matter of course in human relationships that others accept responsibility for having their words accord with what is actually the case. Human interaction and discourse rest on the assumption that others are normally obeying the rule. This is true both for the speaker and the hearer: the speaker need not decide in a highly deliberative way what is the right thing to say in normal occasions, and the hearer need not ask self-consciously whether he is being deceived. If ethical theory is to take account of both what is the case and what ought to be the case in moral action, such common experiences make it difficult to accept any theory that asserts that every action is unique and no general rules can be formulated.

Kant writes, "Truthfulness in statements which cannot be avoided is the formal duty of an individual to everyone, however great may be the disadvantage accruing to himself or to another." This is no arbitrary rule, but is based on his claim, "For a lie always harms another; if not some other particular man, still it harms mankind generally, for it vitiates the source of the law itself." Embodied here is the pressure toward universality that is present in Kant's moral philosophy: "Act as though the maxim of your action were by your will to become a universal law of nature." We are admonished to imagine what would happen if every one acted according to the principle that is now governing our actions: if we choose to lie, we ought to think about what would happen if everyone decided to lie, at least under similar circumstances. But Kant recognizes that certain steps have to be taken in order accurately to apply such general principles to particular cases. These steps, however, can never contain exceptions to the rules. "Such exceptions would nullify their universality, and that is precisely the reason that they are called principles."

For Bonhoeffer, as the selection in Part I indicates, the moral life is conformity to reality, and reality is understood as being created and redeemed in Christ. Reality has to do with concrete relationships in specific situations. Morality is not conformity to abstract principles. Truth refers not simply to "veracity" but to relationships between myself and others. "If my utterance is to be truthful it must in each case be different according to whom I am addressing, who is questioning me, and what I am speaking about. The truthful word is not in itself constant; it is as much alive as life itself." The primary reference for the word truth has shifted from veracity to human relationships. One might choose to use different words to express these different functions of language for the different references or contexts, but Bonhoeffer opts for the word truth in both cases. But Bonhoeffer's more contextual or situational approach is no invitation to a cynical concept of truth, to use words lightly for whatever ends one desires. Rather, there is a theologically and morally normative reference to which words are to be conformed, namely the whole of reality as it has been created and redeemed in Christ. It appears, then, that Bonhoeffer is inviting us to a more demanding and more difficult consideration of what constitutes responsible speech rather than an easier one. Responsible speech refers to that which builds up and sustains the kinds of relationships God has created for man, the kinds of relationships God's will to redemption requires.

Both Bonhoeffer and Paul Lehmann have theological grounds upon which their less rigoristic notions of responsible speech rest. Lehmann's primary theological principle is that God is acting to make and keep human life human, that is, He wills that men become mature. Maturity is integrity in and through our relationships to each other. This is the important positive context within which Lehmann's discussion of truthtelling is to be seen. But he also sets the issue in a polemical ethical context with his distinction between "contextual ethics" and "absolutist ethics." The former "is concerned with relations and functions," the latter "with principles and precepts." For him, the absolutist position insists on a "standard of conduct which can be and must be applied to all people in all situations in exactly the same way." With reference to responsible speech, the absolutist position would require, following Kant, "optimum verbal veracity." Like Bonhoeffer, Lehmann speaks of the "living word," the word which makes it possible for human beings "to be open *for* one another and *to* one another." He illustrates his position with the interesting example of selling a used car, and seems to suggest that even in a business transaction the most important point is being open to and for one another. If one were to challenge this position, it might be profitable to distinguish between the different functions that speech has in different contexts. In more intimate personal relationships, there may be some important lessons in Lehmann's interpretation of truth. But does language function there in the same way as in the use of words in advertising, for example? What criteria would one use to determine the truth of an advertisement if the "living word" theory were the only one available? Or, one can apply Kant's pressure toward universality, and inquire what would happen to human relationships if one could not assume that "optimum verbal veracity" were not the norm. Perhaps such a norm still applies for Lehmann; perhaps his polemic is more against *absolutistic application* of norms without regard to different situations and different persons than it is against the existence of norms and precepts themselves. Needless to say, there is sharp difference between Kant's approach and that of Lehmann and Bonhoeffer, and this difference can lead to serious pondering about the nature of responsible speech.

Bernard Häring writes about truth from the position of a reformer of Roman Catholic moral theology. The manuals of moral theology that have been dominant in the past decades deal with the question of truth under the explication of the commandment, "You shall not bear false witness against your neighbor." A rationalistic way of interpreting this commandment had become more or less standard; there are no significant differences of interpretation among various manuals. The commandment was abstracted from the great themes of God's love and the work of His Spirit in the world, themes that Father Häring uses as the foundation of his ethics and to which he alludes briefly in the first part of the section reprinted here. Thus he writes, "To maintain an adequate moral norm of 'true speech' we must go beyond the mere psychological concept of true speech (conformity of word to mind) and keep in mind the divine primordial pattern and the human end and purpose of the word. The goal is building up of love in ourselves, in our neighbor, and in the community." But his explication of this point of view has continuity with the more traditional manuals. He deals, as the traditional writers have done, with specific issues such as the jocular lie, the lies of children, pathological lying, and various forms of secrets. While the examples he uses to illustrate how his position can be applied to particular situations are briefly stated, they do provide the occasion for thoughtful reflection on the "why" of each situation by the reader.

All of the writings reprinted here assist us in raising the question: How can we be responsible persons in our use of words? They raise practical moral issues: What does my responsibility mean in particular situations? They also raise theoretical questions of ethics: what is the function of general principles and rules? Are particular occasions applications of these principles? Does one begin with the principles (for which reasons can be given) and see how they work out? Or does one begin with the fabric of the context or the situation, discerning what is going on? Where do religious convictions come to bear? Do they provide ultimate reasons for being moral, patterns to which words and acts are to be conformed, or ends toward which speech and deeds are to be directed? The practical issues lead to questions of ethical theory; commitments made to perspectives of theory express themselves in moral decisions and actions.

Immanuel Kant

ON A SUPPOSED RIGHT TO LIE
FROM ALTRUISTIC MOTIVES*

In the journal *France*[1], for 1797, Part VI, No. 1, page 123, in an article entitled "On Political Reactions"[2] by Benjamin Constant,[3] there appears the following passage:

> The moral principle, "It is a duty to tell the truth," would make any society impossible if it were taken singly and unconditionally. We have proof of this in the very direct consequences which a German philosopher has drawn from this principle. This philosopher goes so far as to assert that it would be a crime to lie to a murderer who asked whether our friend who is pursued by him had taken refuge in our house.[4]

The French philosopher on page 124 refutes this principle in the following manner:

> It is a duty to tell the truth. The concept of duty is inseparable from the concept of right. A duty is that which in one being corresponds to the rights of another. Where there are no rights, there are no duties. To tell the truth is thus a duty; but it is a duty only in respect to one who has a right to the truth. But no one has a right to a truth which injures others.

The πρῶτον ψεῦδος in this argument lies in the sentence: "To tell the truth is a duty, but it is a duty only toward one who has a right to the truth."

* From IMMANUEL KANT, *Critique of Practical Reason and Other Writings in Moral Philosophy*, Lewis White Beck, ed. and trans. (Chicago: University of Chicago Press, 1949), pp. 346-50. Used by permission. Kant is the eighteenth-century German philosopher.

It must first be noted that the expression, "to have a right to truth" is without meaning. One must rather say, "Man has a right to his own truthfulness (*veracitas*)," i.e., to the subjective truth in his own person. For to have objectively a right to truth would mean that it is a question of one's will (as in questions of what belongs to individuals generally) whether a given sentence is to be true or false. This would certainly produce an extraordinary logic.

Now the first question is: Does a man, in cases where he cannot avoid answering "Yes" or "No," have a right to be untruthful? The second question is: Is he not in fact bound to tell an untruth, when he is unjustly compelled to make a statement, in order to protect himself or another from a threatened misdeed?

Truthfulness in statements which cannot be avoided is the formal duty of an individual to everyone,[5] however great may be the disadvantage accruing to himself or to another. If, by telling an untruth, I do not wrong him who unjustly compels me to make a statement, nevertheless by this falsification, which must be called a lie (though not in a legal sense), I commit a wrong against duty generally in a most essential point. That is, so far as in me lies I cause that declarations should in general find no credence, and hence that all rights based on contracts should be void and lose their force, and this is a wrong done to mankind generally.

Thus the definition of a lie as merely an intentional untruthful declaration to another person does not require the additional condition that it must harm another, as jurists think proper in their definition (*mendacium est falsiloquium in praeiudicium alterius*). For a lie always harms another; if not some other particular man, still it harms mankind generally, for it vitiates the source of law itself.

This benevolent lie, however, can become punishable under civil law through an accident (*casus*), and that which escapes liability to punishment only by accident can also be condemned as wrong even by external laws. For instance, if by telling a lie you have prevented murder, you have made yourself legally responsible for all the consequences; but if you have held rigorously to the truth, public justice can lay no hand on you, whatever the unforeseen consequences may be. After you have honestly answered the murderer's question as to whether this intended victim is at home, it may be that he has slipped out so that he does not come in the way of the murderer, and thus that the murder may not be committed. But if you had lied and said he was not at home when he had really gone out without your knowing it, and if the murderer had then met him as he went away and murdered him, you might justly be accused as the cause of his death. For if you had told the truth as far as you knew it, perhaps the murderer might have been apprehended by the neighbors while he searched the house and thus the deed might have been prevented. Therefore, whoever tells a lie, however well intentioned he might be, must answer for the consequences, however unforseeable they were, and pay the penalty for them even in a civil tribunal. This is because truthfulness is a duty which must be regarded as the ground of all duties based on contract, and the laws of these duties would be rendered uncertain and useless if even the least exception to them were admitted.

To be truthful (honest) in all declarations, therefore, is a sacred and absolutely commanding decree of reason, limited by no expediency.

Mr. Constant makes a thoughtful and correct remark on decrying principles so strict that they are alleged to lose themselves in such impracticable ideas that they are to be rejected. He says, on page 23, "In every case where a principle which has been proved to be true appears to be inapplicable, the reason is that we do not know the middle principle which contains the means of its application." He adduces (p. 121) the doctrine of equality as the first link of the social chain, saying (p. 122):

No man can be bound by any laws except to the formulation of which he has contributed. In a very limited society this principle can be applied directly and needs no mediating principle in order to become a common principle. But in a society consisting of very many persons, another principle must be added to this one we have stated. This mediating principle is: the individuals can participate in the formulation of laws either in their own person or through their representatives. Whoever wished to apply the former principle to a large society without making use of the mediating principle would invariably bring about the destruction of society. But this circumstance, which would only show the ignorance or the incompetence of the legislator, proves nothing against the principle.

He concludes (p. 125) that "a principle acknowledged to be true must never be abandoned, however obviously danger seems to be involved in it." (And yet the good man himself abandoned the unconditional principle of truthfulness on account of the danger which it involved for society. He did so because he could find no mediating principle which could serve to prevent this danger; and, in fact, there is no principle to be interpolated here.)

If we wish to preserve the names of the persons as they have been cited here, the "French philosopher" confuses the action by which someone does harm (*nocet*) to another in telling the truth when he cannot avoid making a statement, with the action whereby he does the other a wrong (*laedit*). It was only an accident (*casus*) that the truth of the statement harmed the occupant of the house; it was not a free act (in a juristic sense). For to demand of another that he should lie to one's own advantage would be a claim opposed to all lawfulness. Each man has not only a right but even the strict duty to be truthful in statements he cannot avoid making, whether they harm himself or others. In so doing, he does not do harm to him who suffers as a consequence; accident causes this harm. For one is not at all free to choose in such a case, since truthfulness (if he must speak) is an unconditional duty.

The "German philosopher" will not take as one of his principles the proposition (p. 124): "To tell the truth is a duty, but only to him who has a right to the truth." He will not do so, first, because of the ambiguous formulation of this proposition, for truth is not a possession the right to which can be granted to one and denied to another. But he will not do so chiefly because the duty of truthfulness (which is the only thing in question here) makes no distinction between persons to whom one has this duty and to whom one can exempt himself from this duty; rather, it is an unconditional duty which holds in all circumstances.

Now in order to proceed from a metaphysics of law (which abstracts from all empirical conditions) to a principle of politics (which applies these concepts to cases met with in experience), and by means of this to achieve the solution of a problem of politics in accord with the universal principle of law, the philosopher will enunciate three notions. The first is an axiom, i. e., an apodictically certain proposition which springs directly from the definition of external law (the harmony of the freedom of each with the freedom of all others according to a universal law). The second is a postulate of external public law (the will of all united according to the principle of equality, without which no one would have any freedom). Third, there is the problem of how it is to be arranged that, in a society however large, harmony may be maintained in accordance with principles of freedom and equality (namely, by means of a representative system). The latter will then become a principle of politics, the organization and establishment of which will entail decrees drawn from the practical knowledge of men, which will have in view only the mechanism of the administration of justice and how this may be suitably carried out. Law must never be accommodated to politics but politics always accommodated to law.

The author says, "A principle recognized as true (I add, recognized as an a priori and hence apodictic principle) must never be abandoned, however obviously danger seems to be involved in it." But one must only understand the danger not as a danger of accidentally doing a harm but only as a danger of doing a wrong. This would happen if I made the duty of being truthful, which is unconditional and the supreme juridical condition in testimony, into a conditional duty subordinate to other considerations. Although in telling a certain lie I do not actually do anyone a wrong, I formally but not materially violate the principle of right with respect to all unavoidably necessary utterances. And this is much worse than to do injustice to any particular person, because such a deed against an individual does not always presuppose the existence of a principle in the subject which produces such an act.

If one is asked whether he intends to speak truthfully in a statement that he is about to make and does not receive the question with indignation at the suspicion it expressed that he might be a liar, but rather asks permission to consider possible exceptions, that person is already potentially a liar. That is because he shows that he does not acknowledge truthfulness as an intrinsic duty but makes reservations with respect to a rule which does not permit any exception, inasmuch as any exception would directly contradict itself.

All practical principles of right must contain rigorous truth, and the so-called "mediating principles" can contain only the more accurate definition of their application to actual cases (according to rules of policy), but they can never contain exceptions from the former. Such exceptions would nullify their universality, and that is precisely the reason that they are called principles.

NOTES

[1] [The journal *Frankreich im Jahre 1797. Aus den Briefen deutscher Männer in Paris,* published in Altona.]

[2] [*Des réactions politiques* had appeared in 1796 and was translated in this journal.]

[3] [Henri Benjamin Constant de Rebecque (1767-1830), the French writer, statesman, and orator.]

[4] "J. D. Michaelis of Göttingen expressed this extraordinary opinion earlier than Kant. But the author of this essay has informed me that Kant is the philosopher spoken of in this passage."—K. F. Cramer. "That this was really said by me somewhere I hereby admit, though I cannot now remember the place."—I. Kant. ["Such a place is not to be found in Kant's previous works."—Heinrich Maier (editor of the Academy edition of this work). Johann David Michaelis (1717-91), was a biblical scholar and professor in Göttingen. Karl Friedrich Cramer (1752-1807), editor of *Frankreich . . .* , formerly professor of Greek and oriental languages and homiletics at Kiel, had been dismissed in 1794 because of his open sympathy for the Revolution.—EDS.]

[5] I should not like to sharpen this principle to the point of saying, "Untruthfulness is a violation of duty to one's self." This principle belongs to ethics, but here we are concerned with a legal duty. [Ethics as a] theory of virtue sees in this transgression only worthlessness, which is the reproach the liar draws upon himself.

Dietrich Bonhoeffer

WHAT IS MEANT BY
"TELLING THE TRUTH"?*

From the moment in our lives at which we learn to speak we are taught that what we say must be true. What does this mean? What is meant by "telling the truth"? What does it demand of us?

It is clear that in the first place it is our parents who regulate our relation to themselves by this demand for truthfulness; consequently, in the sense in which our parents intend it, this demand applies strictly only within the family circle. It is also to be noted that the relation which is expressed in this demand can not simply be reversed. The truthfulness of a child towards his parents is essentially different from that of the parents towards their child. The life of the small child lies open before the parents, and what the child says should reveal to them everything that is hidden and secret, but in the converse relationship this cannot possibly be the case. Consequently, in the matter of truthfulness, the parents' claim on the child is different from the child's claim on the parents.

From this it emerges already that "telling the truth" means something different according to the particular situation in which one stands. Account must be taken of one's relationships at each particular time. The question must be asked whether

* From Dietrich Bonhoeffer, *Ethics,* Eberhard Bethge, ed., (New York: The Macmillan Co., 1965, paperback), pp. 363-72. Used by permission.

and in what way a man is entitled to demand truthful speech of others. Speech between parents and children is, in the nature of the case, different from speech between man and wife, between friends, between teacher and pupil, government and subject, friend and foe, and in each case the truth which this speech conveys is also different.

It will at once be objected that one does not owe truthful speech to this or that individual man, but solely to God. This objection is correct so long as it is not forgotten that God is not a general principle, but the living God who has set me in a living life and who demands service of me within this living life. If one speaks of God one must not simply disregard the actual given world in which one lives; for if one does that one is not speaking of the God who entered into the world in Jesus Christ, but rather of some metaphysical idol. And it is precisely this which is determined by the way in which, in my actual concrete life with all its manifold relationships, I give effect to the truthfulness which I owe to God. The truthfulness which we owe to God must assume a concrete form in the world. Our speech must be truthful, not in principle but concretely. A truthfulness which is not concrete is not truthful before God.

"Telling the truth," therefore, is not solely a matter of moral character; it is also a matter of correct appreciation of real situations and of serious reflection upon them. The more complex the actual situations of a man's life, the more responsible and the more difficult will be his task of "telling the truth." The child stands in only one vital relationship, his relationship to his parents, and he, therefore, still has nothing to consider and weigh up. The next environment in which he is placed, his school, already brings with it the first difficulty. From the educational point of view it is, therefore, of the very greatest importance that parents, in some way which we cannot discuss here, should make their children understand the differences between these various circles in which they are to live and the differences in their responsibilities.

Telling the truth is, therefore, something which must be learnt. This will sound very shocking to anyone who thinks that it must all depend on moral character and that if this is blameless the rest is child's play. But the simple fact is that the ethical cannot be detached from reality, and consequently continual progress in learning to appreciate reality is a necessary ingredient in ethical action. In the question with which we are now concerned, action consists of speaking. The real is to be expressed in words. That is what constitutes truthful speech. And this inevitably raises the question of the "how?" of these words. It is a question of knowing the right word on each occasion. Finding this word is a matter of long, earnest and ever more advanced effort on the basis of experience and knowledge of the real. If one is to say how a thing really is, *i.e.* if one is to speak truthfully, one's gaze and one's thought must be directed towards the way in which the real exists in God and through God and for God.

To restrict this problem of truthful speech to certain particular cases of conflict is superficial. Every word I utter is subject to the requirement that it shall be true. Quite apart from the veracity of its contents, the relation between myself and another man which is expressed in it is in itself either true or untrue. I speak flatteringly or presumptuously or hypocritically without uttering a material untruth; yet my words are nevertheless untrue, because I am disrupting and destroying the reality of the relationship between man and wife, superior and subordinate, etc. An individual utterance is always part of a total reality which seeks expression in this utterance. If my utterance is to be truthful it must in each case be different according to whom I am addressing, who is questioning me, and what I am speaking about. The truthful word is not in itself constant; it is as much alive as life itself. If it is detached from life and from its reference to the concrete other man, if "the truth is told" without taking into account to whom it is addressed, then this truth has only the appearance of truth, but it lacks its essential character.

It is only the cynic who claims "to speak the truth" at all times and in all places to all men in the same way, but who, in fact, displays nothing but a lifeless image of the truth. He dons the halo of the fanatical devotee of truth who can make no allowance for human weaknesses; but, in fact, he is destroying the living truth between men. He wounds shame, desecrates mystery, breaks confidence, betrays the community in which he lives, and laughs arrogantly at the devastation he has wrought and at the human weakness which "cannot bear the truth." He says truth is destructive and demands its victims, and he feels like a god above these feeble creatures and does not know that he is serving Satan.

There is a truth which is of Satan. Its essence is that under the semblance of truth it denies everything that is real. It lives upon hatred of the real and of the world which is created and loved by God. It pretends to be executing the judgment of God upon the fall of the real. God's truth judges created things out of love, and Satan's truth judges them out of envy and hatred. God's truth has become flesh in the world and is alive in the real, but Satan's truth is the death of all reality.

The concept of living truth is dangerous, and it gives rise to the suspicion that the truth can and may be adapted to each particular situation in a way which completely destroys the idea of truth and narrows the gap between truth and falsehood, so that the two become indistinguishable. Moreover, what we are saying about the necessity for discerning the real may be mistakenly understood as meaning that it is by adopting a calculating or school-masterly attitude towards the other man that I shall decide what proportion of the truth I am prepared to tell him. It is important that this danger should be kept in view. Yet the only possible way of countering it is by means of attentive discernment of the particular contents and limits which the real itself imposes on one's utterance in order to make it a truthful one. The dangers which are involved in the concept of living truth must never impel one to abandon this concept in favour of the formal and cynical concept of truth. We must try to make this clear. Every utterance or word lives and has its home in a particular environment. The word in the family is different from the word in business or public. The word which has come to life in the warmth of personal relationship is frozen to death in the cold air of public existence. The word of command, which has its habitat in public service, would sever the bonds of mutual confidence if it were spoken in the family. Each word must have its own place and keep to it. It is a consequence of the wide diffusion of the public word through the newspapers and the wireless that the essential character and the limits of the various different words are no longer clearly felt and that, for example, the special quality of the personal word is almost entirely destroyed. Genuine words are replaced by idle chatter. Words no longer possess any weight. There is too much talk. And when the limits of the various words are obliterated, when words become rootless and homeless, then the word loses truth, and then indeed there must almost inevitably be lying. When the various orders of life no longer respect one another, words become untrue. For example, a teacher asks a child in front of the class whether it is true that his father often comes home drunk. It is true, but the child denies it. The teacher's question has placed him in a situation for which he is not yet prepared. He feels only that what is taking place is an unjustified interference in the order of the family and that he must oppose it. What goes on in the family is not for the ears of the class in school. The family has its own secret and must preserve it. The teacher has failed to respect the reality of this institution. The child ought now to find a way of answering which would comply with both the rule of the family and the rule of the school. But he is not yet able to do this. He lacks experience, knowledge, and the ability to express himself in the right way. As a simple no to the teacher's question the child's answer is certainly untrue; yet at the same time it nevertheless gives expression to the truth that the family is an institution *sui generis* and that the teacher had no right to interfere in it. The child's answer can indeed be called a lie; yet this lie contains more truth, that is to say, it is more in accordance with reality than would have been the case if the child had betrayed his father's weakness in front of the class. According to the measure of his knowledge, the child acted correctly. The blame for the lie falls back entirely upon the teacher. An experienced man in the same position as the child would have been able to correct his questioner's error while at the same time avoiding a formal untruth in his answer, and he would thus have found the "right word." The lies of children, and of inexperienced people in general, are often to be ascribed to the fact that these people are faced with situations which they do not fully understand. Consequently, since the term lie is quite properly understood as meaning something which is quite simply and utterly wrong, it is perhaps unwise to generalize and extend the use of this term so that it can be applied to every statement which is formally untrue. Indeed here already it becomes apparent how very difficult it is to say what actually constitutes a lie.

The usual definition of the lie as a conscious discrepancy between thought and speech is completely inadequate. This would include, for example, even the most harmless April-fool joke. The concept of the "jocular lie," which is maintained in Catholic moral theology, takes away from the lie its characteristic features of seriousness and malice (and, conversely, takes away from the joke its characteristic features of harmless playfulness and freedom); no more unfortunate concept could have been thought of. Joking has nothing whatever to do with lying, and the two must not be reduced to a common denominator. If it is now asserted that a lie is a deliberate deception of another man to his detriment, then this would also include, for example, the necessary deception of the enemy in war or in similar situations.[1] If this sort of conduct is called lying, the lie thereby acquires a moral sanction and justification which conflicts in every possible way with the accepted meaning of the term. The first conclusion to be drawn from this is that the lie cannot be defined in formal terms as a discrepancy between thought and speech. This discrepancy is not even a necessary ingredient of the lie. There is a way of speaking which is in this respect entirely correct and unexceptionable, but which is, nevertheless, a lie. This is exemplified when a notorious liar for once tells "the truth" in order to mislead, and when an apparently correct statement contains some deliberate ambiguity or deliberately omits the essential part of the truth. Even a deliberate silence may constitute a lie, although this is not by any means necessarily the case.

From these considerations it becomes evident that the essential character of the lie is to be found at a far deeper level than in the discrepancy between thought and speech. One might say that the man who stands behind the word makes his word a lie or a truth. But even this is not enough; for the lie is something objective and must be defined accordingly. Jesus calls Satan "the father of the lie" (John 8:44). The lie is primarily the denial of God as He has evidenced Himself to the world. "Who is a liar but he that denieth that Jesus is the Christ?" (I John 2:22). The lie is a contradiction of the word of God, which God has spoken in Christ, and upon which creation is founded. Consequently the lie is the denial, the negation and the conscious and deliberate destruction of the reality which is created by God and which consists in God, no matter whether this purpose is achieved by speech or by silence. The assigned purpose of our words, in unity with the word of God, is to express the real, as it exists in God; and the assigned purpose of our silence is to signify the limit which is imposed upon our words by the real as it exists in God.

In our endeavours to express the real we do not encounter this as a consistent whole, but in a condition of disruption and inner contradiction which has need of reconciliation and healing. We find ourselves simultaneously embedded in various different orders of the real, and our words, which strive towards the reconciliation and healing of the real, are nevertheless repeatedly drawn in into the prevalent disunion and conflict. They can indeed fulfill their assigned purpose of expressing the real, as it is in God, only by taking up into themselves both the inner contradiction and the inner consistency of the real. If the words of men are to be true they must deny neither the Fall nor God's word of creation and reconciliation, the word in which all disunion is overcome. For the cynic the truthfulness of his words will consist in his giving expression on each separate occasion to the particular reality as he thinks he perceives it, without reference to the totality of the real; and precisely through this he

completely destroys the real. Even if his words have the superficial appearance of correctness, they are untrue. "That which is
far off, and exceeding deep; who can find it out?" (Eccl. 7:4).

How can I speak the truth?

a. By perceiving who causes me to speak and what entitles me
to speak.

b. By perceiving the place at which I stand.

c. By relating to this context the object about which I am
making some assertion.

It is tacitly assumed in these rules that all speech is subject to
certain conditions; speech does not accompany the natural
course of life in a continual stream, but it has its place, its time
and its task, and consequently also its limits.

d. Who or what entitles or causes me to speak? Anyone who
speaks without a right and a cause to do so is an idle chatterer.
Every utterance is involved in a relation both with the other
man and with a thing, and in every utterance, therefore, this
twofold reference must be apparent. An utterance without
reference is empty. It contains no truth. In this there is an
essential difference between thought and speech. Thought does
not in itself necessarily refer to the other man, but only to a
thing. The claim that one is entitled to say what one thinks is in
itself completely unfounded. Speech must be justified and occa-
sioned by the other man. For example, I may in my thoughts
consider another man to be stupid, ugly, incapable or lacking in
character, or I may think him wise and reliable. But it is quite a
different question whether I have the right to express this opinion, what occasion I have for expressing it, and to whom I
express it. There can be no doubt that a right to speak is con-
ferred upon me by an office which is committed to me. Parents
can blame or praise their child, but the child is not entitled to
do either of these things with regard to his parents. There is a
similar relation between teacher and pupil, although the rights
of the teacher with regard to the children are more restricted
than those of the father. Thus in criticizing or praising his pupil
the teacher will have to confine himself to single particular faults
or achievements, while, for example, general judgments of char-

acter are the business not of the teacher but of the parents. The right to speak always lies within the confines of the particular office which I discharge. If I overstep these limits my speech becomes importunate, presumptuous, and, whether it be blame or praise, offensive. There are people who feel themselves called upon to "tell the truth," as they put it, to everyone who crosses their path.

NOTES

[1] Kant, of course, declared that he was too proud ever to utter a falsehood; indeed he unintentionally carried this principle *ad absurdum* by saying that he would feel himself obliged to give truthful information even to a criminal looking for a friend of his who had concealed himself in his house.

Paul Lehmann

THE CONTEXTUAL CHARACTER
OF CHRISTIAN ETHICS*

We have been urging that Christian thinking about ethics starts
with and from within the Christian *koinonia*. In the *koinonia* it
makes sense to talk about the will of God as the answer to the
question: What am I, as a believer in Jesus Christ and as a
member of his church, to do? For it is in the *koinonia* that one
comes in sight of and finds oneself involved in what it takes to
keep human life human. The fruit of this divine activity is
human maturity, the wholeness of every man and of all men in
the new humanity inaugurated and being fulfilled by Jesus
Christ in the world. The description of this activity of God
provides a *koinonia* ethic with its biblical and theological foundations.

1. A CONTEXTUAL CRITIQUE OF ETHICAL ABSOLUTISM

When ethical reflection is pursued in the context of the Christian *koinonia,* the method and materials of ethics acquire a
concrete and contextual character. *A* koinonia *ethic is concerned with relations and functions, not with principles and
precepts.* It will help us to see what is involved in this contrast if
we take up a distinction which is not always made, a failure

* From PAUL L. LEHMANN, *Ethics in a Christian Context* (New
York: Harper & Row, 1963), pp. 124-33. Copyright © 1963 by Paul
L. Lehmann. Reprinted by permission of Harper & Row, Publishers.
Professor Lehmann teaches theology at Union Theological Seminary
in New York City.

which makes for confusion in Christian ethical analysis. The distinction is between *contextual ethics* and what might be called *absolutist ethics*. Is it, for instance, wrong to tell a lie? Is a Christian required always to tell the truth, the whole truth, and nothing but the truth?

Christian ethics, in common with the formative types of non-Christian ethical theory, has, on the whole, tended to give an affirmative answer to both these questions. For a Christian, it *is* wrong to tell a lie. A Christian *is* required to tell the truth, the whole truth, and nothing but the truth. It has not always been noticed, however, that such an affirmative answer has been based upon a conception or standard of truth which is foreign to the focus and foundations of a Christian ethic. Such a conception or standard of truth presupposed, in the main, an intimate and self-validating connection between the human reason and the idea of the Good and so was regarded as ethical in itself. This is really the hallmark of absolutist ethics. Absolutist ethics declares that the proper answer to the question: "What am I to do?" is supplied by an "absolute." And what is an "absolute"? Ethically speaking, *an "absolute" is a standard of conduct which can be and must be applied to all people in all situations in exactly the same way.* The standard may be an ideal, a value, or a law. Its ethical reality and significance, however, lie in its *absolute* character.

But absolutist ethics pays a very heavy price for its claims. The price is abstraction from the complexity of the actual situation out of which the ethical problem arises. There was once a dramatic farce which used to be played, perhaps not uncharacteristically, to crowded audiences on the Chautauqua circuit. Called *Nothing but the Truth* it described the actual predicament in which a person became involved when he set out to tell "nothing but the truth." All human and circumstantial relations became a tangled web of turmoil and misunderstanding, with the result that the leading character's stubborn adherence to this maxim made him thoroughly disliked by everyone else and undermined confidence in the human sense of truthtelling. A friend of mine once told me that he had a colleague who arose upon every issue before the faculty for decision to declare that his conscience required him to vote thus and so. Matters at length came to such a pass that the business of the faculty tended to be obstructed because one never could tell at what point this man would arise to do justice to his conscience. At length the president of the faculty adopted the procedure of calling always upon this colleague first so that his conscience could be got out of the way and the business of the faculty could go forward. Perhaps the most telling confirmation of the "absolutist predicament" is provided by children, and in ways that are both amusing and vexatious. A child I know went through a period of insisting upon eating his food from dishes or with utensils which had been his father's as a child. If assured that this glass or bowl or spoon had been used by his father as a child, he would proceed with breakfast. If the parents demurred, they had a diplomatic tangle on their hands. The Freudian implications of this situation are disconcerting enough, but the ethical hazards are more so. Underneath this diplomatic tangle was a very awkward ethical dilemma. What were the parents to do? Let the child starve for truth's sake? This, and similar dilemmas, suggest what is meant by saying that the price of "absolutist'" ethics is abstraction from the complexity of the actual human and ethical situation. An absolutist ethic can neither escape from nor deal with the very real disparity between the ethical demand and the ethical act, intrinsic to every ethical situation. There is no way of getting precept and practice together except by illusion on the one hand or by hypocrisy on the other.

The ethical discussion of truth from an absolutist point of view has been given classic formulation by Immanuel Kant in a little treatise called *On a Supposed Right to Lie from Altruistic Motives.*[1] Kant's argument is germane to the present discussion not only because of its succinct and forceful character but also because one cannot dispose of the absolutist position without taking quite seriously its claims upon the nature of ethical thinking. The absolutist position has a long and influential tradition behind it which, however much it may have become trivialized, must be fully faced. Kant's treatise was written as a kind of reply to a certain M. Benjamin Constant, whom he identifies as a French philosopher. M. Constant had taken the position that the maxim "It is a duty to tell the truth," if adopted and practiced, singly and unconditionally, would make any society impossible.[2] The Frenchman was not denying that it is a duty to tell the truth. He was arguing, however, for an important limitation upon this duty: it is a duty to tell the truth, but only to one who has a right to it. For example, he argued, it is a crime to tell the truth to a murderer who asks whether or not one's friend is at home. Kant set out to prove the falsity of this contention by asserting that it is a duty to tell the truth *unconditionally*. His point is that if this cannot be regarded as a duty all declarations lose their credence, all contracts become insecure; and *then* there is no basis for society, for society depends upon the inviolability of contracts. Kant, with dubious accuracy, goes on to observe that under certain circumstances even civil law punishes the benevolent lie.[3] He turns the illustration of the murderer against M. Constant's interpretation. If the supposed murderer were to come into the house and be told that one's friend was not there, while without one's knowledge the friend had in fact slipped out of the house, so that the murderer being turned away by the denial encountered the friend along the way and accomplished his purpose after all, the law would in fact regard the denial that the friend was in the house as establishing complicity in the friend's death. As Kant saw it, this legal provision is based upon the fact that truth is a duty which admits of no exceptions. "To be truthful," in his words, "in all declarations, therefore, is a sacred and absolutely commanding degree of reason, limited by no expediency."[4]

Now this is a very formidable claim. And while Kant rests his case rather more upon the necessity of reason than upon Christian considerations, it must be remembered that his whole approach to philosophy and to ethics was not unrelated to the fact that he grew up in a Moravian household. He was a Christian and he thought as a Christian, though not in theological terms. It is understandable indeed that the logic of Kant's position should have become part and parcel of the working maxims by which many people still live and govern their actions as regards telling the truth.

What, then, would a contextual ethic have to offer over against this formidable statement of the absolutist position? Let us try to get at it in this way: Suppose a man has a car which he wants to sell.[5] What does it mean to tell the truth? There would seem to be at least three possibilities open. The owner of the car can refuse to tell the buyer anything. He buys "as is" and at his own risk. Or the owner can take a mediating position, answering the buyer's questions and risking only the buyer's praise or blame, according to the subsequent performance of the car. An absolutist ethic would urge the second of these courses of action: It is the duty of the owner of the car to tell the buyer everything he knows about the car. But there is no guarantee on an absolutist basis that the owner of the car can or could tell everything he knows about it. He might have forgotten something. And the *intention* of the owner to tell the truth would not cover the fact that he actually had *not* told the truth. Here we come upon one of the most ingenious and tested and tried attempts to bring an absolutist ethic into line with the actual diversity and complexity of the ethical situation. This attempt takes the form of an analysis which very closely relates *intention* and *action* in the human ethical situation, and assigns ethical priority to *intention*. Although Protestant thinking about ethics has been heavily affected and indeed afflicted by the doctrine of intention (not least owing to the influence of Immanuel Kant), the doctrine of intention is really intrinsic to the ethics of Roman Catholic moral theology, with which we shall be concerned in a subsequent chapter.[6]

A contextual ethic begins at the opposite point from the one at which Immanuel Kant begins. Kant's dictum that it is absolutely necessary to tell the truth "unconditionally" has been impressively and instructively countered by the position taken in a similarly small treatise by Dietrich Bonhoeffer called *What Does It Mean to Tell the Truth?*[7] In this little treatise Bonhoeffer notes that telling the truth is "a matter of accurate and serious consideration of the actual circumstances. The more complex the circumstances of a man's life are, the more responsible he is; and the more difficult it is for him to tell the truth. Therefore, telling the truth must be learned . . . since it is simply a fact that the ethical cannot be detached from the real situation, the increasingly accurate knowledge of the *situation* is a necessary element of ethical action."[8] On these terms, telling the truth about the car would obviously not be identical with *optimum verbal veracity.* It would be different for a high school adolescent and for a man in middle life; for a man who had two cars and for a man who had to dispose of the only car he had, in order to pay for his wife's burial; for a humanist and for a Christian. But in each case, telling the truth would be a matter of saying, to use Bonhoeffer's phrase, "the right word," or better, "the living word." "The living word," says Bonhoeffer, "is as alive as life itself."[9]

What is the *living word?* It is the verbal expression of the full complexity and totality of the existing, concrete situation. And what is *ethical* about the existing, concrete situation is that which holds it together. And what, it may be asked, holds the concrete situation together? The answer is: that which makes it possible for human beings to be open *for* one another and *to* one another. In so far as the *right* word, or the *living* word, is instrumental to such an openness of human beings to each other, telling the truth is ethically real. If the buyer and the seller of this car come through the transaction to a true consideration of each other's predicament, and so are linked to each other as human beings, then they do not merely transact business. The business transaction becomes instrumental to their discovery of each other as human beings, and whether much or little is told about the car, whatever is told is the truth. It is this *human* factor in the interrelationships of men which is the definitely *ethical* factor. A Christian ethic seeks to show that the *human* in us all can be rightly discerned and adhered to only in and through the reality of a climate of trust established by the divine humanity of Jesus Christ and the new humanity, however incipient, of all men in Christ.

All of us are aware that the problem of telling the truth actually does vary according to the relationships in which we find ourselves. In the relations between parents and children, between husband and wife, between friends and friends, between teacher and student, between friend and enemy—in all these relationships the truth in the words varies. As Bonhoeffer puts it, "Our words must not conform to the truth in principle but concretely. Conformity to the truth that is not concrete is not conformity to the truth before God. . . . One . . . must not forget that God is no general principle, but the Living One who has set me down in a living situation and demands my obedience. Whoever says, 'God,' cannot ignore the given world in which he lives, otherwise he would not be speaking the truth, otherwise he would not be speaking of God who became incarnate in the world in Jesus Christ."[10] It is the fact that God became incarnate in Jesus Christ, as this fact is spelled out by a theology of messianism, which requires of Christian ethics that the diverse relationships in which men find themselves be taken seriously as bearers of ethical reality and significance.

A *koinonia* ethic claims that such human relationships are actualized in the world in consequence of and in the context of the concrete reality of the church. The empirical church violates in many ways the ethical reality which is the true occasion of its existence and without which it cannot be the church. Nevertheless, the empirical church points, despite its ambiguity, to the fact that there is in the world a *laboratory of the living word,* or, to change the metaphor, a *bridgehead of maturity,* namely, the Christian *koinonia.* In the *Koinonia* ethical theory and practice acquire a framework of meaning and a pattern of action which undergird the diversity and the complexity of the concrete ethical situation with vitality and purpose.

In the *koinonia* valid ethical questions and concerns are different from what they may be outside the *koinonia.* For example, the ethical question—in the *koinonia*—is not "What *ought* I to do?" but "What *am* I to do?" because in the *koinonia* one is always fundamentally in an *indicative* rather than in an imperative situation. There is, of course, also an imperative pressure exerted by an indicative situation. The "ought" factor is not the primary ethical reality. The primary ethical reality is the human factor, the *human* indicative, in every situation involving the interrelationships and the decisions of men. In the *koinonia* something is already going on, namely, what God is doing in the situation out of which the ethical question and concern arise to fashion circumstance and behavior according to his will. This is why a contextual ethic does not lead to ethical anarchy or ethical expediency. If what God is doing in the world is to relate men to each other in and through an enterprise of the new humanity, if God is setting the conditions for and bestowing the enabling power of maturity—if this is what God is doing, then it is meaningless to say that if one doesn't tell the truth unconditionally the fabric of society will be shredded by mistrust; it is meaningless to say that if one can claim that whatever occurs to him at the moment to say is the truth, the whole field of truth and falsehood is reduced to anarchy and confusion. Such concerns may have standing in some other kind of ethical climate, but for a Christian ethic they are false concerns.

2. RANDOM INSTANCES OF CONTEXTUAL BEHAVIOR

Almost the first more than casual impact of death upon me occurred in the passing of a lady in early middle life who had come to be virtually a second mother to me. She was stricken, as it seemed, quite suddenly, with a particularly virulent form of carcinoma and died under this ghastly, body-waste disease. When I saw her for the last time, as she lay upon her hospital bed, she said to me, "What do the doctors say? Is there anything that can be done?" At this moment there came to mind the profound and humiliating observation of Dostoevsky, which, it has always seemed to me, ought to serve as the rubric under which the healthy relate themselves to the ill, and in particular as the rubric under which pastoral calls upon the sick are made. "In every misfortune of one's neighbor," says Dostoevsky, "there is always something cheering for an onlooker—

whoever he may be."[11] I knew that this lady would never leave her bed of pain alive. I knew, too, that I was leaving the hospital to take a train for my own work and that I was not in the slightest inclined to exchange places. What should I have replied to her question? How white is a lie? And how black can the truth, the whole truth, and nothing but the truth be? What in such a situation *is* the truth?

Is it telling the truth to say in as sympathetic and tactful a way as possible, "There is no hope!"? Or should one say, "Don't worry! Everything will come out all right!"?

The point at issue here is not the celebrated ethical question of the right of the patient to the truth.[12] The point at issue is, granted that the patient has a right to the truth, what is the truth to which the patient has a right, and how would a *Christian* ethic deal with this right? My own attempt ran something like this: "The doctors are doing all that they can. But you and I have always been Christians. Part of what that has meant has been that we have said in our prayers and confessed in our faith that Jesus Christ is Savior and Lord. I do not claim to understand all that this involves. But if it means anything at all, it seems to me to mean at least this—when in the next days and weeks the going gets hard, remember you are not alone! Jesus Christ has been there before!"

NOTES

[1] Immanuel Kant, *On a Supposed Right to Lie from Altruistic Motives,* in *Kant's Ethical Writings,* edited by Lewis E. Beck, University of Chicago Press, Chicago, 1949.

[2] *Ibid.,* p. 246. Actually, M. Henri Benjamin Constant de Rebecque (1767-1830) was a writer, statesman, and orator, and in this sense also a political philosopher.

[3] Kant's point is that through an accident the benevolent lie can become punishable under civil law. He argues that that which escapes liability to punishment only by accident can also be condemned as wrong by external laws. Benjamin Constant, however, did have legal theory and procedure on his side. Kant may have had in mind certain very special and limited provisions of the German law of his time. If so

it is difficult to understand his attempt in this treatise to rest the case for an unconditional morality of law upon so slender a legal analogy. The likelier interpretation of this passage is that Kant was simply mistaken in his legal interpretation. The law, for example, does punish perjury. But in this case the grounds for punishment have to do with the honor and integrity of the court, not with the unconditional duty to tell the truth. The law also protects the individual against infringement of his right to freedom of speech and against self-incrimination. In these instances falsehoods are not only not punished but allowed, on the ground that the liberty of the individual is a greater good than unconditional truthfulness.

In the present context, Kant's erroneous appeal to law is the more instructive because it underlines the enormous difficulty of ethical absolutism, whether in legal theory and practice or in moral philosophy. Although he is not responsibile for the present interpretation, I am especially indebted to my colleague Professor Harold H. Berman of the Faculty of Law for the clarification of this point.

[4] Immanuel Kant, *Critique of Practical Reason,* Beck edition, University of Chicago Press, Chicago, 1949, p. 348.

[5] This example has been previously used in a preliminary essay dealing with the contextual character of Christian ethics. Cf. "The Foundation and Pattern of Christian Behavior," in *Christian Faith and Social Ethics,* edited by John Hutchinson, Charles Scribner's Sons, New York, 1953.

[6] See Chapter XII.

[7] Dietrich Bonhoeffer, *Ethik,* zusammengestellt und herausgegeben von Eberhard Bethge, Chr. Kaiser, Muenchen, 1949; English translation, entitled *Ethics,* by Neville Horton Smith, The Macmillan Company, New York, 1955 (SCM Press, London, 1955). The translation seems to me to be not altogether a happy one. I have accordingly attempted a translation of my own, noting the reference, however, first in the original and then, in parentheses, in the English edition.

[8] *Ibid.,* p. 284 (327).

[9] *Ibid.,* p. 285 (328).

[10] *Ibid.,* pp. 283-84 (327).

[11] Fyodor Dostoevsky, *The Possessed,* Modern Library edition, New York, 1936, p. 334.

[12] This question has been freshly and instructively discussed by Professor Joseph Fletcher in his Lowell Lectures, *Morals and Medicine,* Princeton University Press, Princeton, 1954 (Gollancz, London, 1955).

Bernard Häring

TRUTH IN CONDUCT
(TO DO THE TRUTH)*

Our most important external "words" are not merely words which fall from our lips, but our deeds, our actions. Through them we express ourselves and place ourselves in objective contact with our neighbor. Therefore our actions above all must be true, which is to say they must flow from the interior attachment to the known truth. They must bear witness to the truth in us. By our deeds men know us as they know the tree by its fruits (cf. MT 7:16). If we wish to be genuine, our inner thoughts, our words, and our actions must all be in conformity.

We must grant that the man ensnared in error is at least relatively truthful and genuine if he acts in accordance with his convictions. And if his conviction, objectively false, is subjectively sincere, he is true by will and intention. Conversely, even externally correct conduct is not authentic if it does not flow from interior conviction. The actions of a culpable unbeliever who has acquired an erroneous conscience often conform to his existing convictions, but for all that his conduct is not true. He is caught up in a lie in his entire existence, exterior and interior.

In terse and lapidary utterance the holy scriptures demand of us that we do the truth, for

he who does the truth comes to the light that his deeds may be made manifest, for they have been performed in God (JN 3:21; cf. I JN 1:6).

* From BERNARD HÄRING, C.SS.R., *The Law of Christ: Moral Theology for Priests and Laity,* Vol. III, Edwin G. Kaiser, C.P.P.S., trans. (Westminster, Md.: Newman Press, 1966), pp. 556-76. Used by permission.

Surely the intent of the words is not that "one act according to one's convictions" in the "enthusiastic" sense of the rationalistic Enlightenment (of the eighteenth and nineteenth centuries). The reference is to that "conduct which is in accordance with revelation,"[1] conduct in accordance with the revealed truth which shall make us free (JN 8:32) and which we not only hear but also do.

As doing evil makes men slaves of sin (JN 8:34), so the truth makes men free. And since we are committed to the truth by Christ who has freed us from sin (JN 8:36) and our relation to Christ depends on our attachment to truth—a bond of heart and hand—it is absolutely essential that truth be the firm foundation of our thought, the basis of our words and acts (cf. JN 1 ff.; III JN 1 ff.). We are firm and constant in the revealed truth only if we "practice the truth in love" (EPH 4:5; II JN 1 ff.).

We are led ever more profoundly into this truth as we act in truth and fulfill the truth—communicated to us by the love of God—through the act of love.

He who does the truth comes to the light (JN 3:21). Birds roost with their own kind, and truth comes back to those who practice it (SIR 27:9)—(American translation).

The Word in the divine Trinity is essentially fruitful in love, in the Holy Spirit. But the Trinity also expresses itself externally in words that are creative. It reveals itself in words proclaiming love, but above all in the great deeds of Christ's love. And in this divine pattern we too can "be" in the truth and bear witness to the truth, but only if we "practice the truth in love" (EPH 5:15). The revealed word in us manifests itself effectively as divinely true only if it is fruitful in love. But the more we live from the truth in love, the more does the heavenly truth penetrate our hearts. As the knowledge of truth and love grows and ripens, so also does the doing of truth and love. Knowing and doing go hand in hand.

Truth in practice is opposed to all sterility in works of faith and love, but most directly to actions which contradict the convictions of faith and the manifest will of God. The contrary of this truth in action is hypocrisy which is conscious dissimulation in deeds which do not flow from attachment to truth but from the straining for the mere appearance of reality. It is the lie in deeds.

4. Truth in Words (To Speak True: Truthfulness in the Narrow Sense)

a. TRUTHFULNESS AND ITS RETINUE

The true speech of man must be patterned on the divine Word as that which it reflects and imitates. It must be viewed in this light, both from its origin within us, which is the mental word (our knowledge) and from its end and purpose, which is the way to love, and the exchange of love.

For Saint Augustine the inner mental word, the word of knowledge, must profoundly make us like to the Logos, the Word of God:

"The word that sounds outwardly is the sign of the word that gives light inwardly; which latter has the greater claim to be called a word."[2]

As the Eternal Word assumes human flesh, so the audible word must in some measure be an incarnation of the inner or mental word:

"When, therefore, that is in the word which is in the knowledge, then there is a true word, and truth, such as is looked for from man; such that what is in the knowledge is also in the word, and what is not in the knowledge is also not in the word. Here may be recognized, "Yea, yea; nay, nay" (MT 5:37).

"And so this likeness of the image that is made approaches as nearly as is possible to that likeness of the image that is born, by which God the Son is declared to be in all things like in substance (*substantialiter similis*) to the Father."[3]

It is true that we cannot exhaustively express our own inner mental word, the word of knowledge, by our external word (for that matter even our inner knowledge can never comprehensively grasp the rich full meaning of reality) and often we are not even permitted to reveal it fully. However, the divine likeness must be preserved so fully within us that nothing in our external word may ever be found which is not in our inner word of knowledge.

"God the begetter, . . . has in some way spoken by His own co-eternal Word all things that He has in His substance; and God His Word Himself, . . . Himself has nothing either more or less in substance than is in Him, who, not lying but truly, hath begotten the Word."[4] God the Father expresses Himself fully only in the Word, in His Son; in creation and revelation, however, He grants us participation in His truth only by degrees.

The Word of God, the Son, cannot lie. "This Word can never have anything false, because it is unchangeable, as He is from whom it is. For 'the Son can do nothing of Himself but what He seeth the Father do.' "[5] But Christ is absolutely truthful, even though He proclaims the mysteries of His Heart only gradually and not at all, even though He does not cast "pearls before swine" (MT 7:6). He, all truthful, praises the Father, the source of all truth, for having hidden from the wise and prudent what He revealed to the little and humble ones (MT 11:25). Hence the primordial source and pattern of every true utterance lays down the norm of truth for us: nothing in our utterance (words) may contradict what is in our mind (our thought). But we are not obliged, or even permitted, to express all that is in our mind (our knowledge).

To maintain an adequate moral norm of "true speech" we must go beyond the mere psychological concept of true speech (conformity of word to mind) and keep in mind the divine primordial pattern and the human end and purpose of the word. The goal is the building up of love in ourselves, in our neighbor, in the community. Speech (in this term we include all signs and actions insofar as they "express" something for our neighbor) must be community-forming and community-sustaining. Intellectual (spiritual) and moral fellowship can exist only in the

harmony of word and love. The word which does not flow
from the love for the good and for one's neighbor becomes
contradictory because it cannot be the basis of fellowship. Only
the word which serves the good and enriches the treasure of
love in the world is like to God in His truth and fulfills its
commitment to the ideal of the divine pattern.

The divine pattern, ultimate norm and guide of truth, forbids
us to turn truth to evil use by damaging our neighbor. But this is
not to say that we should not with all our might engage against
evil. The authentically truthful man will not play fast and
loose with truth. He cannot deal with truth in a heartless and
calculating manner but must be taken up with it, heart and soul.
Every word of truth must be guided by prudence, by discretion
which makes clear to us whether or not the word which is
formally true is truly edifying here and now, whether it bridges
over differences, closes gaps, heals wounds, binds the members
of the Mystical Body together, testifies to truth; or on the contrary, ravages and divides it, shuts it out from men's hearts.
Only love possesses this unfailing insight, the discernment
which always perceives truth in the splendor and service of
love.

The interior attachment of truth and love expresses itself in
straight-forwardness, uprightness (*simplicitas*), which are a
realization of the words of Jesus: "Be therefore wise as serpents, and guileless as doves" (MT 10:16). Frankness and
simple genuineness of character manifests itself in one's language and in one's whole deportment. Its opposite is duplicity,
discord, and perfidy.

Frankness or the spirit of candor does not pervert truthfulness into a means of currying favor and popularity. On the
contrary, the candid man is ready to sacrifice his own advantage
by taking up the cudgels for truth in the service of the good.

Sincerity and candor are bound up with openness of heart
which has nothing to conceal. For the upright man purges his
soul of all which—as far as he is concerned—should reasonably
be kept secret. But even the sincere and upright man, for all his
openheartedness, must conceal many things because of consid-

eration for his neighbors. Therefore openness must be bound up with reticence, which, as far as is possible, spares the sensitivity of others, and gives thoughtless, cunning, or malicious men no occasion to mar the good work of those whom our imprudent speech has placed in an unfavorable light.

Silence is the deep fountain of the correct and fruitful use of speech. One who does not know how to keep silent in order to uphold the great truths and problems which support our human existence is likewise not capable of being an authentic witness through his speech for the divine truth. From the depth of silence words have their profoundest meaning. Loquacity robs words of their gravity and depth. It often leads to indifference to truth and to the perversion of reality to the prejudice of our neighbor. Without the "faculty" of silence, truth loses the insight and luster of love and the dynamic authority of witness.

b. THE LIE

The positive (affirmative) precept to serve the truth (which by comparison with the negative prohibition of the lie is the more important and comprehensive) binds at all suitable and proper times and according to the measure of the subject's powers and the circumstances. The negative precept, "You shall not bear false witness against your neighbor" (EX 20:16) obliges always and under all conditions: the lie is intrinsically evil and therefore never permitted.

The sacred scripture condemns lying categorically and without any reservation:

Flee from lying (EX 23:7, Vulgate).
You shall not lie or speak falsely to one another (LV 19:11).
Put falsehood and lying far from me (PRV 30:8).
Delight not in telling lie after lie, for it never results in good (SIR 7:13).

Especially numerous and incisive are the passages which single out for condemnation lying connected with harming others (EX 20:16; PRV 6:16 ff.; SIR 4:25).

In the New Testament Christ links lying basically with the

152   ON BEING RESPONSIBLE

devil, "the father of lies" (JN 8:44 ff.). He demands of His
disciples simple and upright speech (MT 5:34 ff.). Saint Paul
bases his condemnation of the lie—residue of the old unregen-
erate man—and its utter perversion on its irreconcilability with
the essential character of grace in us (COL 3:9 f.) and our
membership in the Mystical Body of Christ (EPH 4:24 f.).
Saint Peter regards the lie as directed against the Holy Spirit. If
the punishment of Ananias and Sapphira is extremely severe, it
is not because they withheld the purchase money of their land,
but because they lied (ACTS 5:1 ff.). The passage is significant
because it is not actually concerned with a "damaging" lie and
yet the chastisement as well as the language of the Apostle
justifies us in considering the offense a grave one. The couple
obviously aggravated the heinousness of their lie by contriving
to deceive the Church authorities. The Apocalypse allots the
"liars" their portion in the pool of fire (AP 21:8). The lie
excludes men from the celestial Jerusalem (AP 21:27; 22:15).
Paul also lists the lie in one of his catalogues of sin together
with grave sins (I TM 1:10).

Tradition.[6] The most ancient Hellenic Christian tradition regarding the lie derives from Greek philosophy and from certain
passages of holy scripture. In Greek philosophy (apart from
Aristotle and Sophocles) there is hardly any notable representative who condemns the lie as absolutely unlawful. The biblical
passages pertinent to this background, in turn, tell of certain lies
of the patriarchs without expressly condemning them. In consequence of this Greek and biblical background there is a degree
of hesitance and vacillation in primitive Hellenic Christianity
regarding the morality of lying. *Origen* and *Chrysostom* are
particularly obscure, as are *Hilary* and *Cassian* who draw in-
spiration from them. These Fathers, appealing to the example
of the patriarchs, sought to justify at least the use of the officious lie—under certain circumstances—if it proved of advantage to one's neighbor.

In contradiction to this position the doctrine that every lie is
absolutely forbidden was defended by Saint Augustine whose
teaching determined all subsequent tradition. Already in his

early work, *De Mendacio,* he decisively repudiated the doctrine that any lie is lawful, though subsequent reflection led to misgivings about his presentation. He felt that he had not been decisive enough regarding the theoretic bases of the book. He was particularly concerned with the question of the will to deceive. Does the will to deceive belong to the nature of the lie? "It is obvious that a false utterance with the will to deceive is a lie."[7] But here his later teaching is already clearly in evidence that it is not simply the express will to deceive which constitutes the lie, but rather the deliberate false utterance which implicitly also contains the will to deceive.

"Wherefore, that man lies who has one thing in his mind and utters another in words or by signs of whatever kind."[8]

"But whoever shall think there is any sort of lie that is not sin will deceive himself foully, while he deems himself honest as a deceiver of other men."[9] In his later work *Against Lying* (*Contra Mendacium*) Augustine is even sharper in defense of this position. Here he makes every effort to resolve the difficulties arising from the sacred scriptures and from practical life with its many sources of friction. *Saint Jerome,* who in his commentary on Galatians had justified the officious lie in serious situations, seems to have been won over to Augustine's point of view in the famous controversy between the two great doctors. Subsequently theology follows the teaching of Augustine throughout: unequivocally it declares that any consciously false utterance is unlawful. Every lie is evil.

Luther, after his apostasy from the Church, was the first who ventured to depart from this tradition with a sweeping defense of the lie:

"A good hearty lie for the sake of the good and for the Christian Church, a lie in case of necessity, a useful lie, a serviceable lie would not be against God."[10] Despite this bold statement, H. Grisar rather overstates his case when he accuses the Reformer of constructing an entire "theology of the lie."[11] Most Lutherans adhere to the position of their leader, whereas Calvin and the "Reformed Church" faithful to the ancient Christian tradition condemn every lie as evil.

Since the time of *Hugo Grotius* and *Samuel Puffendorf,* there has been a wide acceptance in Protestant circles of the distinction between *mendacium,* the lie, or withholding of the truth which another has the right to know, and *falsiloquium,* or false speech, which is the consciously false utterance in instances when the other party has no right to the truth. The latter was considered morally indifferent. Practically speaking the purely mental reservation defended by some Catholic theologians in the seventeenth century did not differ from this *falsiloquium.* Accordingly it was deservedly condemned by the Church.[12]

Unfortunately in more recent times a number of Catholic moral theologians who deserve well of theology in other respects have sought to distinguish a morally justifiable false utterance from a lie. They defended such utterances as acts of necessary defense. Thus with some differences testify Tanquerey[13] (who maintained, though incorrectly, that his conoept did not objectively differ from the "perceptible mental reservation"), Vermeersch,[14] Lindworsky,[15] Ledrus,[16] Laros.[17] Laros says: "The patent violation of the right to truth by the inquiring party must enter the definition of the lie."[18]

Though we realize full well that all these moralists wish to restrict the justifiable use of the *falsiloquium* to an absolute minimum, their opinion itself must be rejected. The obligation to truthfulness is not derived from the individual right of a specific individual to my utterance, but from the divine primordial source of truth, from the value of one's own uprightness, and not last from the right of the community to absolute trustworthiness of speech. It is certainly true that the basic renunciation of every conscious false utterance may at times demand the greatest sacrifice. But the Christian—perhaps only the Christian—can find this sacrifice meaningful and obligatory because he sees truth in the splendor of the holiness and love of God.

c. THE LIE: MORTAL OR VENIAL SIN

There is no doubt that the obligation to truth as such is grave. Theologians are likewise in agreement that the malicious lie (under this classification we include not only the damage done in the material order, but also—and even more so—the damage to faith and the knowledge of moral values and principles) is grave by its nature (*ex genere suo*).

As to the question whether the lie as infringement on truth (apart from any involvement of love) is grave sin by its nature (*ex genere suo*) or only venial sin, the views of theologians differ. Most theologians of more recent times hold that a lie as untruth is only a venial sin. Obviously the venial sin may be rendered gravely culpable through the motive or circumstances or some other reason, such as scandal.

The whole of tradition confirms this position at least in the sense that jocose lies and so-called useful lies are as a rule considered venial faults.[19] But since all theologians concede that a lie is a grave fault where a decisive position regarding truth is involved, we should not take umbrage at the formulation of Mausbach: "A lie, like theft, detraction or calumny, and similar faults, is of its nature a grave sin (*ex genere suo*)."[20] For this opinion merely expresses more pertinently than the other view that the obligation to truth as such is very serious; and therefore if this basic principle is not flouted, our practical judgment of a concrete instance of lying need be no more severe than that of the milder view: the lie, apart from the malicious or damaging lie, is in itself only a venial sin. The holy scriptures (cf. especially WIS 1:11; PRV 12:22; SIR 20:23 ff.; PS 5:7) speaking of the lie in general use terms which can imply grave culpability. And yet it is clear from other passages that the very converse is true regarding the so-called lies of necessity or the useful lies of the patriarchs, the Egyptian midwives and others. The sacred account does not treat these as involving subjectively grave culpability.

Indeed on the part of God the prohibition of any and every untruth is to be considered strict and rigorous. Wherefore we cannot hold with Kern[21] that a lie generally speaking is not against the order of love, but only beyond it (*non contra sed praeter ordinem caritatis*). More correctly we should say that in the last analysis it is due to human frailty and imperfection that ordinary petty lies—speaking very generally—are only venial faults. This experience is expressed by Augustine and Aquinas in union with the whole ancient tradition.[22] But a distinction is in place: we may well agree that within the moral-pastoral context reflecting human experience the ordinary lie is a venial sin and not in conflict with the order of love. However, this is not the same as to lay down as a basic abstract principle: the lie as such is not in actual conflict with the order of love. The basis of formulation of the principle is not the antithesis of laxism or of rigorism but the fundamental problem of the nature of venial sin itself. Does venial sin ultimately arise from the imperfection of the act which generally must be prudently assumed when a petty object is involved, or from the fact that certain things in themselves do not directly oppose the commandment of God and hence to an extent merely lead one somewhat astray.[23] The lie as such is diametrically opposed to the will of God who is Truth itself. Wherefore the Christian must also assume a decisive position basically and in principle in opposition to the lie. To reject truth and its demands in principle is quite different from an occasional lapse, an actual lie due to excitement, personal difficulty or need, excess of sympathy for our neighbor,[24] none of which is the "fundamental" lie.

As our prudential norm we must hold strictly that ordinary lies regarding matters which involve no special value are to be considered practically only venial faults. This rule which does not diminish the seriousness of the combat against the lie holds above all in regard to the reception of the holy sacraments.

A special problem is posed by the jocose lie. If one actually wants to lead another into error, the jocose lie is really a sin. If our neighbor is harmed, humiliated, or disgraced, the jocose lie might under certain circumstances fall under the condemnation of the pernicious or damaging lie. Often, on the contrary, the jocose lie as such aims only at amusement or recreation of others and if the truth is clearly evident from the entire context, it is my opinion that there is no lie at all. For we are not permitted to take a part of the whole discourse out of context, but must consider the meaning of the conversation as a whole. Accordingly most jocose lies would not have to be considered as actually lies at all, though this is not to say that such a type of wit is to be commended.

Frequently the officious lie told to relieve one's neighbor from distress or misery without harming anyone, is not *subjectively* culpable. Though every lie is objectively sinful there are instances when one does not consider or intend the infringement of truth but only the rendering of service. Nevertheless it should always be borne in mind that the good cause has no need of our lie (JB 13:7).

The falsification of information is an especially aggravated form of lying fraught with grave consequences. Nothing so readily undermines or destroys the confidence of men in their fellows as such perversion of the communication media.

As we showed when treating commutative justice, the material and spiritual harm knowingly caused by lying obliges the guilty party to make good the damage wrought by this sin against truth and justice.

d. THE LIES OF CHILDREN

The fanciful stories of children who are—let us say—under five years of age should not in general be censured as lies since the lively play of fantasy is not yet adequately distinguished from objective insight. In this period of the child's life training to truth should consist above all in the kindly introduction to examination of the "untruthful" utterances. In the subsequent years—and in part also in very early years—children's lies are due above all to anxiety, to the imitation of lying practices of adults, or to a reaction springing from their previous experience of distrust or lack of confidence. Therefore those who undertake the guidance of children in such matters must first look to themselves and examine their own conduct. Education to truth can succeed only if it is based on the exemplary pattern of truthfulness of parent or teacher, on confidence and kindly restraint in correction and punishment. Chastisement, even though deserved, should be altogether omitted at times as recognition of uprightness and sincerity when the child admits a fault.

e. PATHOLOGICAL LYING

It would not be correct to maintain that a psychopath bears no moral responsibility whatever for the lies he may tell. But it is true that the neurotic and especially the psychopathic person manifests a strong propensity for lying. And to a certain degree they are not capable—or at least not at all times—of discriminating between truthful and mendacious utterance. Apart from the many delusions to which they are subjected, many a lie scarcely enters their conscious awareness as morally reprehensible in itself, even though there may be some awareness that their assertions are awry. Often in fact the moral barriers and psychic inhibitions against lying which are normal safeguards in mentally sound individuals break down almost completely in psychopaths. The result is a veritable obsession for lying and deception, for exalting themselves by lies (megalomania to the point of delusions of grandeur). The asocial passion for lying and the mania for fantastic fabrication and self-glorification can become so entwined and confused that eventually the sorry psychopathic "liars" can no longer clearly distinguish between truth, fantasy, and conscious lies. For them the boundaries of truth, imagination, and lie are blurred. In consequence moral responsibility is diminished in proportion to the extent or degree of their mental illness. As to their correction and cure, the educative procedure must stress above all the concern for truthfulness. They must be given the same kindly understanding as that which is given to children. But they must be led step by step to sense the moral malice of lying.

5. The Secret

a. THE BASIS AND JUSTIFICATION OF THE SECRET

The all-truthful God did not disclose the mysteries of His love at every turn of history and to every individual.

I praise thee, Father, Lord of heaven and earth, that thou didst hide these things from the wise and prudent, and didst reveal them to little ones (MT 11:25).

Even to His privileged friends the Lord says:

Many things yet I have to say to you, but you cannot bear them now (JN 16:12).

For those to whom the revealed truth is committed the Savior lays down this norm:

Do not give to dogs what is holy, neither cast your pearls before swine (MT 7:6).

Reverence for truth in its divine source must caution us against manifesting it without reason where there is no preparation or disposition to receive or accept it fruitfully, where the right response to it will certainly not be given, or where we cannot actually bear witness to it. In the communication of truth the acceptance and response are of capital importance. Many delicate problems can be discussed with a mature and moderate man who appreciates the value of just and honest criticism if heat and passion are avoided. Even abuses and grievances can be seriously pondered in such an atmosphere, whereas public discussion of the same matters in open forums might result in disaster.

A further reason for keeping certain things secret is reverence for the intimate realm of the soul—one's own and others. Indeed if the good we do should be guarded from the prying gaze of others—when this is possible—then it is surely simulation or falsehood, to say the least, to make a vulgar display of our most intimate impulses for good which have hardly gone beyond the stage of impulse, since we have hardly fully approved of them or sustained them in trial and temptation.

Man has the right to the mask of exterior calm and self-mastery. The soul which unmasks its inner self to the gaze of all and indulges in free converse about its inmost thoughts cannot come to itself in rich spiritual fruition.[25]

The soul should be open, completely open only to God (and of course this includes also the tribunal of penance). It should also be noted that if we were to expose the depth of our intimacy (our temptations and aspirations) indiscriminately to any and every one, we would quite often cause scandal, nip incipient resolution in the bud, and place the purity of our motives in peril.

Even more urgently do reverence and love forbid us to pry into the intimate life of our neighbor or to divulge secrets entrusted to us.

The secret is above all a stern imperative arising from harsh and evil reality. We must always reckon with our own frailty as well as with the susceptibility of our neighbor. And above all with the reality of the war between good and evil in and about us. We may never deliver the weapons of combat to the enemies of the good through our indiscretion. Even in earthly enterprises the lack of discretion can cause very serious damage to ourselves and our neighbors, to entire families and communities. Our moral teaching must take a very serious view of human sinfulness and frailty. For this reason the moral laws are in great part "ordinances of exigence in an evil world."

Nevertheless, since the knowledge of human sinfulness and frailty is a basis—and indeed not the least in significance—of the secret, it follows that this knowledge must always be animated by loving understanding, must always remain open and sympathetic, for in our natural and supernatural life we are committed to a loving understanding and fellowship. We cannot stand alone. We have need of others whom we can trust and in whom we can confide when occasion demands. If this were not possible, we should fail in many ways. Our cares and trials and struggles would prove too much for us. However, in the most intimate and serious concerns of our life, we can confide only in men who are discretely silent. From this it is evident that the proper sense of silence and the sacred vigilance over committed secrets—rather than degenerating into a closed and forbidding reserve—will always be open and sympathetic to the confidence of others.

b. THE VARIOUS KINDS OF SECRETS

1. The natural secret includes all hidden truths or facts whose revelation by the very nature of the case would here and now violate justice or charity.

2. The promised secret embraces all hidden truths or facts which one has lawfully promised not to disclose, even though apart from the promise there may be no obligation to secrecy. The promise follows the nature of the object: if the secrecy is meaningless or even in conflict with a higher good the obligation of the promise ceases.

3. The committed secret embraces all the knowledge which one has obtained under the explicit or implicit condition of secrecy. The most important type in this class is the professional secret (of physicians, midwives, lawyers, notaries, etc.). The strictest and most sacred of professional secrets is protected under the seal of the confessional, and next to it is any secret entrusted to the priest as a spiritual guide or director. Complete secrecy is an indispensable prerequisite for fruitful spiritual activity in the care of souls.

c. PRINCIPAL OBLIGATIONS REGARDING SECRECY

It is forbidden (1) to pry into the secrets of others, (2) to misuse or exploit secrets, (3) to betray, to divulge, or publicize them.

1. It is a grave sin (*ex genere suo*) to pry into the secrets of others, without just cause, for the purpose of using the information in violation of justice and charity. If the motivation is only curiosity and there is no desire to exploit the knowledge sought, the fault is not too readily to be considered grave.

Unauthorized eavesdropping or spying on others is a gross impropriety. It is gravely sinful to tape record what are probably indiscreet remarks in an unguarded conversation without the knowledge and consent of the speaker in order to trap or expose him. Our judgment would be quite different, of course, if such action were taken only to protect oneself or others from grave and unjust damage.

For adequate reasons, just and proportionate, (e.g., good of souls, aversion of injustice threatening ourselves, our neighbors or the community, etc.) it may be permitted, at times even required, to probe into the secrets of others. However, it must always be borne in mind that the means must be honorable. (Obviously, if a confidential relationship is disturbed or destroyed in such an effort, it may well be questioned whether the evil resulting may not be greater than the good one hopes to accomplish.)

To read the letters of others without authorization is generally speaking a violation of justice in a very sensitive area. Nevertheless the state does have the right to restrict this privileged and secret form of communication to avert the menace of grave danger (e.g. in times of war). In instances when censorship of private correspondence is established the authorites may make no use of the information gleaned in this manner unless it is demanded by the common welfare. And it goes without saying that the officials concerned are bound by the professional secret regarding the contents of the letters subjected to the censorship.

Parents and teachers have the right to exercise control over the correspondence of their charges if they have serious reason to fear that privacy is gravely abused. In fact parents have a far-reaching right of controlling the correspondence of their minor children.

As to the attitude of spouses in this matter, it would be ideal indeed if husbands and wives could dispense entirely with secrecy in their private correspondence. But a certain prudent reserve is always in order. Surely it is not necessary that every letter be laid open to view before both spouses. For this reason neither spouse is allowed to read the other's letter against his or her will. But if a well-grounded suspicion of immanent danger exists (e.g. of an adulterous liaison on the part of one of the spouses) it is permissible to read the letter which probably contains the evidence of such sinful communication. In fact under certain circumstances it would even be permissible to intercept the letter. However, such actions obviously must be

guided by loving prudence, lest the evil be worsened rathe..
corrected.

If the statutes or customary grant the religious superior the
right to read the letters of religious subjects, obviously the superior is strictly bound to secrecy regarding the contents of the
communication. If in the course of reading he should come
upon matters of conscience or family secrets which are outside
the realm of his official duty, he must discontinue the reading.

We may make only such use of secret information acquired
from others as justice and love permit or require. Hence it is
obvious that we may use secret information in order to protect
from bodily or spiritual harm the individual about whom this
secrecy is concerned. But of course no use may be made of
information, acquired in the sacrament of penance, which
would violate the seal of the confessional. In every instance of
official secrecy serious effort must be made to avoid any under-
mining of public trust in professional secrecy or in the profession itself.

Under certain circumstances we may also use secret information about the affairs of others in order to protect ourselves and
our neighbor from harm, provided that thereby trust and confidence is not undermined and misused. But unjustly acquired
information regarding secret matters may not be used if the
circumstances are such that this use is tantamount to a continuation or exploitation of the sin by which the secret was first
obtained.

3. To disclose or publicize a natural secret without authorization is a grave sin by its nature (*ex genere suo*). *A fortiori* such
violation of the professional secret is also a grave sin by its
nature.

If one has merely promised secrecy in instances where there
is no natural or professional secret, such disclosure is usually no
more than a venial sin, if indeed the promise binds under sin at
all.

The damage done by violation of the professional secret must
always be repaired *in justice*. Other violations of secrecy in
general oblige to restitution "only" in charity, unless justice is

ₕh use of unjust means.

.ch is founded in charity, has also its limits in ₗigation to secrecy ceases, (a) if the one con‐ ₒly permits or is obliged to permit its disclosure, (ᵦ₎ ₗtter has ceased to be secret because of disclosure by otheᵣ. ₒc) if disclosure effects a greater good than secrecy itself.

If one is obliged to render an account of a certain matter to a superior or to a court of law, he is not freed from the obliga‐ tion because of a conflicting promise of secrecy.

The mere promise of secrecy, when no higher good is in‐ volved, cannot oblige one who has made the promise to expose himself, without good reason, to disproportionately great dam‐ age or even risk of his life. We might go a step further and assert that not only is there no obligation to keep such a prom‐ ise, often there is not even a justification for doing so. (These views differ from those of many ancient authors.)

If safeguarding a secret in certain areas would cause dis‐ proportionately great damage to the community or to an inno‐ cent party, the matter must be disclosed even though the prom‐ ise of secrecy was confirmed with an oath. However, here we must always bear in mind that professional secrecy above all is an important factor in the common welfare and therefore out‐ weighs or counterbalances many advantages of a lesser order.

To discuss a secret matter with a person who is responsible and discreet in speech in order to be advised on a weighty problem or to be relieved of great mental strain or anxiety is ordinarily permissible. But in any instance the secret itself may not be endangered.

Physicians are faced with a knotty problem of professional secrecy when dealing with abortion and other crimes which must be prevented. Surely the physician is not bound to secrecy if through exercise of his service on his own part (hence not through the confidence of his patient), he comes upon an in‐ stance of an abortion performed by an unscrupulous man from whom one may anticipate still further immoral action. The diffi‐ culty is compounded if the physician learns of the crime only through the confidential physician-patient relationship. It seems certain to me that in this instance he is not permitted to betray the confidence by reporting the patient. But he would be allowed—all the while offering the greatest possible safeguards to the patient confiding in him—to pursue a criminal who constituted a menace to the common welfare to the point of having him reported and properly arraigned. In my opinion the physician who had ferreted out such a case would even be justified in exerting moderate pressure upon his patient to permit a judicial arraignment.

But in no instance may the physician consider himself an agent of the state, of its departments of criminal investigation and police power. His service and his professional secrecy is directed first of all to the sick. It is a service to life. And yet we may not justly expect of him that he should reward a "confidence" that violated his sense of duty with silence.

Thus, for example, if the civil law should prescribe that the physician would have to report every case of miscarriage and every abortion, in my opinion he would be obliged in some measure to comply. However, he would not be under obligation in the instance when a patient came to him in confidence after such an operation. For disclosure even in such cases would make it impossible for the patient to consult a conscientious physician with the result that the vile craft of unscrupulous quacks would only be encouraged.

d. VEILED SPEECH (MENTAL RESERVATION)

The secret is to be safeguarded through silence in language and deportment. Ordinarily an indiscreet inquirer should not be answered at all, though he may be rebuffed or diverted by a counter-inquiry. However, in many instances silence which attracts special attention or a rebuff betrays the very secret it should protect. Nor is a lie permitted to safeguard the most important secrets. In consequence quite frequently there is no other way left open except a manner of speech which, though not untrue, nevertheless conceals more than it discloses. It is possible even in using words to "be silent," to veil, to conceal. Of course this is not the original or primary meaning and purpose of the word. Therefore among the true disciples of Christ the oath and veiled speech may not be given too much leeway. Their speech should rather be the simple, Yes, yes, No, no (cf. MT 5:34 ff.). But veiled speech, like the secret which it serves, is at times a necessity, an "order of necessity" in an evil world, a consideration for one's own and others' frailty.

Christ Himself used expressions which in some way resemble what we call "mental reservation." On many occasions in addressing the Jewish people He spoke only in parables whose full meaning He revealed only to His disciples (cf. MT 13:10 ff.). But even to them His words were often veiled. Let us note the much cited response to the disciples regarding the last day. It is the classical instance: "But of that day or hour no one knows, neither the angels in heaven, nor the Son, but the Father only" (MK 13:32). The meaning in its bearing on the question itself is, "the Son of man as Revealer of the mysteries of God," does not possess "communicable" knowledge. The questioners, keeping in mind the full context of the Savior's words, the occasion and circumstances, and particularly the Master's mission, could rightly grasp His meaning. But of course prepossessed as they were with their petty curiosity, they could readily miss the deeper sense (cf. JN 2:19 ff.). With such a mentality they could take as simple ignorance what was tantamount to a rebuke for curiosity and a directive to be concerned with the deeper mysteries of salvation.

Veiled speech or the "response with deeper meaning" (*hintergruendige Antwort*), in order to be morally justified, must always have a proportionate reason and a discernible deeper meaning. The reason must be love under some aspect or other. This required background of deeper meaning is designated in the traditional moral theology by the term of "perceptible mental reservation" (*restrictio non pure mentalis*). Even veiled speech must be true, which is to say the thought in the background, which is precisely the occasion of the words used, must correspond to the external expression in some way and under some aspect, so that the interior and exterior word are in accord.

Veiled discourse has precisely this as its purpose, not to disclose the full thought, but consciously to conceal a phase of it which was misused by another (usually the inquirer), or which would unnecessarily distress or damage another. But this concealment is part of a discourse which is in itself true, though of course it does not express that which the inquirer—because of his unwarranted anticipation—will take out of it, but which he could understand if he rightly grasped the situation and above all his own position as indiscreet inquirer.

Truthfulness consists in the agreement of our thought and the meaning of our words expressing the thought.[26] If in our discourse there is no thought (no interior word) corresponding to our speech (the exterior word), then the discourse is a lie. If the inner word is merely reserved in the mind and in no way contained in the exterior word, then we have what is called a *purely mental restriction*. This is in no way better than a lie and justly condemned by the Church's magisterium.[27]

However, the discourse—true but veiled—or the perceptible (*broad*) *mental reservation* makes use of a mode of speech which can have a multiple meaning. This meaning lies either in the current significance of the words or in the special situation of inquirer and speaker (in the manner of speaking, the use of gestures, or in other signs, etc.). Among these multiple meanings one corresponds to my true thought, but nevertheless does not betray the secret which is to be kept from the inquirer. To this meaning I relate my thought (here we have the mental background). This inner reference to a suitable or proper meaning—even though it is not the obvious or surface meaning—of the veiled discourse is nothing else but the perceptible (broadly such) mental reservation.

Hence it is clear that the mental reservation—which implies the correspondence of the mind to a true and proper meaning of external terms and signs—becomes impossible and absurd if under the actual circumstances the discourse can have no valid meaning, if indeed an objective listener cannot detect at least the multiverse significance or the imprecision of the language used.

The purpose of veiled discourse is not deception as such. It is not to mislead others so much as to protect a truth whose disclosure here and now would violate love of neighbor. Misleading one's neighbor (who plays the role of indiscreet inquirer) may nevertheless be permitted if under the circumstances this is the lesser evil and if the deception is not the inevitable or necessary result of the veiled discourse as such.

The multiverse discourse as veiled speech must always be an exception—only reluctantly accepted or tolerated as dire necessity in an evil world by the disciple of Christ. He will not have recourse to it for every petty reason, above all never because of egotistic or avaricious motives. Judiciously used, it is a manifestation of love for truth. Ineptly, inopportunely used, it leads to mendacity. The use of veiled discourse in a manner which does not betray an inviolable secret, nor trample truth underfoot is a meaningful act of Christian prudence in accordance with the admonition of the Lord: "Be therefore wise as serpents, and guileless as doves" (MT 10:6).

In critical situations in which the truth must be kept inviolate it surely is possible that the Christian can become perplexed and confused to such an extreme that in groping for veiled speech he will hit upon words which are concretely and in fact much like pure mental reservation, objectively the equivalent to a lie (M. Laros and others of like mind would speak of this as permissible false speech). The perplexed conscience which in case of necessity can see no escape from its dilemma (violation of secrecy or false utterance) except through false speech in order to protect an inviolable secret should not be judged as guilty of a lie. The disposition toward truth is such that the so-called false discourse should be considered veiled speech or broad mental reservation. However, this mild verdict applied practically in cases of perplexed conscience may not be taken from a concrete context and distorted into a kind of principle which would prove flexible enough to justify the slightest deviation from truth. Christian prudence in even the most critical situations will find a way to avoid having a lie laid to its charge, but will trust in the guidance of the Holy Spirit (MT 10:20).

Even though it does not deviate formally from the norm of

true utterance, veiled speech is not in place in instances when (1) one must confess the true faith, (2) or is obliged in charity or in virtue of one's office or position to inform or instruct others regarding errors or dangers which may beset them, (3) or is lawfully questioned in court or in the tribunal of penance (in matters falling within the competence of the official or confessor), (4) or draws up a bilateral contract.

The problem of the mental reservation confirmed under oath presents very serious difficulties for the moral theologian: is one permitted to confirm a mental reservation (an equivocal response) for proportionately grave reasons? Very many moralists reply in the affirmative, provided that the mental reservation is a truly "perceptible" one and no scandal is involved. However, a caution is in place. This view of theologians is the result of an extreme—we might call it an almost inhuman—stress of the law in certain countries and historic epochs. The accused was interrogated even under torture to extort information of every conceivable kind. In civilized states in which the accused has the right to decline to answer in all just and reasonable matters the problem cannot arise at all.

To confirm under oath and without good reason an equivocal statement which one foresees will mislead another seems to me to be strictly and absolutely a mortal sin. However, many moralists have held that such an act is no more than a venial sin.

It is difficult to determine in individual concrete instances whether or not a specific form of speech is in conflict with the moral demands of truth. This is to say that it is not easy and often not even possible to form a judgment, *a priori,* regarding the permissibility of certain veiled utterances apart from the concrete situation. The reason is obvious: quite often only this concrete situation gives to the speech this or that particular meaning, ambiguity, or multiple sense.

The following examples should serve to clarify our teaching:

1. Ordinarily one may respond to an unwarranted or unauthorized question regarding a professional secret: "I don't know

anything about it" (with the mental reservation "to communicate to others"); or with a clearer rebuff of the indiscreet questioner: "I know absolutely nothing about it."

2. To an unjust or unwarranted demand in the courts one may answer: "You are asking too much"; or "With the best intention in the world I can't say anything about it"; or in extreme cases, "I know nothing about it." The reservation "about which I could be rightly interrogated" is "perceptible" through the situation which involves the clear circumstance of illegality of interrogation.

3. The faithless spouse nagged beyond endurance by the question, "Did you commit adultery?" may use a mental reservation in order to save his marriage by responding: "How can you ask me such a question?" or "I object to such suspicion" or (after a good confession) "I do not have such a sin on my conscience" or better "Let's spare ourselves such suspicion and such questions."

4. According to the customary forms of polite speech one may call ill-prepared meals good, for in some manner they are "good." Similar forms are justifiable to encourage the sick.

NOTES

[1] R. Bultmann, "Aletheia" in *ThW* I, S 248.

[2] Augustine, *De trinitate* lib. 15, cap. XI. PL 42, 1071.

[3] *L.c.*, PL 42, 1072.

[4] *L.c.*, lib. 15 cap. XXI. PL 42, 1088.

[5] *L.c.*, lib. 15, cap. XIV. PL 42, 1073.

[6] Cf. in relation to the following paragraphs, A. Kern, *Die Luege* (Graz, 1930), S 17 ff.

[7] Augustine, *De mendacio* cap. IV, 5. PL 40, 491.

[8] *L.c.*, cap. III, 3. PL 40, 488.

[9] *L.c.*, cap. XXI, 42. PL 40, 516.

[10] Philipps *Briefwechsel*, I, S 369 f. in A. Kern, *Die Luege* S 57.

[11] H. Grisar, *Luther* (Freiburg, 1911), II, S 460. Translation: *Luther*, (St. Louis: B. Herder, 1915) vol. IV p. 108 ff. Cf. also J. Lortz, *Die Reformation in Deutschland*, (Herder; Freiburg in Br., 1941), II, 248.

[12] Innocent XI (1676-1689) condemned the following position: Si quis vel solus vel coram aliis, sive interrogatus sive propria sponte, sive recreationis causa, sive quocunque alio fine iuret, se non fecisse aliquid, quod revera fecit, intelligendo intra se aliquid aliud, quod non fecit, vel aliam viam ab ea, in qua fecit, vel quodvis aliud additum verum, revera non mentitur nec est periurus. D 1176. Cf. also 1177.

[13] A. Tanquerey, *Synopsis theologiae moralis,* 9 ed.; III, 381-83.

[14] A Vermersch, S.J., "De mendacio," *Greg.* 1 (1930), 11-40; 425-74.

[15] J. Lindworsky, S.J. "Das Problem der Luege bei katholischen Ethikern und Moralisten," in O. Lippmann, *Die Luege.* (Leipzig, 1927), S 69 ff.

[16] M. Ledrus, S.J. "De mendacio," PRM 32(1943), 5-58; 123-71; 33 (1944), 5-60.

[17] M. Laros, *Seid klug wie die Schlangen und einfaeltig wie die Tauben* (Frankfurt, 1951).

[18] *L.c.,* S 82.

[19] Cf. Augustine, *Enarrationes in Psalmos* 5. PL 36, 86; II-II, q. 110, a. 4.

[20] J. Mausbach, *Kath. Moraltheologie;* 5 Aufl. III, S 244. This position is still maintained in the revision of Ermecke, 10th edition, III, 596.

[21] Kern, *Die Luege,* S 117.

[22] A Landgraf, "Suendhaftigkeit der Luege nach der Lehre der Fruehscholastik," *ZKathTh* 63 (1939), 157-80.

[23] Cf. vol. I, 352 ff. on the distinction between mortal sin and venial sin, which is closely bound up with our position on the present problem.

[24] Cf. Augustine, *De mendacio* cap. XVII. PL 40, 510s.

[25] R. Egenter, *Das Edle und der Christ* (Muenchen, 1935), S 61.

[26] II-II, q. 109, a. 3. [Augustine, *Enarrationes in Psalmos* 5. Eds.]

[27] D 1176 f. Cf. note 12 above.

III

ON BEING RESPONSIBLE IN LOVE

INTRODUCTION

For some time the word "morality" has been associated in the popular mind almost exclusively with sexual activity. Even in newspaper jargon, if a man is brought to court on a "morals" charge, we know there is a sexual offense involved. Fortunately, we are being freed from this too narrow idea of morality to a broader view which understands that morality quite properly pertains to all fields of human decision and action. To be sure, the "new morality" is generally discussed around the issues of premarital sexual intercourse, homosexuality, abortion, adultery, and divorce. The ethical concerns of many students, however, have gone beyond this preoccupation with sexuality; in a recent conference on the new morality at a state university, sexuality was only briefly mentioned.

The tendency to fix upon sexuality either as *the* question of morality, or as such a unique question of morality that the ethics of sex are discussed without reference to other aspects of behavior or more inclusive patterns of values, can highly distort the moral issues involved. The three readings included in this section set the particular questions of sexual morality in wider frameworks of moral reflection. In the lecture by Bishop Robinson sexuality itself is not the focus; the focus is on love and law, a general problem in morality and a particular issue in Christian morality. Sex is alluded to within this framework as an instance of the general issues involved. In the two chapters written by Roger Mehl, we see sexuality set in the context of what it means to be a person in various human relationships. Themes of responsibility and fidelity provide some of the structure within which sexuality is discussed. Marc Oraison's chapter represents a Roman Catholic position informed by modern psychology and by the basic theological renewal of Roman Catholic ethics. The essays have in common a view that relationships of sexuality are to be seen in a wider framework of human relatedness, values, and possibilities for the total fulfillment of life.

The "new morality" stresses, as Robinson points out, the situation in which action takes place. As has been indicated in earlier introductory sections, how one interprets that situation makes a lot of difference. One popular account of situational morality ends a paragraph on sexual relations with the well-known opinion of Mrs. Patrick Campbell, that whatever you do is all right just as long as you do not do it in the street and scare the horses. Although the paragraph is not as trivial as its closing illustration, it does point to a potential oversimplification of what the "situation" is. Sexual relations, like all relations, exist in continuity with other patterns of human relatedness, through time and across the space boundaries of human communities. While particular actions take place in particular moments—whether that action is voting, deciding how to spend money, or sexual intercourse—these actions are in continuity with past actions and have effects that move into the future. To make any decision requires that one, in a sense, draw a time line around one's considerations: one cannot anticipate all the future consequences, and one is not bound by past actions. Where one draws that time line, however, is important in the interpretation of what constitutes the situation in which I will decide and act. Is the time box an evening in my life, when my date and I are mellowed by a good dinner, fine wines, lovely music, moonlight coming through the window of my car, and knowledge of erogenous zones? Or is the time box bigger? Does it include my past relationships to this particular date—my commitments to her or to another, my personal sense of integrity or consistency in moral activity (which may be consistency as a seducer or as consistently chaste, or something else), my anticipations for the future for myself, my date, and whatever life we will have together after this evening?

What is the space or social line that limits my "situation"?

Again, one isolates the important relationships from those that are unimportant for a particular decision or action; to attempt to interpret a particular relationship in the light of its almost infinite continuities with other interactions would lead to confusion. Clearly on that lovely evening I am primarily in relationship to my date. Physically there are no others present. But my relationships with other persons are only temporarily blocked from attention. I remain in some kind of relationship to my parents, to the religious community to which I belong or have belonged, to other women or other men, to values and beliefs that I have attested to, and perhaps even to God. It is not only to the horses on the street that I am related.

This time-space delimitation is already an interpretation of what my situation is, even though it appears to be more a descriptive than a normative one. It can be interpreted, however, in terms of the central concept of this book, responsibility. To whom am I responsible? For what am I responsible? Am I responsible only to myself for the maximum gratification of physical pleasures? Am I responsible only to the other person for the preservation of his or her notion of what constitutes moral integrity or for the fulfillment of his or her desires? If I accept responsibility for the consequences of sexual activity, is possible pregnancy the only consequence that is involved in moral considerations? To what extent does the acceptance of responsibility require some expression of commitment of one person to the other? What kind of commitment is a responsible one: a word of love to smooth the way for seduction or to ease the conscience? A public pinning to show seriousness of relationship without indefinite tenure of intention? An engagement? A marriage acclaimed before the state, God, and "this company"?

Choices about sexual life may indicate orientations toward life that are more pervasive than what happens in sexual relations alone. They may indicate loyalty to certain values, or integrity in certain patterns of life that are more general in their exemplification and application than sex. Here, as in the discussions of responsibility in speech, we can see how some of the general types introduced in the first part of this book apply.

One might say that in sex, as in other things, one is man-the-rule-obeyer. What rules one decides to obey is another matter. One can even conceivably have a philosophical defense that would substantiate the view that "you ought on every possible occasion seek to gratify your sex drives by copulation with a woman." A comparable rule could be devised for a woman, of course. But most of the rules about sex are quite antithetical in content to this, and it is more meaningful to outline a pattern of life in accord with the more prevalent rules. One might conduct himself according to the rule that premarital and extramarital sexual relations are always wrong. We might note here some points mentioned in our other introductions. Such a rule might appear in the context of "legalism," it might be seen not only to be inflexible, but also arbitrarily established and substantiated only by the irrational authority of a tradition or an institution. And one's obedience to it might be motivated more by fear of disobedience to the rule and desire for self-righteousness than by any reasonable grounds for the rule itself. The rule, however, might be seen in another context, namely, as an authoritative guideline for behavior for which moral and religious reasons can be given, and which is adopted in light of these reasons and the loyalties that direct and inform them.

Whatever pattern or model of behavior one employs for the moral life, it will refer to a much wider framework of life than sex alone. To be such, there may be times when one model is more effective than another, and certainly no one behaves perfectly consistently according to ideal constructs designed as a way of arranging a vast body of ideas and behavior. Life is more dynamic and complex than typologies and models. But surely an intelligent and conscientious person might reflect upon the consistency of his approaches to moral action in various spheres. Perfect consistency may not only be impossible; it may not even be desirable. But pressure for consistency might help clarify not only questions of behavior in a particular set of circumstances, but also questions of ethical theory.

We noted that one can have a rule to be chaste or a rule to

copulate as often as possible. This suggests that rules can serve quite different values. But actions may be framed not just in terms of rule-obedience, but also in terms of end-realization as well. One could argue that in relationships between the sexes, in the whole of married life, and in one's vocation, the primary guiding value is self-realization. One seeks in all actions to realize most fully one's potentialities as a human being. Obviously this general value requires more specific content if it is to be helpful in moral understanding. For example, is the self to be realized interpreted primarily in terms of physical desires? If not, what is the relation of this aspect of the self to other aspects of the self, e.g., to the fulfillment of the human spirit, to use a vague term? How is the realization of oneself related to other people? Are they to be used as means for one's own actualization without regard to their fulfillment in human relationships? Can self-realization refer exclusively to oneself, or is it dependent upon a mutuality between persons, upon the wider interpersonal and institutionalized relationships of which one is a part? If this is the case, how do others contribute to self-realization? By limiting and restraining us on some occasions, and by sustaining and fulfilling our conception of our needs on others? Is there a utopian element in any understanding of self-realization, since what we become is not fully ours to determine?

One could take a quite different perspective on what is good and go through a similar series of questions. The primary value might be self-sacrifice, instead of self-realization, based upon certain religious convictions. But without further specification such a general end would be as ambiguous as self-realization. (Indeed, the two may not be as antithetical as first appears.) If we live always in accord with the Pauline injunction "Seek not your own good, but that of the neighbor," our behavior will depend upon what we determine our neighbor's good to be. To determine what his good is can be at least as complex as the determination of what the self is that is to be realized. Is his good primarily the gratification of his physical needs? Certainly if he is in dire hunger, without a decent place to live, and physically suffering from lack of medical attention, that is, if his survival is in question, one answer is seemingly clear: meet his physical needs. But is that answer adequate when survival is not the question, or when the neighbor is known to be a fraternity stud? Probably not.

These briefly stated questions point to the wider framework within which questions of sexual behavior are set. How we behave in "love" (a term that also requires development) depends in part on how we view the pattern of human relationships, the preferred values that we have, the images we have of ourselves and of others, the dominant inspirations of our lives. It is both interesting and important to observe that the pattern of relationships is complex, that the values we hold do not fall into automatic harmony with each other, and that our aspirations for ourselves are revised according to experience, including our relationships to others. A relationship with another person that persists through time obviously involves more than what we do together in bed. Compatibility and fulfillment refer not only to sexual activity, but also to sharing a meaningful world, to living according to routine expectations of mutual duties, to patterns of faithfulness in various areas of life. Our understanding of our own good may have to be qualified by our understanding of the good of another which we feel obliged to attend to; indeed, the two might be in clear conflict on some occasions. Our aspirations for ourselves are revised as we live with certain crucial choices we have made: to drop out of college or to go on to graduate school; to marry this girl or this man; to choose to become a social reformer rather than a physician or an accountant. They are revised as new doors are opened to us, on the basis of good luck or our own achievements. The relations between a man and a woman alter as they share life with one another, in friendship, in courtship, engagement, and marriage. Persons change through time, the situations in which they live change through time, the patterns of fidelity and fulfillment change through time.

The selection of readings was made with the intention of setting considerations of love between man and woman in a wider moral framework. Readers may wish to compare Bishop J. A. T. Robinson's chapter, "The New Morality" in his famous book, *Honest to God,* with the chapter on "Law and Love" that is included here. In the former his intention was more polemical; he was prophetically exposing the problems posed when an "old morality" is defended by conservative ecclesiastical institutions and theologies. In the reading included here he is relating a centuries-old polarity in Christian thinking, love and law, to issues of morality. He is also seeking to relate the traditional substance of the Christian faith to a moral framework adequate for society. Although love has priority in this chapter, it is not seen to be antithetical to law. It has its positive value-forming functions in particular situations, but this does not exclude wider responsibilities for the loving man. "The plea for the priority of love fully recognizes the obligation upon Christians in each generation to help fashion and frame the moral net which will be to preserve the body and soul of *their society.*" While Robinson criticizes legalistic views of sexual conduct, he is aware that love can provide the basis for "working rules." "I recognize to the full that all of us, especially young people, have to have working rules. But my point is that when these are questioned, as they are being questioned, the Christian is driven back to base them not on law ("Fornication is always wrong") but on love, on what a deep concern for persons as whole persons, in their entire social context, really requires." Love is primary, but law and rules are not jettisoned; the "dykes of love in a loveless world" are not to be weakened. Put in other words, faith and love free men from false bondage to legalistic rules, but love has its order, and freedom in love has a proper direction.

Roger Mehl is a thoughtful French Protestant theologian whose understanding of what it is to be human is influenced by the personalistic and phenomenological tradition that is presently shaping French philosophy. He is concerned to perceive clearly what the fundamental structure of human relationships is and what it really means to be an "embodied" person. His thinking is also profoundly informed by the Bible and theological reflection. In the chapters included here, Mehl draws upon these two perspectives to set sexuality in a wider human context. When sex is separated from other intentions in human relationships, it becomes an abstraction that is untrue to what it means to be human. His case against adultery, for example, is built not upon arguments of the potential disorder to society, but upon what it is to be a "being of relationships." In his relationships, a person preserves his identity or singularity "only in forming or in discovering within himself, through these very relationships, an inward being that cannot be surrendered to all and sundry, that must be held back." There is in these relationships a unique self and a unique mutual giving of the self. "It is an exclusive relationship where the mystery of the one is offered to the mystery of the other, where man discovers himself in discovering his wife." Sexual involvement is a unique form of human fidelity, but the notion of fidelity of which it is a form is more pervasive than sexual involvement, more constitutive of what it means to be human. True fidelity for Mehl, as for Marcel, is not static and coercive, but is "active and creative. . . . It desires to fulfill the other in fulfilling itself." Thus in marriage there is a mutual development of each other, a reciprocal belonging, a caring for each other. Sexuality is expressed and confirmed within these wider aspects of being human.

Traditional Christian teaching has described three purposes of marriage: procreation, mutual love between those married, and a "remedy for sin." In Roman Catholic teaching, procreation has been primary; this accounts for the Church's traditional opposition to contraception. Modifications of this completely negative stance toward contraception—such as permitting intercourse during "safe" or infertile periods in the woman's menstrual cycle as a means of birth control—have been made in light of the value of the second purpose of marriage (mutual love) and in light of the total well-being of the children (which is jeopardized if their number exceeds the economic and emotional resources of the family). Thus priority in the relationship between mutual love and procreation is a matter of contemporary debate.

Among those who have sought to stay within the Catholic tradition while seeking to widen the considerations of the nature of marriage is Marc Oraison. In so doing, Oraison relates sexual union to great themes of Christian belief, and particularly to the redemption or "resurrection" of the world. He calls for an "integral view on marriage" that will be a harmonious synthesis of all the personal elements of life, including sex. Sex is only one occasion, though it "has a quality of supreme intensity," in which selves are related to each other in marriage. "The mutual and true giving of self goes on through the days, all through the minutest details of life." There remains in Oraison what may appear from a modern Protestant perspective to be an undue division of life between the instinctive and the spiritual union. But in many ways he seeks to avoid this manner of thinking more than some traditional writers have done. This integral view can be seen when he writes that "sexual intercourse should be viewed graciously, and not under precept, by each partner as a fulfillment of the other partner's well-being for the good of their community. The joy of their union and even its delight should above all consist for one partner in the rebound of the joy and delight experienced by the other, through the complete oneness of the couple."

John A. T. Robinson

LAW AND LOVE *

I began my first lecture by saying that my intention in these three talks was to make an attempt at *interpretation* between the "new morality" and the old in what threatens to be a disruptive debate. My contention was that each side must try to understand and respect the other as having an equally genuine concern for the fundamentals on which Christian morality rests. For, as I see it, they represent complementary rather than contradictory attempts to do justice to the great polarities which lie at the heart of the Christian ethic. Each tends to start at the opposite end from the other, and each for a particular individual, or even perhaps for a whole generation or culture, may be the way in. But we cannot afford to allow a sterile antagonism to develop between them: for each needs the emphasis that the other would cherish.

I began by examining the tension that must always exist in Christian ethics between the fixed and the free, the constant and the changing, the absolute and the relative. I suggested that what the new morality is saying to us—and I believe it needs urgently to be said at a time of unprecedentedly rapid social change—is that we need not fear flux: God is in the rapids as much as in the rocks, and as Christians we are free to swim and not merely to cling.

I want now to look at another aspect of the same polarity, the

* From JOHN A. T. ROBINSON, *Christian Morals Today* (Philadelphia: Westminster Press, 1964), pp. 20-33. Copyright © SCM Press, Ltd., 1964. Used by permission. Bishop Robinson has been an outspoken British participant in the debate over "The New Morality."

tension between law and love. No Christian can ever set these in bare opposition or fix on one to the exclusion of the other as the sole focus of his ethic. Nevertheless, there is a real danger, as recent sparring has shown, of one side supposing that the other *is* denying what it has no intention of denying—because it begins from a different point. And, before we know where we are, the charges of legalism and antinomianism[1] are being flung around. Phrases like "the Cambridge antinomians" and "South Bank religion," with both of which brushes I have the misfortune to be tarred, are further evidence of the slogan-thinking with which the press has fed us this year.

But let us try to see what both sides are saying, coolly and charitably. The old morality (if we must use these labels) starts from the position, which no one could deny, that the Old Testament comes before the New. In that sense law has a priority over love. Love builds on law, and it comes to fulfil it, not to destroy it: the second mile of love presupposes the first mile of law. And still for each man, as for the Jew, law is the tutor which brings him to Christ; and even when he is "no longer under law but under grace" (Rom. 6:14) he is still "under the law of Christ" (I Cor. 9:21). St. Paul continued to insist that "the law is in itself holy, and the commandment is holy and just and good" (Rom. 7:12) and repudiated with vehemence the charge of antinomianism. The Christian can never say that he is beyond or outside the sphere of law. He needs it for himself, he needs it for his children, and he certainly cannot dispense with it for his society.

I hope that is a reasonably fair statement of the case, and there is certainly nothing in it that I would want to dispute or deny.[2] I would ask only that the opposite emphasis, the other way into the same complex of Christian truth, should be heard with equal understanding, and not simply dismissed for the "damage" it can do.

This other way in starts from facts which equally the old morality would not wish to deny. It insists that the Christian *is* under grace and not under law. It insists that the law is but a tutor, and not the master. It insists on the priority of love in every sense except the temporal—for on this one command is made by Jesus to hang all the law and the prophets (Matt. 22:40). The second mile in fact changes the basis of the first *as law*. Love is the end, the *telos,* of the law not merely in the sense that it fulfills it (which it does), but in the sense that it abolishes it as the foundation of the Christian's relation whether with God or man. Of that the Epistle to the Galatians can leave us in no possible doubt: it is the *magna charta* of the freedom with which Christ has set us free. Moreover, any ethic which is genuinely Christian will always be open to the charge of destroying the law and the temple. Jesus faced this charge; Stephen faced it; Paul faced it. Antinomianism is always a false accusation, but I should immediately suspect there was something sub-Christian about an ethic which did not provoke it. I am honoured that my university is now associated with it!

With all this, as I said, I imagine no Christian would want to disagree. All that the so-called "new morality" is concerned to do (and, of course, it is nothing new at all) is to start from this emphasis, without denying the other. The heat in fact is generated on both sides by the denial of the denials—which really is rather absurd, though it may be unavoidable. For, in fact, each side, in order to safeguard the element which it feels is being threatened, can easily be led into statements which destroy the proper tension. Inevitably one will be provoked into utterance by distortions or one-sidednesses which it detects in the other, and this will lead to counter-charges. But rather than get caught up in this, let me try to say simply what those of us who are dubbed antinomians are seeking to get accepted. And since one of the charges is that we are primarily impelled by the pressures of the contemporary situation and by the impossibility of "selling" the old medicine because it is unpalatable, I should like to base what I have to say firmly on the compulsions, as I see them, of the New Testament. I believe that the Holy Spirit *is* speaking to the churches through the deadness for so many today of the old morality. But he is speaking as always, if it is really he, by taking the things of Christ and showing them to us. What he is showing us is what we have heard from the beginning. There is fundamentally nothing new here, though as always, when we feel its power, it is fresh and explosive.

I suppose that what we want to see accepted as a starting-point is that the Christian ethic can never honestly be presented as law plus love or law qualified by love, *however much safer that would be.* There is no question that law has its place, but that place is at the boundaries, and not at the centre. This was the revolution which Jesus represented for the Pharisees. His teaching was not a reform of legalism but its death. As Professor Paul Ramsey puts it in his *Basic Christian Ethics,* "A faithful Jew stayed as close as possible to the observance of the law even when he had to depart from it. Jesus stayed as close as possible to the fulfillment of human need, no matter how wide of the . . . law this led him."[3] And this, of course, as the Scribes well saw, is terribly dangerous doctrine. It needs its checks and balances: it cries aloud for letters to the church press! And to these "the new morality" says: "Fine—as long as no attempt is made to substitute law again for love as the centre and basis of it all." But that is what precisely it sees happening, in exhortations, however earnest, to return to "the Law of God" as the foundation of the moral life.

But this is what the New Testament refuses to allow us to do. As Professor C. F. D. Moule has recently insisted, writing on "The New Testament and Moral Decisions," the ten commandments are not the basis of Christian morals, on which an ethic of love goes on to build.[4] Of course, the commandment of love does not contradict or relieve men of the obligations of the old: it summarizes them and immeasurably deepens them. In fact, in the Sermon on the Mount Jesus takes several of them, pointing through them and beyond to the unconditional claim of God upon man and of person upon person they were framed to safeguard. But in the process he destroys them *as law.* As St. Paul said subsequently, "Against such things there is no law" (Gal. 5:23)—nor, he might have added, for them either.

Jesus's treatment of the fourth commandment, for instance, effectively subjected it to the concern for which it stood, in a way that undercut it as law altogether. "The sabbath was made for man, not man for the sabbath" (Mark 2:27). It was no longer a case of starting from the law and reforming it to make it more loving. As Paul Ramsey comments again, "Jewish ethics was a legalism modified by humanitarianism, which meant also a humanitarianism *limited* by legalism."[5] Jesus' ethic was unconditional neighbour-love, and weighed against that the law was not less important, but nothing. Against the counter-claim of "doing good," the Sabbath regulation, as regulation, was null: law and love were simply incommensurable. But, in terms of the real purpose of the Sabbath rest, Jesus claimed that his actions were not its negation but in the profoundest sense its fulfillment: "Ought not this woman, a daughter of Abraham whom Satan bound for eighteen years, to be loosed from this bond on the Sabbath day?" (Luke 13:16).

Not in the case of every commandment might there be such a clash of practice, but the principle was the same. More often it was a matter of simply "going beyond"—though so far beyond that one was soon quite outside the sphere of law. Equal retribution—an eye for an eye and a tooth for a tooth—can be translated into law; but turning the other cheek can never be. Murder and adultery can be codified as crimes; but to make anger and lust indistinguishable from them is not only bad law: it is to destroy the basis on which law operates. Equally, to say that all divorce involves adultery is not a new law: indeed, it is palpably untrue as law, and merely confuses perfectly valid legal distinctions. Rather, it is to say to the Jew, who regarded adultery heinously (at any rate by a woman) but divorce lightly, that all divorce is morally (though not legally) adultery. If you divorce your wife because you do not like her face, you are making her, morally, an adulteress. And this, I think, explains the famous Matthean exception, "except for the reason of fornication" (Matt. 5:32). For if she has already committed fornication, you cannot, technically, make her an adulteress: she has already made herself one. I see this clause as a rather heavy-handed addition to clear Jesus of what would otherwise be a logical contradiction.

But the clause is also a reminder that this particular injunction in the Sermon on the Mount has been treated by the old morality entirely differently from any other.[6] To go no further afield, Jesus makes two closely parallel statements about adultery—first, that all *lust* is the moral equivalent of adultery, and, secondly, that all *divorce* is the moral equivalent of adultery. No one has thought to treat the former as legislation; but the latter has been erected into a law (of the Church if not of the State) according to which divorce is always and in every circumstance wrong (or, if Matthew's exception is allowed, in all circumstances but one).

Now it is important to recognize a distinction at this point. Clearly, both a Christian society and Christians on behalf of the society they live in must have rules and laws about divorce. There is nothing wrong in that. They are bound, as I said in my last lecture, to construct a moral net. And within the pages of the New Testament we see that happening in the Christian community (at this stage, of course, only for its own members). The web is very embryonic, and we are not in a position now to reconstruct it. It is interesting to note, however, that at three points at least the rulings for which we have evidence certainly would not have passed the Convocations of Canterbury and York!

If, as is usually assumed, Matthew's exception (whatever may have been its original intention) reflects the discipline at least of his church, then divorce was presumably definitely permitted to Christians on grounds of adultery. But the official mind of the Church of England is different. Again, St. Paul allows Christians on conversion to divorce their pagan partners if these will not live with them (I Cor. 7:12-16)—hardly a permission to commend itself today either to Church or State. (In fact, Paul's permissiveness must be contrasted with the regulations in the Old Israel where under Ezra the Lord's people were *compelled* to divorce their pagan spouses (Ezra 10). And, finally, the practice of cohabitation in celibacy of which we get such a fascinating keyhole glimpse in I Cor. 7:36-38, so far from being a better thing than marriage, as St. Paul asserts, would today be regarded as a cause of scandal—certainly in a vicarage!

All this is but a way of saying that while the Church, like the

State, must have its rules, they are certainly not timeless. Indeed, even today the main branches of Christendom, Roman, Orthodox, Anglican, and Protestant, all have different divorce disciplines. Nevertheless, some law there must be, and we should not be surprised to see the teaching of Jesus formed within the New Testament into material for that sort of code, both for catechetical and disciplinary purposes.

What is quite different is to regard the teaching of Jesus itself as a code, to see it as laying down for all Christians at all times, or indeed for any Christians at any time, what they should do. It is the encroachment of this view upon the thinking of the Church that "the new morality" would see as more dangerous *in the long run* than the hazards of its opposite. Not that it underrates the hazards of its opposite, and I certainly appreciate the harm done by irresponsible talk (though most of it, I believe, has in fact come from irresponsible and alarmist reporting). The deeper one's concern for persons, the more effectively one wants to see love buttressed by law. But if law usurps the place of love because it is safer, that safety is the safety of death.

I said earlier that Jesus's purpose was not to provide an ethical code but to proclaim the Kingdom. And this is the point to which I believe we must constantly return if we are to evaluate his moral teaching aright. For in his sayings we find a concentration upon the vertical of the divine imperative which would otherwise be inexplicable. This is not, I am convinced, as Albert Schweitzer thought, for a reason external to the ethic itself—because Jesus reckoned the horizontal line of history to be so short as to be negligible. Rather, it is because the claim of the Kingdom, of men's "ultimate" relation to God, was the "one thing" with which at all costs they must come to terms if they were to find life. To that all else was secondary. And this explains why Jesus did not concern himself, as any moralist must, to adjust or reconcile the conflicting claims which any real-life situation raises: "Who made me a judge or divider over you?" (Luke 12:14). His concern, rather, was to uncover with piercing clarity what the unconditional claim of the divine *agape* meant when translated into love of neighbour. Consequently, his illustrations always isolate the single neighbour, confronting a man in this sharply focused instance with the total demand of love, *as though no other claims existed.* To quote Paul Ramsey again, "Not only all prudential calculation of consequences likely to fall upon the agent himself, but likewise all sober regard for the future performance of his responsibility for family and friends, duties towards oneself and *fixed* duties to others, both alike were jettisoned from view."[7] "We may scarcely be able to perform it in regard to a single . . . neighbour. It was never intended to be performed as a new law for the adjudication of neighbour-claims in a settled society. Nevertheless, 'we are able to be transformed by it.' "[8]

Regarded as a code of conduct, prescribing what one should do in any situation, the Sermon on the Mount is quite impracticable. It tears the individual loose from any horizontal nexus. In any given precept it rules out of consideration all other interests, all other values, all other people. It never weighs conflicting responsibilities or helps a man to balance his commitments. It simply says, "Give to him who asks you," with never a thought for the stewardship of money. It commends the widow who throws "all her livelihood" into the treasury without asking who is to support her henceforth. It does not take into account —it does not reckon to take into account—the fact that there is always more than one neighbour to be considered, always more than one claim upon one. For instance, while I was preparing the material for this lecture, someone asked to borrow one of the chief books I was consulting. "From him that would borrow turn not away." Your claim or his? I did not in fact lend it to him.

Even the complete waiver of one's *own* rights is seldom a simple matter affecting oneself alone. As Brunner puts it, "If, as a good Christian," an industrial worker "is willing to endure the injustice of his position—so far as *he* is concerned—for the sake of others he ought not to do so."[9] And even more, what of other people's rights? What should the Good Samaritan have done if he had arrived on the scene while the robbers were still at work? Should have tried to beat them off—or should he himself have passed by on the other side? Or, to quote Professor

John Knox, "Jesus said: 'If any man smite you on one cheek turn the other also'; here the situation is relatively simple—you and your enemy. But Jesus did not say: 'If any man smite one of your friends, lead him to another friend that he may smite *him* also.' Not only is it clear that Jesus could have made no such statement, but also that he would have felt that the involvement of the interests of others . . . transformed the whole moral situation and placed our obligations with respect to it in a radically different light."[10]

What "A" does in that situation Jesus simply does not say, though from the parable of the two debtors "it is evident that love which for itself claims nothing may yet for the sake of another claim everything, that anyone who unhesitatingly and times without number renounces 'what is due' when he himself alone bears the brunt of such a decision may nevertheless turn full circle and insist with utter severity upon full payment of what is due to others."[11]

But the point is that the moral teaching of Jesus is not to be judged by its adequacy as a code. As such it is entirely inadequate. It says nothing whatever, for instance, about how a man is to pursue what after all occupies most of our waking hours (when we are not being slapped in the face or asked for our coat), namely, our everyday work, or how one is to be a good citizen and a positive and useful member of society.

It is worth noting that, in contrast, the earliest summaries of the Church's ethical teaching *are* concerned with precisely such things. They are practical injunctions on the basic Christian virtues in a pagan world—about how Christians are to get on with their work and support others, the responsibilities of wives, children, slaves and masters, the Christian's reputation in a non-Christian society, his duties towards the government authorities, etc.[12] Many of the injunctions (for instance, about not returning evil for evil, loving one's enemies, etc.) are in fact clearly dependent on Jesus's teaching. But the maxims of the Christian catechesis are, as Dodd points out,[13] in contrast with the Sermon on the Mount, practical rules for day to day living. No one has suggested they are impracticable, though they are clearly only possible "in the Lord."

Now it is significant that we do not at once feel that the ethics of the Epistles are a great let-down after the ethics of the Gospels, that there is a disastrous drop in spiritual temperature, such as we often sense in the sub-apostolic age. There is nothing more astringent than the moral tone of I Peter. But if the Sermon on the Mount were intended to be a perfectionist ethic which Christians were to fulfil literally at that level or not at all, then the ethics of the Epistles, prescribing for Christians very much involved in the compromises of the world, would appear an intolerable accommodation.

I think this comparison and contrast helps us to see more clearly what the sayings of the Sermon on the Mount are meant to be. They are, as it were, the *parables* of the Kingdom in its moral claims, flashlight pictures of the uncompromising demand which the Kingdom must make upon anyone who would respond to it. As Dodd puts it, "The ethical teaching of the Gospels . . . is not so much detailed guidance for conduct in this or that situation as a disclosure of the absolute standards which alone are relevant when the Kingdom of God is upon us. These standards, however, are not defined in general and abstract propositions, but in dramatic pictures of action in concrete situations; and they are intended to appeal to the conscience by way of the imagination."[14] The Sermon on the Mount does not say in advance, "This is what in every circumstance or in any circumstance you must do," but "This is the kind of thing which at any moment, if you are open to the absolute unconditional will of God, the Kingdom, or love, can demand of you." It is "relevant" not because it solves our moral problems (that is the kind of relevance we are always asking for), but because "it transforms us" (and that is the kind of relevance we don't ask for, but which in the end is what changes us and the world). In other words, Jesus's purpose was not to order the fruit, but to "make the tree good" (Matt. 12:33).

Brunner, I think, put the matter very well when he wrote, now over thirty years ago:

The Commandments—both of the Decalogue and of the Sermon on the Mount—are God-given paradigms of love. . . . Each of these commandments does two things: it makes the one Command concrete, and it also abstracts from the concrete reality. It stands, so to speak, in the center between the infinitely varied reality of life and the unity of the divine will of love. It shows us what love would mean in this or that more or less "special" but still general case, and it commands us to do this very thing. Then is this the beginning of casuistry? No. It is of the utmost importance to note how unsystematic, how "casual" are all the commandments which are scattered through the New Testament.[15] Here and there a plunge is made into human life and something is "lifted out" in order to make the meaning of love clearer. But the matter which has been singled out is not held fast as such; it is allowed to slip back again. Care is taken to avoid the possibility of even *apparently* dividing life up into various "cases" or "instances" which, as such, could be prejudged in a legalistic manner. *None* of the commandments in the Sermon on the Mount are to be understood as laws, so that those who hear them can go away feeling, "Now I know what I have to do!" If it were possible to read the Sermon on the Mount in this legalistic way the absolute and binding character of the Divine Command would be weakened, the sense of responsibility for decision would be broken, the electrical charge of the moral moment would be released.[16]

That is the note which "the new morality" is concerned shall not be muffled if the distinctively Christian contribution is to be heard. It is not, I believe, an irresponsible or an immoral witness. And to insist on this at the centre is not to doubt the necessity of law in its place. The plea for the priority of love fully recognizes the obligation upon Christians in each generation to help fashion and frame the moral net which will best preserve the body and soul of *their society*. We have seen the Christians of the first century seeking to relate the command of *agape* to their bewildering new environments, Jewish and Gentile, in the Graeco-Roman world. From their obedience we can indeed learn what the Spirit may be saying to the churches of the twentieth century. But we shall not do it by treating their formulations (any more than those of the Old Testament) as a

permanent code—or by attempting to solve the perplexities of
our generation with "the Bible says."

For, not only do "new occasions teach new duties," but "time
makes ancient good uncouth." This is most obvious in the case
of social ethics—if only because the early Christians were simply responsible *to* power, whereas we are also responsible *for*
power—and what power! But it is true also at the most personal level. Take, for instance, the much debated problem as to
the *limits* of pre-marital sex for engaged couples (and I deliberately put it in this way). You can only find things of very dubious relevance in the Old Testament—where the social context
was so utterly different and offences against women were primarily offences against property.[17] Jesus really said nothing about it
(his only recorded utterances are about adultery or prostitutes).
And to settle what is a responsible and searching question by a
sweeping reference to "fornication and all uncleanness" (Eph.
5:3) is to invite the recent comment of an atheist that these
questions are too serious to be discussed at the religious level.
For *porneia,* as its derivation implies, always has associations in
the New Testament with promiscuity, if not with prostitution. It
"describes the relationship in which one of the parties can be
purchased as a thing is purchased and discarded as a thing is
discarded and where there is neither union of, nor respect for,
personality."[18] To assume that this applies to all relationships
between engaged couples is to prejudge the moral issue in an
utterly insensitive and irresponsible way.

This is not in the least to suggest, as proponents of the "old
morality" have been quick to do, that advocates of the "new"
treat this matter laxly or lightly. Some, indeed, to whom this
label has been attached have done so, and I would want
strongly to dissociate myself from them. I believe the nexus
between bed and board, between sex and the sharing of life at
every level, must be pressed as strongly as ever by those who
really care for persons as persons. But these are the kind of
terms in which I believe this question has to be sorted out for
young people—as, for instance, Hugh Montefiore does in his
admirable and conservative essay in *God, Sex and War.*[19] And,

of course, I recognize to the full that all of us, especially young people, have to have working rules. But my point is that when these are questioned, as they are being questioned, the Christian is driven back to base them not on law ("Fornication is always wrong") but on love, on what a deep concern for persons as whole persons, in their entire social context, really requires.

Finally, the account I have given of Jesus's moral teaching will, I hope, help to dispel what is surely one of the most superficial charges against "the new morality," namely, that it is individualistic. The "paradigms of love" do indeed frequently strip the individual down to the bare relationship between him and God and the single neighbour. But that is not because Jesus or anyone else thinks that a system of ethics can be based on such deliberate abstraction. Moral decisions are inextricably corporate and social—and even more so for the Christian, since, as Professor Moule has reminded us in that same article in *The Expository Times*,[20] the normal "organ of perception through which the Holy Spirit may be expected to speak with distinctively moral guidance is the *Christian worshipping community listening critically.*" Moreover, most of those who are concerned with the emphases now labelled "the new morality" have come to them through engagements in the problems of *social* ethics. This is particularly true of Professor Joseph Fletcher,[21] whom I quoted extensively in *Honest to God*. Indeed, I would humbly suggest that those who suppose we are advocating an individualistic love ethic which has no place for law or justice might refer to the essay on "Power" in my earlier book, *On Being the Church in the World*.[22]

"The new morality" is not in the least interested in jettisoning law, or in weakening what in *Honest to God*[23] I called "the dykes of love in a loveless world." But it also believes it has something to say which is not an incitement to immorality or to individualism, and for which it craves a quiet, unemotional and honest hearing.

NOTES

[1] *"Antinomian:* one who maintains that the moral law is not binding on Christians" (*The Concise Oxford Dictionary*).

[2] See G. A. F. Knight, *Law and Grace* (1962); A. R. Vidler, *Christ's Strange Work* (rev. ed. 1963).

[3] British edition 1953, p. 56.

[4] *The Expository Times,* September 1963, pp. 370 f.

[5] *Op. cit.,* pp. 56 f.

[6] Cf. H. Oppenheimer, *Law and Love* (1962), pp. 72 f.; D. A. Rhymes, [*No New Morality* (1964) Ed.], pp. 56-71.

[7] *Op. cit.,* p. 39.

[8] *Ibid.,* p. 43. The last phrase is cited from M. Dibelius, *The Sermon on the Mount* (E.T., 1940), p. 135.

[9] *The Divine Imperative* (1932; E.T., 1937), p. 431.

[10] *The Christian Answer* (ed. H. P. van Dusen, 1945), p. 173; quoted P. Ramsey, *op. cit.,* pp. 170 f. See further J. Knox, *The Ethics of Jesus in the Teaching of the Church* (1962).

[11] P. Ramsey, *op. cit.,* p. 171.

[12] Cf. C. H. Dodd, *Gospel and Law* (1951), pp. 18-22.

[13] *Ibid.,* pp. 51 f.

[14] *Ibid.,* pp. 60 f.

[15] Cf. Joseph Sittler, *The Structure of Christian Ethics* (1958), pp. 49-53.

[16] *Op. cit.,* pp. 135 f.

[17] See on this whole question the excellent discussion in W. G. Cole, *Sex and Love in the Bible* (1959), ch. VII.

[18] W. Barclay, *Flesh and Spirit* (1962), p. 24.

[19] "Personal Relations before Marriage" (ed. D. MacKinnon, 1963), pp. 61-98.

[20] September 1963, pp. 372 f.

[21] Cf. e.g. his *Morals and Medicine* (1955).

[22] 1960, pp. 43-58.

[23] P. 110.

Roger Mehl

THE MYSTERY OF THE SEXUAL LIFE*

These remarks on the many-sided—and equivocal—relationship of the body to the person were necessary in order properly to situate the problem of the sexual life. The sexual life makes evident the impossibility of limiting oneself to the instrumentalist conception of the body. It is impossible for sexuality to be without finality. The sexual function is a physiological one, presenting analogies with other functions (e.g., digestion) that psychoanalysis has revealed. It is relative to the body, to that aspect of the physical body which science has only begun to explore: glandular secretions and hormonal balance. But at the same time, it cannot be detached from the highest, most personal manifestations of the ego. The term, "love" bears witness to this decisive and irreducible ambiguity. It unalterably designates a comportment that involves both animality and a kind of spirituality.

It is true that some have wished to detach the sexual function from all significance that can be openly acknowledged by authentic man, to take away from the sex act its dignity. But what has been the cost of this reduction? First of all, it has led to a ruinous dualism in terms of the human person, an impossible dualism of soul and body that holds up the soul and the body as two opposed and uncommunicating substances, as if the soul and the body were not involved in each human situation.

* From ROGER MEHL, *Society and Love: Ethical Problems for Family Life,* James H. Farley, trans. (Philadelphia: Westminster Press, 1964), pp. 142-60. Used by permission. Professor Mehl teaches ethics at the Faculty of Protestant Theology, University of Strasbourg.

Next, sexuality has been deprived of all significance in relation to the person. It has been permitted a meaning only in relation to the *species,* as if human sexuality had no other role than to assure the perpetuity of the species. Through his sex the human being would be simply the preserver of the species. In attaching pleasure to the consummation of the sex act, nature would have found a solid guarantee for the perpetuation of the species. If this view were correct, expressing the entire finality of sexuality, it would be at variance with our mores, our social institutions, the most fundamental advances of civilization. Monogamy would be called into question, for if it is only a matter of the preservation of the species, one can conceive of institutions less burdensome than the monogamic conjugal family. We would have to recognize either that this type of family is only an accident of history or that it is not linked with sexuality.

But there is more: this view affirms the preeminence of the species over the person. Man is at the service of the species, which is an affirmation that is at the root of all racism. This is an affirmation that is in fundamental contradiction to the Christian doctrine of the creation of man. The account in Genesis clearly emphasizes that although animal is created as species, man is created as personal being. His relationship with his helpmate is, from the very first, a personal relationship in which dialogue plays the leading role. To be sure, man has a sexual nature like the animal (at least the higher animal). But whereas sexuality remains purely instinctive in the animal, submitted to a seasonal rhythm that imperatively commands the manifestations of it, "it is freely," as Jean Jacques Rousseau put it, "that man rises to the level of animal instinct."[1] This is an excellent way to put it, for it reminds us that man does not start from animal instinct, which he strives with all the artifices of culture and language to sublimate more or less deeply. Rather, on the contrary, it is in starting from a properly human relationship, of a personal nature, that man and woman encounter the sexual relationship, not as a point of departure but as a result. The adolescent is normally first attracted by the femininity of a young girl long before he has the desire for sexual possession. The love of man and woman is born only exceptionally of a sexual encounter. Love precedes the sexual encounter, and it frequently happens that if instinct alone has carried the man toward the woman, love will not be born. Prostitution has never given birth to love; rather, it is love that leads toward the sexual encounter. Erotic literature, however little psychological truth it contains, witnesses to this very thing. Although the animal is guided by a powerful instinct that permits only a minute margin for the consideration of the individuality of the partners, man follows a completely different path. It is, indeed, a question of rising to the level of animal instinct, namely, of rediscovering it by starting from something different from it, of causing it to emerge from a more complete, more concrete, and more personal experience than that which it would give to us spontaneously.

Immorality and inhumanity begin at the moment where the sexual relation is conceived of as primary and when its fulfillment is an end in itself. For the profligate, the sex act ends on itself; not being rooted in a human encounter created from trust, affection, generosity, and the giving of oneself, it can only be indefinitely repeated with the most diverse partners until one is surfeited and disgusted with it. It is out of this disgust with the sex act that all sorts of spiritual aberrations have arisen in the course of history. It explains the obsession with a love of angelic purity, i.e., with a love that is not consummated. It also explains the obsession for spiritual espousals that were such a temptation in many Oriental religions, but that also infected nascent Christianity and is rediscovered in many sects and para-Christian utopias.[2] One is thrown necessarily into these aberrations as soon as one starts from man as animal, and with this animality as a base, tries to build a human coronation.

However, man has not been created animal, but a person destined to live in communion with his counterpart, capable of generosity and a giving of himself. He is not at all oriented toward a primordial satisfaction of his needs. Hunger offers another example of this. It is a need even more powerful than the need for sexual satisfaction. Yet in humanity it is satisfied at the end of a process that includes the concern for proportion, dignity, beauty, culinary refinement. There is a concern for sharing bread with others in a meal that is a communion in friendship and regard for the other. The maternal instinct is the same way: the mother, in one sense, only reproduces the actions and attitudes of the animal in regard to the child. It is true that the child has all the external marks of the animal. In certain respects he is essentially a digestive tube. Yet he is also a child, that is, a being with whom the mother maintains personal relationships, whom she does not suckle without smiling on him. He is a being who has, in her eyes, a destiny; he is born from her womb, to be sure, but he must be born anew at each instant in human life. He is a being who has received, or who should receive, baptism.

In the same way, we should see that the relationship between man and woman is at first a relationship of two beings who are each other's fellow creatures. Man and woman must begin from their reciprocal friendship in order to rise together toward that mysterious sphere in which the animal existence is lived in a human manner.

Scholars reduce man to animal by abstraction, in order to keep their work from becoming too complicated. Yet contrary to their statements, instinct, with its powerful dynamism, is not primary; if it were, all that would be erected on it would be, in the final analysis, only an artificial superstructure that each individual or social crisis could sweep away. A civilization that is based solely on the repression of instincts inevitably changes into an aphrodisiac civilization. Sublimation builds itself on repression, but allows what has been repressed to show through, and under its sublimated forms the savagery of instinct reappears in aberrant and pathological forms. Even though Freud was right in unmasking all the hypocrisy of repressions and in reminding us that there is an animal in every man, he was in error in not having sufficiently emphasized that there is a human libido, a libido rediscovered at the end of a humanization.

It should be pointed out that it is an analysis of man that cuts man off from his humanity. It is always possible to slip into such an analysis, because man can be treated as nature and not as being, because nature is, in man, always the reverse of his being, i.e., his relapses, and because it is easier to observe the relapses than to grasp the act by which man accedes to being. It is easier to describe a human nature that comes undone, as it were, than to describe a human nature in the process of building itself up.

This explains the origin of the constant ambiguity that hangs over the description of sexual love. The very term "eroticism" is charged with this ambiguity:

It can designate first of all [writes Paul Ricoeur] one of the components of human sexuality, its instinctual and sensual component; it can also designate the art of loving built on culture and sexual pleasure. As such, it is still an aspect of tender affection, as long as the concern for reciprocity, mutual gratification, and giving prevails over egoism and the narcissism of possession. But eroticism becomes errant desire for pleasure when it is dissociated from the body of tendencies linked by the concern for an interpersonal, durable, intense, and intimate bond. It is then that eroticism becomes a problem. Now, we have learned from Freud, principally from *Three Essays on the Theory of Sexuality,* that sexuality is not simple, that the integration of its manifold components is an indefinite task. This disintegration, when no longer considered as a failure but as a technique of the body, makes eroticism the counterpole of tender affection; in tender affection the relation to the partner triumphs, but yet it can include eroticism in the meaning of the sensual component of sexuality; in eroticism, however, the egostic cultivation of pleasure obliterates the possibility for an exchange of giving.[3]

This dissociation of sexuality and tender affection, this isolation of sexuality regarding all intention of encountering the fellow being of the other sex as a person, obviously remains a permanent possibility. It is the counterpart of the intellectual vice of abstraction. It is the analogue of an intellect that is not disinterested, but that is dilettante, refusing all commitment because it has beforehand suppressed all conditions for a commitment. There is a profligacy of the spirit, an intellectual eroticism, just as there is a sexual eroticism.

It is because man ex[
tutes a major temptation[
evil and to weight it dov[
him to speak of sexual l[
uality, occasionally inter[
account of the first sex [
love, much in the mann[
courage to admit: "As f[
delight of love lies in the[
woman know from birt[
evil." This is truly a stra[
and woman in sexual lov ... ...ger concerns they themselves.
It no longer has any aim except their communion in evil.

ON BEING

204

all prohibitions that a civ[
(prudish because aphr[
We said "in the [
of The Song of S[
the theologica[
to it in ord[
quite si[
i.e., [
me[

Although man, once he has liberated Eros from all ties with the person, rarely engages himself in this satanic course, he nevertheless suffers a repeatedly disappointing experience of the poverty of Eros. Sexual pleasure, when it is not tied to tender affection for a person loved in body and soul, does not possess the secret of its renewal. The imagination is drained trying to renew it: "Here is man," writes Paul Ricoeur, "engaged in an exhausting struggle against the psychological poverty of pleasure itself, which is scarcely susceptible of attaining fulfillment in its biological savagery. Eroticism will then construct its myth in the period of self-indulgent dissociation and within the limits of affective finitude."[4] Civilization, in its aphrodisiac aspects, seeks to renew the sources of pleasure, to vary the conditions of it, and to heighten the intensity of it through refined preparations. Its incessantly renewed effort witnesses to its failure. Man is thrown back toward solitude by pleasure itself.

It is understandable under these conditions how humanity, taught by the failure of the sexual myth, has come to disparage love, to consider sexual instinct degrading, and why it has been loaded down with all sorts of restraints and prohibitions. We can understand why, in these conditions, the best service that poets and novelists can render to a humanity fatigued by its own eroticism, is to sing, if in extremely crude terms in the manner of a Giono, the marvel of love and tender affection, of the gratuitousness of this gift, of the liberty of a love released from

...lization both prudish and aphrodisiac
...disiac) has laid upon it.
...anner of a Giono," but also in the manner
...lomon. The Song of Solomon, far from having
...and allegorical meaning that is ordinarily given
...r to justify its presence in the Biblical canon, sings
...ply of human love, of demythologized conjugal love,
...f love freed from its religious concerns, from its sacred
...aning (which it borrows in order better to hide itself and
sublimate itself in the pagan hierogamies). In commenting on
The Song of Solomon, Daniel Lys writes: "Eros has an end in
itself. It is not utilitarian, and this is why it is fidelity (exactly as
the love of God is fidelity). . . . If love does not have an end in
itself, the other is only an object subordinated to the end pursued. This object is worth nothing in itself. It is valuable only
insofar as it helps attain the end desired. It is abandoned when
another, better, presents itself."[5]

At the beginning of this chapter we protested against an interpretation of sexuality that seeks its utilitarian justification in
its social function (procreation, the preservation of the race or
of the species, the temporal extension of man in a lineage). This
protest was made not because we contest that marvelous aspect
of sexuality which enables us to go beyond ourselves through
procreation. Rather, it is because in putting this function first,
man risks seeing in woman nothing but the mother of his children. He risks degrading her into an instrument that permits the
survival of his line. There is a bourgeois ethic of love that is no
less perverse than the ethic of the profligate, viz., that ethic
which, sometimes inspired by a certain puritanism, wishes to see
in woman only the *genetrix*. But it is obvious that, in this view,
all women are the same, provided that they give an heir and,
above all, a male heir. It is equally obvious that love would then
lose all personal character and that, by this very ethical bias,
one reintroduces into sexuality that profound dissociation from
tender affection, friendship, and respect.

"Human sexuality," writes Th. Bovet, "is integrated . . . into
an order of things in which it has its place. It has its own

meaning as a creative function which is fulfilled in the order of love."[6] Of what creation is it first of all a question? It is a question of the creation of the other and of the self in the mystery of a communion in which solitude is not, to be sure, conquered once and for all, but in which it appears as provisional and not absolute.

The assertion that sexual relations must not take place outside of marriage is frequently presented to us as a sort of social necessity, as a discipline that is initially imposed on us by the group as a safeguard of order and that eventually we impose upon ourselves as proof of the strength of our will over the impulses of our instincts. These are sound arguments, but they are also insufficient. The ethical foundation of the prohibition of adultery is far more profound.

Each human being is involved in a multitude of relationships in which his personality is built (or possibly destroyed). He is a being of relationships. But man preserves his personal singularity in these relationships (which expose him and make demands on him) only in forming or in discovering within himself, through these very relationships, an inward being that cannot be surrendered to all and sundry, that must be held back. And the more intense our relationships with others become, the more we feel the necessity and the value of reserve and modesty. This is why we make a selection among our relationships that marks the limits of our availability to others. We choose our friends, certain intimates to whom we surrender a part of this hidden mystery of ourselves. But none of our friends can know us perfectly.

However, this hidden being, which is our own mystery yet which we suspect that we ourselves know only imperfectly and whose revelation we await in some way, cannot be maintained unexpressed. Otherwise it wilts and dies. We cannot make our own private use of it by some type of refined egoism. Narcissism is the trap of the discovery of the self. This hidden being, which must be revealed to ourselves and which must be made fertile, must also be offered to someone. In friendship we find something of this giving of the self, but in friendship it is not without reserve and reticence. The occasion of this unique giving of the self, of this revelation of the self in the bosom of the conjugal couple, is love. The relationship of man and woman in the midst of the conjugal couple is nothing other than the realization of this unique mutual giving of the self. It is an exclusive relationship where the mystery of the one is offered to the mystery of the other, where man discovers himself in discovering his wife.

This unique and irrevocable experience does not have, it is true, a purely sexual character, but the sexual aspect is a necessary part of it. An unconsummated marriage is not a true marriage. It does not create between the "conjoints" this unique and exclusive intimacy. For sexuality has a way of expressing all the mystery of our incompleteness, all that expectation of the other that witnesses to the fact that man is fully himself only in the unity of the couple (he was created male and female!). Because sexuality is thus tied to the giving of the self, and to the extent that it is so, it participates in this intimacy of being. It is aberrant only to the extent that it is not integrated into this intimacy and that it, consequently, cannot participate in this giving, in this unique and unreserved generosity that binds man to woman.

Sexual relations between man and woman have human significance only as the sign and the fulfillment of a personal relationship so profound that it must be unique. It is precisely this necessity which explains the bond between love and fidelity. It explains why love in its intention wishes itself faithful. And this fidelity, which is first of all fidelity to the other, is also fidelity to oneself. Man respects his own intimacy only in his fidelity to his wife. Infidelity signifies not only that the individual does not respect the person who has given herself to him but that, in a certain sense, he ceases to respect himself, since he considers himself as perpetually offered to the other. Infidelity signifies that the individual denies his own intimacy in favor of a permanent and quasi-public availability that kills it in its very mystery.

The exclusiveness of fidelity is, undoubtedly, difficult to understand. Against it plays that incessant renewal and transformation of a being who has a history. And this history bears witness that all the individual's other choices are not at all irrevocable. Fidelity implies a renunciation, a sacrifice, a determined will no longer to give to new encounters that the individual might have the same meaning that one special encounter (and why *that* one?) had at one sole time in his life. Has not a mistake been made? Has not one's generosity itself hidden reality? It is impossible, even to faith, to strip this decisive encounter of every element of contingency. A psychological analysis would unveil quite a bit of illusion in it. The person whom I have known (in the Biblical sense of the term "to know," extremely significant in the light of what we have just said)—was she truly the one with whom my life could blossom forth? Such a question never brings an entirely satisfactory reply.

Let us try, however, in continuing with the preceding line of thought, to understand what sexual love (which, because it is sexual, is also personal love) requires as its necessary complement of exclusiveness.

One thought in particular seems instructive. It is aimed not at love itself but at all forms of human relationships. All human relationships are selective. When they are not, they sink into banality. This banality means that all beings have become equal and interchangeable. It is undoubtedly good that one can be attracted by the humanity of each being and that all human relationships are, in principle, stamped with a sort of benevolent urbanity and attractiveness which are codified and institutionalized by the rules of good manners. It is also good that the relationships of the man with all women carry that quiet homage to their femininity which we call courtesy, indeed gallantry. But what would a human being be who remained only on this level, whose relationships with his fellow beings were marked only by the necessary respect of politeness?

On the basis of this refined and civil life we can isolate certain elective and selective affinities. Now, the mark of every elective relationship is that it is at the same time exclusive. It can have depth only at this price. One cannot be the friend of everyone. We would justly mistrust the quality of a friendship that would be distributed without choice, that is, without exclusiveness. True friendships, those which not only resist all the tests of life but are expressed in generosity and trust, are rare. Fidelity in friendship means that one's word has been given to another, a word that can no longer be taken back or shared. Fidelity is the gift of something unique: one's word, one's good word.

All these remarks are located on the plane of psychology and intersubjective experience. Even though they give a sufficient justification to the institution of monogamy and remove its character as a contingency of civilization, they still cannot persuade us that sexual love must normally have the nature of an irrevocable giving. Persons change profoundly in the course of their life. Why should love follow these changes?

As Otto Piper has clearly shown, the mystery of the sexual life could not be truly understood apart from the intended purpose of man as Scripture reveals it to us. Scripture, indeed, far from limiting sexuality to the fulfillment of a biological function, shows us that it is tied to a knowledge of ourselves and of the other: "Both knowledge of the unity of the partners and awareness of the differences between the sexes are implied in the mystery of sex. The assurance that in spite of their strangeness they have merged into unity gives the partners a feeling of happiness. . . . The sexual differentiation may become the cause of hatred between the sexes, because the individual in being so terribly proud to be a Self resents the loss of his (or her) ability to lead an independent life."[7] Sexual relations abolish the distances between the sexes that biological and psychological individuality make us accept as absolutes. The married couple form one sole flesh; in Biblical language this term "flesh" designates, in this respect, a personal unity: "They are no longer two, but one." And in this unity there is a divine blessing, which is to reduce the tendency to see the unity only as a sensual delight. This blessing is why man and woman live in expectation of mutual fulfillment precisely on condition that the act of coition be not for each the occasion of an egoistic enjoyment, which would enclose each one in his or her isolation and which would turn their personal relationship into a relation of subject to object. The immoderateness of the sexual life has, as an inevitable consequence, the deterioration of personal relationships such as we see in Don Juanism and, in the extreme, in prostitution. Love requires fidelity, just as this unity must be respected and preserved, exactly because the sexual relationship gives birth to a new personal unity, richer than that of the constituent individuals. It is enriched from the fact that their contradictions have been surmounted. It is even richer because it will be the expression of a double generosity and of a double reception.

This unity has a value in itself in the Biblical perspective, and it is striking that for Plato the erotic relationship is only the point of departure for a higher knowledge, the lowest degree of an ascending dialectical movement that is presumed to lead us to the love of the good, the beautiful, and the true, as if personal knowledge were not the highest knowledge there is.

From the Biblical viewpoint, because of the discovery of a new personal unity that is transcendent in relation to the individual characteristics that constitute it, all other human relationships, including those which bind us to our parents, are not reduced in value but are placed on a second level. It is because of his wife that a man must leave his father and his mother (Gen. 2:24; Matt. 19:5). Man will attach himself exclusively to his wife, and this tie will be stronger than the tie, no matter how strong, that attaches him to his friends. The latter no longer have quite the same openness in relation to the married friend. It is the sign of a very marked spiritual inferiority in pagan antiquity, as in present-day Islam, that the man belongs to his friends, to public life, and to his children more than he belongs to his wife. This signifies that the sexual relationship is not lived in all its depth and that the wife is considered more as an instrument than as the partner of a personal unity.

The Old Testament has a more reliable appreciation of the authenticity of this personal relationship when it insists on respect for the unity of the flesh that is established by the first sex act (Ex. 22:16; Deut. 22:28; 22:13-21, 23 ff.). If we consider this sex act only as an experiment, an initiation, we would prove quite simply that we do not understand what it is all about. We would disregard this new being, born in a reciprocal generosity. But this unity does not depend solely on our will to constitute it. It is an objective fact that goes beyond our egoistic intentions and our frivolity. This is why Paul did not hesitate to say to the Corinthians, who interpreted Christian liberty as the possibility of surrendering themselves to all types of sexual adventures: "You surely know that anyone who links himself with a harlot becomes physically one with her (for Scripture says, 'The pair shall become one flesh')" (I. Cor. 6:16, NEB). The relationship with the prostitute is not sought as a personal relationship, and yet it creates, whether or not we are aware of it, a unity that will dominate and mark us. Does this mean, then, that fornication would be a deadly sin, more serious than cowardice or avarice? In a certain sense yes, because sexual wantonness involves the individual beyond the point where he means to involve himself, and it also involves the other person. This is why the apostle can conclude: "Shun fornication. Every other sin that a man can commit is outside the body; but the fornicator sins against his own body" (I Cor. 6:18, NEB). The sin consists not only in treating the person of the other as a means, but also one's own person, since fornication makes use of one's person as if it were independent, that is, as if it had no intended purpose and no vocation at all. Paul links in extremely narrow fashion that body which is the source of sexual activity and that body which belongs to God: "Do you not know that your body is a shrine of the indwelling Holy Spirit, and the Spirit is God's gift to you? You do not belong to yourselves" (I Cor. 6:19, NEB). Let us not hesitate to correct the teaching of the apostle, not at all in the name of our own wisdom, but in the name of the apostolic teaching itself: other sins are as serious as fornication, carrying with them a kind of debasement of the person and of the other. They are a prostitution of the self. Falsehood is undoubtedly among this number. Yet it is nonetheless true that fornication remains as one of the most glaring forms of contempt for the other and for the self.

It is precisely because the sexual relationship is a relationship of mutual *belonging,* and that this belonging gives birth to a new personal unity, that it could not involve several partners. For, inevitably, this repetition would end by turning the sex act into an act that is sought for itself, in a sort of ignoring of the person as such and in the forgetting of the belonging thus created. The libertine is right whenever he speaks of his sexual adventures as a type of amusement or pastime, that is, as the opposite of a commitment. They are for him only the opportunity to obtain some petty vanity from his success, that is, he attaches little importance to his partner.

But such is the mystery of the sexual life that it ties us and affects us beyond the feelings and emotions that it leads us to experience. If there is a metaphysic and a theology of sexuality, it is precisely because it involves us in an existence in which our motives and conscious intentions are bypassed. We have the illusion that we are absolute masters of our actions and that our actions have no other meaning than that which we give to them. In reality, this description fits only our technical activities; in each specifically human act there is an interrelationship between the person initiating the action and the action itself. The action becomes a part of the acting person; man and woman, in the sexual encounter, are overtaken in their conscious or unconscious intentions. This is what Scripture means when it speaks to us of this new flesh to which man and woman, without having wished it, have given birth. The child that can be born from their encounter is only the objective realization of that beyond themselves which they have unveiled.

What we have just said regarding the sexual involvement could, moreover, be repeated for all other forms of human fidelity. In giving his word to someone, the individual is transferred beyond that which he had desired. But his word has been given, a yes has been pronounced that leads his individual liberty to be compromised under forms that he had not foreseen and that he was incapable of foreseeing. But in the sex act he pronounces an even more decisive yes, one that mortgages the future even more, because it is the yes not of one's calculating intellect but of one's incarnate being, that is, of one's true being.

NOTES

[1] J. J. Rousseau, *Discours sur l'inégalité*, I, 85.

[2] Cf. the book of Henri Desroche, *Les Shakers américains* (Paris: Editions de Minuit, 1955).

[3] "La Sexualité. La Merveille, l'errance, l'énigme," in the review *Esprit*, November, 1960, No. 11.

[4] *Ibid.*

[5] Daniel Lys, "Le plus beau Chant de la Création," in *Etudes théologiques et religieuses*, 1958, No. 4, pp. 114-16.

[6] Th. Bovet, *Le Mariage, ce grand Mystère* (Neuchâtel: Delachaux et Niestlé), p. 65.

[7] Otto Piper, *The Biblical View of Sex and Marriage* (Digswell Place: James Nisbet & Co., Ltd., 1960), p. 48. (This book is a complete revision of *The Christian Interpretation of Sex*, published by James Nisbet & Co., Ltd., 1941.)

Roger Mehl

MARRIAGE AND ENGAGEMENT*

The problem of the sexual life is resolved by access to love in
fidelity; it is not necessarily resolved by marriage. For there
exist, in fact, many types of marriage. There is the marriage that
serves the partners (or one of them) only as a form of discipline and restraint, more or less tolerable. There are marriages
that constitute simple acquiescence to social conventions and
that, consequently, ignore the sexual problem entirely. There
are also marriages, although more rare, where the sexual life is
consistently repressed and where a laborious and sterile search
is pursued for a love falsely called spiritual. The institution of
monogamic marriage is not, in itself, a solution to the problem
of love. It simply offers a social and legal setting, more favora-
ble than polygamy, for the blossoming of a personal love and
for the creation of a receptive household for children. We
should not be afraid to speak of the ambiguity of the institution
of marriage, where social control is aimed at guaranteeing intimacy and where discipline is aimed at stemming the tumultuous
force of Eros. "It is a fact," writes Paul Ricoeur, "that man has
attained his humanity and has humanized his sexuality only
through the discipline, costly in many respects, of the conjugal
institution. . . . Marriage is, in our civilization, always to some
degree under the mark of duty. Many people are defeated by it.
Marriage can protect the duration and the intimacy of the sexual bond, and therefore render it human. But it can also be

* From ROGER MEHL, *Society and Love: Ethical Problems for
Family Life,* James H. Farley, trans. (Philadelphia: Westminster Press,
1964), pp. 161-81. Used by permission.

what ruins for many both its duration and its intimacy."[1] If marriage does not instruct love and does not permit it to become fidelity, then it is no longer anything but a social institution, just as relative as all the others. It does not hinder, and perhaps even favors, the debasement of love into habit, a debasement that is described with sadness and truth by one of the heroines of a novel by Paul André Lesort: "Even then, when he made me pregnant with this child, we no longer came together except out of habit. Pure habit, a need for going through the motions between us, and no longer anything of ourselves in the motions."[2]

There is no obligatory fidelity. It is more than a duty. This is why marriage leaves room for fidelity without guaranteeing it. There are some marriages that continue out of habit, even with a sort of mutual reliance, without fidelity. Fidelity requires more than a stable environment, more than an honored institution. It is even hostile, in a certain sense, to this stability and immobility. It seeks growth. It wants the joy of mutual assistance and sharing, of common discoveries, and of the building of a common destiny.

Exactly because of the ambiguity of the institution of marriage, Christian thought has endeavored to go beyond the institution in the social sense of the word in order to make a sacrament of it. Protestant theology is rarely involved in this course, or has proposed this solution only with reservations,[3] having, in general, a very narrow definition of sacrament. A sacrament, by definition, is instituted by Christ: it is the mediation, through a symbol, of divine grace concerning our salvation. Marriage, however, even if happy, is not the symbol of our salvation.

The definition of sacrament in Roman Catholic theology is broader, permitting a consideration of different types of sacraments. For Roman Catholic thought, a sacrament is not necessarily related to an event in the historical ministry of Christ. Ever since Thomas Aquinas, the Roman Catholic Church has taught that each sacrament has a form, consisting normally of the sacramental words pronounced by the priest, and a content, which is the tangible object serving as the symbol. This definition applies imperfectly enough to marriage, since the blessing pronounced by the priest does not have sacramental value and the sacrament is administered by the spouses themselves. The form and content of the sacrament is thus contained in the mutual agreement of the spouses. The Lord has elevated to sacramental dignity the legitimate union of man and woman, attaching to this union a grace which sanctifies the conjoints. When a man and a woman, under the conditions prescribed by the Church and knowing that they are obedient to the will of God, decide to unite together in an irrevocable fashion, they consummate the sacrament of marriage.

We do not see any necessity to quibble with Roman Catholic theologians over the fact that their definition of sacrament can be applied only with some difficulty to marriage. For no theology possesses, on the basis of Scriptural witness, a truly satisfactory definition of sacrament in general.

Rather, we think it more useful to consider the intention that is expressed in this attempt to elevate marriage to sacramental dignity.

It is a question, first of all, of recalling that marriage is willed by God, that his blessing is attached to this bond which unites man and woman. Through marriage a grace of God comes to man. Marriage is for his good: in it is realized the profound goal of man, outside of personal solitude, in the unity of the couple. Valid in itself, this unity leads to procreation, which in turn extends mortal man's power over the future. It permits him to make of the father-son relationship, which is a decisive experience of humanity, a relationship with someone other than himself, a relationship in which he even recognizes himself. Undoubtedly one of the greatest errors of certain philosophical anthropologies is that they have not taken into account man's calling to paternity: Marxism defines man through work alone. The account of Genesis, on the other hand, links procreation and work. And in any event, the creative aspect of work is, in the final analysis, often only a pale reflection of the procreativity of man.

In the second place, since marriage is willed by God and by

grace given to man, it cannot be isolated from the spiritual destiny of man, that is, from his redemption. We should be careful to avoid any dissociation between the natural and the supernatural (which is often found in Roman Catholicism), between Order of Creation and Order of Redemption. It is in Christ, in the redeeming Christ and through him, that God has created all things (Col. 1:16). Nothing authorizes us to think that a temporal grace is not also a spiritual grace. When the Old Testament speaks of blessings, it is remarkable that earthly happiness and temporal prosperity are implied as well as eternal life. They are in a constant ambiguity. Nothing could be more false than to set happiness over against salvation. To be sure, the blessings of the Old Testament do not have a self-sufficient meaning. They refer to the fulfillment that they proclaim. The benevolence of God, who wishes both happiness and salvation for his creature, appears more clearly when the fulfillment has taken place.

This is why Paul does not hesitate to place side by side the union of Christ with his church and the union of man with woman in marriage. But this parallel has meaning only when referred to the history of salvation. This means simply that marriage does not have redemptive significance by itself. It is ambiguous, and can lead to our ruin as well. Whoever unites himself to a prostitute becomes one flesh with her. As a fornicator, he will not inherit the Kingdom. But whoever is already united by faith to the Lord can, through that alone, sanctify the spouse (I Cor. 7:14).

Therefore the unbelief of one of the conjoints never constitutes a reason for repudiation or divorce. A true union between a Christian and a non-Christian, where Eros is not aberrant but is integrated into a personal communion, can lead the nonbelieving conjoint to discover the source that strengthens the life of the other and, ultimately, of the couple itself. This is understandable even on the psychological or moral level.

Indeed, this is why the church, in principle, should not dread mixed marriages or even forbid them, as does, also in principle, the Roman Catholic Church. To be sure, the churches are right in pointing out very strongly the psychological, moral, and spiritual dangers and difficulties that mixed marriages involve. The delicate and often painful problem of the religious education of the children should also be pointed out. But they should also recall that there is sometimes a promise and a hope bound to mixed marriage, on condition that the believing conjoint has an adult faith.

The institution of marriage acquires its true significance only at the cost of a tie between the Order of Redemption and the Order of Creation, of a tie, therefore, between the love that God has for man and man's own carnal love, i.e., at the cost of Eros being taken in charge by Agape. Marriage does not possess its true significance in and of itself. Certainly, one can give monogamous marriage credit for a certain stability, a discipline of passions, and a greater dignity accorded to women. But legal and social restraint, although it might stabilize mores, does not create an ethical existence. There always exists a deep heteronomy between the institution of marriage and that which it claims to codify. Fidelity is not at all engendered by discipline. Few examples attest more clearly than fidelity to the reality of what Paul calls the end of the law. This fidelity, to be sure, can be sustained by customs; by the sanctions, however uncertain, of public opinion; by feelings of reliance, esteem, and affection that are born of the common life; by the growing old of Eros; and by a certain lack of imagination and audacity on the part of the married couple. These realities, although humble and equivocal, cannot be scorned; they are very precious supports. But they do not constitute the foundation of marriage. It would be dreadful to see in fidelity only a cooled passion. True fidelity is active and creative. It does not let itself become the prey to habit. On the contrary, it desires to fulfill the other in fulfilling itself. It is the love for the other beyond what the other is at the present time. It is the anticipation of the manifestation of the other.

This is why fidelity has an affinity with faith. It believes that what we are, my spouse and I, has not yet been totally manifested. Thus one can establish a link between God's fidelity in relation to us and conjugal fidelity. The fidelity of God signifies that God shows an incredible patience toward us, looking at us through the promise he has given to us, i.e., he sees us in Jesus Christ. So in the same way conjugal fidelity is faith in that promise which is given to each of the conjoints and to the couple itself. The exchange of promises in the religious marriage should not be considered as the essential fact of the ceremony. For these promises, taken in themselves constitute an untenable wager: I count on the persistency of my present feelings, I wager against the deteriorations of time, I deceive myself regarding my constancy.

In reality, these promises which are exchanged are against common sense if they are not based on an awareness of God's fidelity toward us. The state, which cannot call forth this fidelity, is quite right in reducing the contents of these obligations and in limiting them to a certain number of mutual services and forms of assistance. And it is also right in not affirming the indissolubility of marriage (which is, however, what the Roman Catholic Church requires of the state in opposing all civil legislation authorizing divorce). When the married couple cannot count on the fidelity of God, their commitments cannot go beyond the limits of what is reasonable. This is to say that a marriage based on fidelity is scarcely possible outside of the church. Within the church the limitations imposed by the marriage law cease to be artificial and intolerable disciplines, and the intimate relationship between man and woman appears as the symbol and the declaration both of the communion and of the liberty of the Kingdom. In saying this, we do not ignore the fact that there are, on the outside of faith, faithful couples whose fidelity is all the more admirable since, to human eyes, it is ignorant of its own foundation. But the existence of such couples should not lead us to put confidence in human possibilities.

It is evident that the idea of making of marriage a sacrament is not devoid of meaning, on the condition, however, that no *opus operatum* is tied to this sacrament, that it is not reduced to a magical-juridical mechanicalism. The error of the Roman

Catholic Church consists precisely in making of the marriage sacrament an absolute obstacle to divorce. Most assuredly, it is necessary to condemn divorce resolutely, as Jesus did (Matt. 5:32). But, in fact, divorce is brought about in the same way that infidelity toward God is brought about. As God forgives infidelity toward himself, so the mocked partner forgives the infidelity that comes to him. We cannot insist too much on the power of a forgiveness that is capable of annulling the past. But it also happens sometimes that forgiveness is beyond our measure of faith, or that forgiveness is not received as such and, consequently, does not become an object upon which the forgiven person can begin a new life.[4] There are also breaches that are final. Jesus warns us that "every one who looks at a woman lustfully has already committed adultery with her in his heart" (Matt. 5:28). This adultery certainly does not mean that divorce is the irreparable result, that the course of fidelity is henceforth closed. We should at least understand that fidelity cannot be secured by constraint, no more than faith can. Thus, after all humanly possible attempts at reconciliation have been tried, why should a conjugal union be continued that is already void of meaning and that is no longer anything but hypocrisy? Why continue a relationship that in many cases, through the irritation it provokes, hinders the man or the woman from rediscovering not only a balanced moral life but even access to divine forgiveness, and that can be for the children the cause of a scandal or of psychological troubles?

Although one can legitimately reproach the Protestant churches for sometimes too lightly authorizing the remarriage of divorced persons, thus bringing contempt on the divine blessing, they cannot be reproached for not having made divorce impossible. Divorce is the result of sin. It must be understood as such, and it must also be understood that, in principle, this sin is [due to] one of the two partners. But it is impossible for us not to recognize the sin in its social and moral consequences, to act as if these consequences did not exist.

In emphasizing the sacramental significance of marriage, that is, the necessary tie between the fidelity of God and that of the conjoints, and in insisting on the fact that conjugal fidelity is a grace, we do not absolutely prohibit recourse to all forms of human wisdom that can help us remain in this fidelity. Quite the contrary, it is in the certitude that all is grace that we can and must work out our own sanctification. This is why Christians have been quite wrong in depriving themselves of the assistance of Eros and in not maintaining its force. Its presence is necessary in a Christian marriage. And Karl Barth is right in criticizing Anders Nygren for being too eager to combat Eros and to reduce its value, as if Eros were not a part of God's good creation.[5] A Christian marriage is not a marriage of convenience; it is a marriage of love and passion.

In our age it is no longer necessary, happily, to be on guard against that bourgeois idea that would prefer marriage to come later in life (for the man!), as a sign of the abatement or even of the weariness of a previously immoderate sexual life, as if one had reached a time in life when a more settled existence is possible, the sensual life having been satisfied in other ways. On the other hand, our age can, perhaps, find something of value in one minor element of this supposed wisdom of our fathers. Is it not necessary to guard against the hasty marriage that follows after the first spark of love? For this first spark can be purely sentimental and naïve. It can be more the excitement of the young man who discovers with wonder, not the one who will be his wife, but rather *the* Young Woman, and who hastens to marry, not his wife but, in her person, every young woman and all femininity. Eros, in its first phase, is still undifferentiating. It carries the person toward the other sex in general. Imagination colors the first encounter with all possible charms. One will marry then; one will repent afterward. A maturing of Eros is necessary, an initiation of the young person to the other sex. A preliminary generic knowledge must be acquired before choosing and being chosen (the initiative must not be one-way).

This is why it seems wise not to discredit *flirtation,* as Protestant moralism has so often done. The medieval church encouraged gallantry and the chivalrous spirit, which are only stylized forms of flirtation. But it is necessary that both sides know what flirtation is and that no one be fooled by it. They should understand that flirtation is both serious and wonderful, and that it nevertheless remains a game. It must, therefore, be accompanied by humor and by a certain levity, without sentimentality becoming involved in it. Our ancestors, who understood it well, used the happy expression *"conter fleurettes"* [literally, "to recount little flowers,"—tr.] A sort of roundelay, a sort of dance where each sex becomes acquainted with the other, that's flirtation. Consequently, it must not have too secret a character. Although nascent love passes through a period of secretiveness, flirtation is carried on in a collectivity of young men and women. But once again, like all games, flirtation has a set of rules. And the first rule is lucidity. This lucidity is likely to saturate the game with guilt feelings, which can be shaken off only by a complete honesty. Flirtation can prevent marriage from being a manifestation of puerility.

And yet marriage does not presuppose a serious weighing of the future. It is not the result of a calculation in which one puts all the odds on his side after duly making inquiries. It is a great risk to run and it should be run gladly. The joy will be all the greater in proportion as we are not hypnotized by the singular gravity of our commitment. "An individual without a sense of humor," Dr. Bovet says, with humor, "should never get married."[6] It is this humor, which is true only to the extent that it is based on the deep assurance of faith, which will permit a confrontation of the first difficulties of common existence, the first clashes of character and taste, the manifestations of the profound otherness of the partners, without dramatizing them. It is this humor which will stem the envenomed, but quite natural, outbursts of jealousy and will spare love from becoming tyrannical and possessive.

Although it is true that the honeymoon, which is the apprenticeship of life together, requires a certain discretion on the part of the couple's friends, it is not at all true that a happy household is necessarily the one in which each of the conjoints breaks all ties with friends from before the marriage, in which the man and woman renounce, in particular, their friendships among the other sex (such a renouncing can lead to each of the partners reproaching the other later on for having forced the renouncing.) There is, undoubtedly, a peril attached to these friendships. But it is necessary to risk and at the same time to free oneself from it by giving no illicit aspect to the friendships.[7]

Marriage is fundamentally an acknowledgment of reciprocal belonging. Through marriage the individual, in this very acknowledgment, commits the secret of his existence to the care of the partner. He will belong only to her. Betrayal exists already when one confides to a third party, of whatever sex, an innermost anxiety, an existential inquietude that could not be acknowledged to the other spouse. But, this being said, friends remain a precious thing, who by their dependable presence preserve the couple from a sort of psychologically inevitable boredom, and who, above all, aid the couple to avoid withdrawing into themselves and to avoid practicing a collective egoism. Friends help the couple to remain open to the calls of the world, of culture, and of politics. It is conversation that saves the home, yet this conversation must be given fullness by preoccupations other than domestic and culinary ones. It is necessary that the marvelous diversity of the world find its place in the home and that the dialogue of the married couple be open to others. The hospitality of the home is one of the conditions for its health.

To be sure, this health is preserved only insofar as the hospitality does not become a whirl of social relationships with the many "obligations" that such sociability involves. For then the invasion of the home by friends and its involvement in external relationships would mean that the couple cannot endure their own privacy, that it has become meaningless for them. And soon they will attempt to have their own individual relationships outside the home, to give to these relationships an aspect of private domain.

Even when this peril is overcome, when the couple themselves assume the many worldly relationships that are often the result of the social or socioprofessional situation, it is advisable carefully to watch that the home does not become a sort of extension of the professional life. Just as it would be false for the husband not to keep his wife abreast of his professional problems (largely the case in the middle class of the nineteenth century), so it would be false to turn the home into a place for professional appointments. It would be wrong to value the home only for the conveniences that it offers for transacting business and for fostering good relationships with clients and colleagues.[8] It should be remembered in this respect that if society is not the extension of the family, neither is the family the extension of society. The family is the particular society entrusted with the guardianship of private life.

Whether or not it will remain this will depend obviously on the individuality of the conjoints. It is the absence of individuality in one of the partners (or sometimes in both) that creates rapidly and permanently that particular type of boredom peculiar to the family. The call to others then becomes a compensation for this boredom. To be sure, it is exceptional when both partners have the same degree or the same type of individuality. In a couple there is nearly always a dominant element. It becomes serious when the dominant element, in asserting his (or her) superiority too strongly, becomes destructive of the other, when, for example, the wife is reduced to the function of admiring her husband. The husband undoubtedly will be pleased by this, but only for a certain time. The admiration that his spouse has for him, and that perhaps she alone has for him, will profoundly bore him. On the other hand, a wife who exercises a perpetually critical function toward her husband will produce in him, besides discouragement and various types of inferiority complexes, an irritated boredom.

Although it is true that a couple, because the members are one flesh, must have its own personality, this can only give birth to the development of the personality of the partners: there must be, in the couple, a sort of mutual development, each one having clearly marked the potentialities in the other and, where possible, the particular calling of the other. This calling underlines the particularity and the limitations of the other partner. It is necessary that each of the spouses has ambitions for the other that are compatible with his calling and limitations. Many conjugal disappointments derive from the fact that one of the conjoints has excessive ambitions for the other, which secretly makes him grieve over his inability to realize them. This is to say that there will be mutual development only where the partners are first of all accepted for what they are, with the very limitations of their particular vocation. The dictum "Accept your spouse as he or she is" would be equivocal if it meant a renunciation of any progress. But we can be allowed to wish for this progress only in the direction compatible with a character and a vocation. If I am by nature a conscientious and intelligent subordinate, and not one who takes bold initiatives, my wife must not require me to become a leader. Such a requirement would be disastrous and would leave feelings of resentment and disappointment in the hearts of both. The man and wife must not settle down into a routine life, but they must be encouraged with prudence and discernment to acquire more authority and more prestige in the realm that is their own. The concern for social promotion must not be the principal ambition of the couple. The happiness of the home can be destroyed by the very demands of a civilization of work that, in the near future, will have less and less need of inferior workers and will exercise a very strong pressure for social promotion.

There is a form of acceptance of the other that is particularly difficult in the couple: this is the acceptance of the other in his growing old. We say intentionally the aging of the other; for although the acceptance of our own growing old is sometimes quite facilitated by nature (which proportions our energies and our ambitions to our strength and our age) and encouraged both by the growing old of our contemporaries and by a sort of fatalism as old as humanity, we accept with more difficulty the aging of our spouse. The difficulty seems to be the greatest for man, who stupidly would like his wife to remain always young.[9] This ambition is not completely puerile, since it expresses the obscure awareness of a Biblical teaching, viz., that the woman is the glory of her husband. Rather, the puerility consists in not having perceived that the wife is this glory in all ages of life, in not being attentive to the special charm of youth, to that of young adulthood, to that of maturity, to that of middle age. The frequency of divorces that come after fifteen or twenty years of marriage is the statistical expression of this type of resentment which some conjoints nourish toward the other because the other grows old.

It is certain that the acceptance of the growing old of the other presupposes something different from resignation and fatalism. It presupposes the sort of faith by which one can discern in the person of the other a reality different from that which is shaped and sometimes disfigured by time, the subject upon whom the divine promise is pronounced, the new being whose existence is attested by baptism. This requirement that we accept the growing old of others is valid for all our interpersonal relationships. How much more reason is there, then, to accept it in the husband-wife relationship, the exemplary relationship of all human relationships!

The growth of the personality of each partner in the bosom of the conjugal union is subordinated to a condition that is both psychological and moral: it is necessary that each of the partners escape from the influence of his own family and that he free himself from the emotional fixations inherited from early childhood.[10]

We should admire the wisdom of the redactor of Genesis, who could not be supposed to have had a knowledge of the secrets of depth psychology, yet who nonetheless has given this fundamental rule: "Therefore a man leaves his father and his mother and cleaves to his wife" (Gen. 2:24). It is necessary to insist on the physical sense of this verb "to leave." The concern of our modern societies should be to give to each young couple housing that is *theirs,* where they can live in independence from the parents. But this physical break should be accompanied by a psychological break as well. This is the price of reaching adulthood. Not only should the home be able to make its decisions without assistance (even if it includes the advice of preceding generations), but the husband and wife should belong to each other more than they belong to their parents. The man who remains too much a son will not be a true husband and he should not consider his wife as a new mother. The question is even more delicate since, psychologically, conjugal love is not always dissociated from paternal love and maternal love. Many men treat their wives as children. The protection that is given to the wife takes on the air of paternalism, and the wife, in turn, especially when she is childless, envelops her husband in an anxious and possessive love that does not permit him to assume the risks of life and to take the initiatives of an adult. The spouses love each other and yet are "poorly loved" (Francois Mauriac). And their love will curiously develop into resentment, each one reproaching the other for not having permitted him (or her) to become an adult.

Much healthy stress is put on the continuity that the family, through the forming of a lineage, introduces into the midst of society. This is undoubtedly an essential aspect of its function. But it is necessary to see that the family also creates a discontinuity. It forms cells that are separated in time, groups that do not reproduce each other exactly in the course of generations. Thus it breaks traditions at the same time that it maintains certain others, thereby participating in the necessary renewal of humanity.

The fulfillment of the couple, the fulfillment of the conjoints in the interior of the couple, constitutes an essential activity of humanity, which is something we too often forget in a civilization of work. It is a slow task that is never totally finished, not even in the evening of life. It requires unceasing renewals, but it is also the assurance, for the couple, that it truly has a future before it, even when it has finished the education of its children, which sounds for it the hour of retirement.

Engagement

We could certainly have spoken of engagement at the time of dealing with flirtation. The occurrence of engagement emerges sometimes slowly or suddenly out of a period of flirtation. But flirtation and engagement are far from having the same meaning or the same finality. Flirtation is that game of love by which young men and women acquire a mutual knowledge, a generic knowledge. An engagement no longer belongs to the realm of games. It involves a choice and a form of commitment. And it should, in the normal course of events, lead to marriage. If we speak of engagement after having spoken of marriage, it is because its meaning is defined by that of marriage. The engagement is a promise of marriage, but not a trial marriage.

The status of engagements is paradoxical enough. The fiancés are not husband and wife, although their reciprocal fidelity can be as great as that which binds husbands and wives. They know that they must wait, that it would not be good for them, having chosen each other, to be man and wife right off. They know that it would not be good for their first encounter to be a sexual encounter, for then they would give a kind of priority and primacy to the inclination that is undoubtedly present and that has attracted them to each other, but that should submit to a maturation. It should become filled with friendship, tenderness, and psychological and spiritual understanding before being able to exert itself, precisely in order to lessen the risk of it becoming aberrant.

On the other hand, it is neither necessary nor desirable for the engagement period to be very long, as has been the case in the past. If the engagement period is a time of expectation, this expectation, when it is prolonged for too great a time, risks uselessly intensifying the desire. It is a time truly unique in human existence. It is the time of the promise, where what will be us is already mysteriously given under the form of a promise—and where, at the same time, nothing irrevocable is yet completed. Although the engagement is not a trial marriage, it should however, be a period of testing in which the fiancés verify the authenticity of their feelings, the soundness of their choice, and in which they have a glimpse of each other not only as individuals but as representatives of a certain family tradition, of a certain social milieu. In an age where the barriers of social class undoubtedly play a more effaced role in the choice of a mate than in the past, the engagement period takes on a special importance. For it is an illusion to think that one marries solely an individual being, that it is possible to disregard the social and intellectual milieu of which this individual, whether he knows it or not, is the representative.

To say that the engagement period is a time of testing is to imply that there is a possibility that the result of the testing can be negative, and that the engagement can be broken. Protestant moralism has often encumbered engagements with an excessive seriousness, considering their ruptures as being as grave and degrading as divorce. This is a prejudice that destroys the true meaning of engagements. Certainly, a commitment is involved in the engagement that, as such, is not conditional, and the breach of this commitment is painful, all the more so because it is very rarely the doing of both fiancés at once. It will leave one of them, if not both, the memory of a broken communion, of an impossible love, impossible because not shared, of a love offered and not received. Now, it is the essence of love to be shared; it is not wrong to speak of an unhappy love, when it is unrequited. But it is sometimes the proof of an authentic courage, of a true honesty, of a true faith (God should not be tempted by asking him to sustain us in an experience that is beyond our forces), to break off an engagement that does not promise happiness, to break it off with simplicity in the hope that a true friendship, sincere and affectionate, can one day be reborn.

Yet in order for this to be possible it is necessary for the engagement not to have been encumbered with too great an air of solemnity. Middle-class society gives quite readily, but wrongly, a publicity to engagements that is a bit too noisy, thus prejudging the future. Inversely, secret engagements are not to be recommended; it is good for the fiancés to know themselves committed to each other from a certain moment, and that their friends respect with discretion their privacy. It will be invaluable help to the fiancés not to know themselves engaged only in the secrecy of the heart, but of being recognized as such in the circles in which they run. There is middle ground between premature solemnity and uncertain clandestineness.

Modern psychologists rightly insist on the fact that the harmony between a man and a woman is not only of the feelings and of spiritualized affectivity. There is, more deeply, a sort of sexual assent. In this semiconscious realm certain irremediable incompatibilities can exist despite feelings. Moreover, it is certain that the sexual life of the man follows a rhythm different from that of the woman. In the woman, frigidity is frequently the mark of a sexual incompatibility that is difficult to overcome. Is this a motive for transforming the engagement period into a trial marriage? Many psychologists and physicians are of this opinion. But the proposed remedy seems to us to be quite dubious, and worse than the danger run: the end result would be to give a primary place to sexual Eros and to consider it in and of itself as animal function; whereas when it is integrated into the person and colored with tender affection, it is capable of evolving and even of changing.

On the other hand, this suggestion would deprive marriage of its fundamental quality: it would no longer be an absolute beginning in our life, the entry into a new existence. In the full sense of the term, one would deflower it. Also, without disregarding the risks pointed out by psychologists and physicians (risks that should be explained in "schools of preparation for marriage"; for in this area explanation can liberate), it is advisable to remember that as act and wager of fidelity, marriage necessarily involves certain risks, and that marriage could not fall to the level of a reasonable calculation without losing that which gives it its dignity and its charm, its character of human adventure, the greatest adventure that it is given to man to run.

NOTES

[1] Paul Ricoeur, "La Sexualité. La Merveille, l'errance, l'énigme," *Esprit,* November, 1960, No. 11.

[2] P. A. Lesort, *Le Fer rouge* (Paris: Ed. du Seuil, 1957), p. 56.

[3] Cf. Henry Leenhardt, *Le Mariage chrétien* (Neuchâtel and Paris:

Delachaux et Niestlé, 1946). We follow his analysis of the Roman Catholic conception. In a recent book, Ernst Kinder (*Die Ehe,* cf. in particular p. 29) shows, with much persistence, that although the New Testament does indeed establish a relationship between marriage and the order of grace, marriage does not appear in the New Testament as a means of grace. Quite to the contrary, marriage has need of the saving powers of grace. Marriage is not the means of appropriating grace and salvation. It is the object of it, or at least a privileged object.

[4] Who is able to decide if the forgiveness, in such a case, is an authentic forgiveness? It might be simply a form of pride, humiliating to the other more than allowing the other access to joyous liberty. Cf. the play by Gabriel Marcel, *Un homme de Dieu* (Paris: La Table Ronde, 1950, 2d ed.).

[5] Karl Barth, *Kirchliche Dogmatik* III/2, 339-41.

[6] Th. Bovet, *op. cit.,* p. 130.

[7] On this point, see Th. Bovet, *ibid.,* pp. 103-104, who underlines the necessity of being conscious of the fact that an erotic current continues to exist in these friendships.

[8] We think these remarks are perfectly applicable to the pastoral household, which too often suffers from a permanent invasion of members of the congregation and which, because of this, progressively loses the virtues that it should have.

[9] It is a fact that widowers always marry wives a great deal younger than themselves, whereas during the time of their youth they wished to marry someone from their own generation.

[10] Cf. Th. Bovet, *op. cit.,* p. 11.

Marc Oraison

THE IDEAL MARITAL UNION *

Having considered the concrete conditions proper to man himself, to his organism, his social adjustment and his own proper
ends, we are now in a position to evolve a more exact concept
of what the ideal union between man and woman should be.

Primordially "divided," as it were, into two distinct persons
destined to beget a third person through their own union with
each other, the human being spends his earthly and temporal
life seeking an unachieved and often even jeopardized unity, a
stability as yet unattained, a fulfillment he feels is peculiarly
fated to be his. In a natural and well-ordered view of things, the
dynamic unity for this quest shall depend on the married couple
as such.

THE NEED FOR ACTING AS ADULTS

The ideal couple receives its definition in the complete, definitive, and free (*i.e.,* responsible and spontaneous) exchange of
gifts between two adult and well-developed persons of complementary sexes.

A truism? Of course, but some of these notions always require our reexamination.

Sex is not just a certain physical, anatomical and functional
conformation. It is a condition involving and influencing the

* From MARC ORAISON, *Man and Wife: The Physical and Spiritual
Foundations of Marriage* trans. from the French by André Humbert
(New York: The Macmillan Co., paperback, 1958), pp. 69-86. Used by
permission. Father Oraison is a French theologian who is also a Doctor
of Medicine.

entire person in the emotions, in the ways of thinking and judging, in the whole frame of reference within which the person chooses to view the world and live. Sex represents a person's psychological approach to the implementing of relationships and of all activity. A man is not really a man, capable therefore of really and effectively loving a woman, unless he has fully and consciously acquired certain powers of initiative, conquest, strength of leadership, without faltering before the demands such powers make upon him, but also without straining them to the point where they become a sort of "will to power" tantamount to the reassertion of an inferiority complex. On the other hand, a woman is not fully capable of playing the part of a woman unless she has fully understood and accepted womanhood with its features of active receptivity, of need for support coupled with the special gift of intuitive perception so indispensable to the equilibrium of the mated pair; above all, she must understand and accept motherhood: her exalted part in the glorious task of procreation, a part burdened with the most exacting demands.

It is therefore necessary for both persons, man and woman, to enjoy maximum release from the confused unconscious yearnings of frustrated childhood emotionalism. Such release will forestall a constant, if unwitting, tendency to seek in their married life compensations for this or that deficiency which might have plagued their early emotional life within their respective families. In other words, each partner must consider the other as a person really *other* and distinct, one to whom the gift of oneself is complete and mutual, not as an ill-defined part of a person who might fill the void created by the frustration of some childhood emotional need. The power of each to love should be at the peak of spontaneity, immune to any instinctive self-regard—an attitude which is all the more deceiving since it always takes on the more or less vivid appearance of what is called "love," though it is nothing more than an unreasonable, self-centered demand.

THE NEED FOR BEING REALISTIC

It is also essential to the proper balance of a married couple that neither mate should fall victim to idealism or to illusions about the other. This means that the bright joy of their mutual "find" should not so dazzle them as to leave them blind to the irreducible element of frailty in every human being on this earthly pilgrimage. There persists in each of us so great a thirst for success, so deep a desire for the absolute, that we remain quite impervious to the reality of failure or of conflict in daily life. If we possess but for a fleeting moment the joy of love in all its purity and grandeur, we irresistibly tend to settle down in it and to believe it is with us to stay, by virtue of its own power, acquired, solid and lasting. This is perhaps the most cruel and stubborn illusion to which we fall prey. In point of fact, our joys exist only so long as we keep creating them, and they crumble away the moment we fail to keep activating them with creative energy, with a constant effort to extend ourselves, to move forward, forgoing the moment just past, thrilling though it was, in order to prepare for the next moment which is always more fraught with demands and weighted down with difficulties.

No doubt the most subtle danger is that of a certain idealism which tends to assign to sexual union, for its own sake, first rank in the scale of values, especially spiritual values, in marriage. Again, in actual fact there is no couple, granted its parties are sincere persons, that has not been aware as much of the immeasurable significance of sex as of its terrible inadequacy. This is because sexuality alone is not everything; but it is also a consequence of the strong tendency, deeply rooted in each one of the spouses, to be sluggishly self-centered and powerless to wrench oneself free from narcissism or self-love. Each partner in varying degree is forever busy looking for self in the other, most of the time unwittingly and in good faith; but if two people should hurry into married life with blissful disregard of the fact that they have this weakness, they would be heading into a spiritual impasse, or riding for a tragic fall. Not only their spiritual relationship but their sexual instinct itself, as we shall see, would be saddled with this burden of selfishness; and their very reflexes would be at odds, now impelling them to altruistic love and to gift of self to one another, now holding them back with invincibly selfish reactions. In order to prevent all this, a call must be made at the very outset of married life upon the quiet and objective kind of courage it takes to admit the basic fact that man is selfish, a fact which is quite unpalatable to anyone's self-esteem. Psychologists might describe this weakness as a result of arrested development in instinctive emotional life, or as an inability to attain at all levels of human activity, whether spontaneous or half-conscious or deliberate, the freedom to give oneself and to separate oneself from one's own egotistic desires. It is this freedom which constitutes the supreme balance in human personality.

That specific frailty of man is the basis for the struggle St. Paul describes in his *Epistle to the Romans* (7:15-20). A disregard of the practical importance of this real weakness, which is partly moral decay and partly a regressive yearning, would be the surest preparation for soul-searing setbacks, as much in the moral as in the emotional complexes of a married couple.

THE NEED FOR BEING CONSTRUCTIVE

Union in marriage can be thought of only as a matter of long and arduous construction on the part of two people and as a result of their joint efforts. Such an observation may seem to be a commonplace; but the point demands emphasis.

It seems, indeed, that in current evaluations of marriage—not so much ones expressly stated as those underlying the habitual behavior of people—marriage is quite often considered as "a settling down," or as a terminus. How very many young people there are who have in their student days, for example, led a life morally and spiritually well-directed toward the vaguely foreseen eventuality of marriage, with an unhampered disposition some day to give themselves to another generously and completely; but who suddenly, when the hour has come to implement such a disposition, merely "settle down" to marriage in an attitude, as expressed by these words, which might be proper enough with reference to financial status or ownership but is not quite right in the domain of the spirit! For imperceptibly, yet all too quickly, it affects the overall mental and moral tonicity or health of the couple, singly and jointly considered. Their horizons narrow, their contacts with the world of their past experience are virtually cut off: something which is understandable and, as we see it, would imply no detriment if only it were attended by their joint finding of new frontiers. But instead they begin to live for themselves, to shut themselves in a kind of "egotism for two"—later expanded to three or more. They adopt what is wrongly called the "family spirit," which might more accurately be described as a spirit of clannishness or even of caste. Married life comes to be valued only as a "comfortable" reality, whose provisory character they are unwilling to face, and which they take the habit of defending, fiercely if need be, against attacks from the outside. And, too, these young couples begin to practice a "nicely regulated" married life which alternates between material preoccupations, and concern over teaching the children good manners so they will honor their parents; and Sunday Mass which they would not miss for the world because it offers the chance to meet others like themselves and provides a vague sense of insurance against an equally vague "eternal fire." Who can deny that a goodly number of "nice young couples" finish—the word "finish" has been deliberately selected—just that way?

The most terrible thing about all this is that in a sense they are right, because they should indeed shape and guard the conditions that shall give equilibrium to their family and home. But it is all too natural and easy to become so absorbed in this quite necessary task as to lose sight of the fact that it is not, in short, the be-all and end-all of marriage. There is a natural tendency to forget that something or everything might some day turn into an enigma defying solution by any human equation, and that some preparation might be advisable for such a contingency. There is a natural inclination to forget that married life is a kind of training course for another and fuller life which is pitched in a much higher and more vibrant key, and that here really lies the essence of the dynamism and joy of marriage.

The penalty of such forgetful disregard is the inevitable re-birth in the mates of those selfish reflexes against which they had waged such a brave battle in their youth. In the married couple caught under the dead weight of its temporal condition, and bogging down in a dominant concern with this condition, each partner is bound to become ensnared again gradually and unconsciously in a selfishness over which there was never a complete individual victory, and against which there is now no joint striving.

The ideal marriage, reflecting the comprehensive teaching of the Church, is a starting point and not a terminus or a resting place. Wide awake and determined, the partners ought deliberately to set forth on a future course of mutual training with the courage to see beyond the vistas of time while yet encompassing and using time within a sound and sensible range of view of things. It becomes a question of shaping oneself into an offering dedicated to a primal community, the aim of which is dynamic, destined to promote in each of its members the orientation of the self toward complete altruism and toward the entrance through death and the Cross into the Resurrection. It is literally true that no marriage could be truly Christian unless it were visualized and lived out in this perspective.

The child itself through the demands it makes upon the parents should contribute to the development of the higher and longer view of marriage. This ought to be so not only because in its earliest existence the child preoccupies the parents in care, worry and time, but the more so because it is a personal being to whose service the primal conjugal community is of itself ordained. Considerations like this can have far-reaching effects as to how much the child's personality should be respected, and might change a few so-called traditional, authoritarian and glib concepts in education. They could also lead to creating for the parents eventual demands in self-sacrifice of the cruelest kind. For example, what mother can accept clearly and calmly the incalculable consequences of her passing the fifties and do so without tending in the least to consider her last sixteen-year-old son as just a boy who is escaping from her? This strange young man who blindly and sometimes incoherently demands his own proper and legitimate autonomy reminds her of an inescapable truth—a truth which comes to mind with dreadfully brutal impact unless one has made long preparation to accept it—the truth that the time has come for her to think of old age, and so of death. If I am to believe the lessons of my own dealings with young married couples, rare indeed are the families who are able to absorb without a trauma the impact of this very hard stage in life's conflict. The only palliative to the harshness of such blows is found in lifelong conjugal training in spirituality.

Now marriage, as understood according to the Christian concept of the world itself and of man's destiny, cannot be anything but a temporal reality. We have established that it is the means within the bounds of time on earth for the preparation of humanity's access to the Kingdom of Eternity and, by virtue of its sacramental quality, for the building of the Kingdom of God. Thus marriage is not itself eternal, as can be readily discerned. For if marriage stamped the union of two persons with a mark of eternity, remarriage would be impossible and unthinkable in the event of death striking down one of the mates. This was precisely the objection with which the Sadducees sought to test Christ, though not in an attack on marriage but as an expression of their disbelief in the resurrection. All three synoptic evangelists[1] tell the same story of Our Lord's availing Himself of His enemies' sarcastic cunning to confound them all with a teaching that opened wide the traditional frames of reference on the subject, with the transcendent logic of mystery.

"For at the resurrection," says Jesus as quoted by Matthew, "they will neither marry nor be given in marriage" (Matt. 22:30). This means that sexuality, which is the specific character of the marital union, will no longer be exercised, precisely because the reproductive function of sex will no longer have reason to exist. It does not mean that persons will not be marked in the most intimate recesses of their psychological being with the characteristic differences of sex. The joy of unity in sexual union will be transcended by the infinitely more direct and total joy of participation in the unity of God Himself. The impermanence of the enjoyment derived from sexual relations arises from the twofold fact that sex is on the one hand a function of reproduction and that, on the other, in the definitive Kingdom of Eternity the sum total of human persons destined to populate the heavenly Jerusalem shall have been attained. Joy then will no longer be derived from a transient union linked with the power to procreate, but from the fullness of reciprocity in the eternal contemplation of the Oneness of God. In this, sexuality as such will no longer have any part to play.

Marriage is in a way an apprenticeship to Divine Love with creative cooperation as the occasion for its practice. If the mates wish to remain consistent in their adherence to the Christian view of human destiny (a view that is founded on the power of the mystery of resurrection), as they showed they wanted to do on the day of their union before the Church, they must be profoundly imbued with the idea of the transience of sexuality as a generative function. It will follow that from the very outset of their marriage they will have reasons to avoid falling prey to the violence of instinct. They will be intensely motivated to seek in their marriage something quite different as its primary value, and hence to engage jointly in practicing a certain asceticism with regard to their sexuality. Keenly and deeply alive to the real significance of their union in the warmth and light of the Charity of the Mystical Body they will find it less difficult to advert to this self-denial, accept its necessity and affirmatively practice it.

THE NEED FOR AN INTEGRAL VIEW OF MARRIAGE

Though, as we have pointed out earlier, sexuality and its exercise gives to the conjugal union its specific character, it is not, from the point of view of communality, the goal of marriage. Proof of this can be found in the recognition granted by the Church to unconsummated marriage, the union in which the partners mutually agree not to exercise the sexual function. Such a marriage is a valid contract, provided abstention from intercourse has not been set as a prior condition of the partners' mutual consent to become married; and only the most exceptional reasons justify this kind of union, for procreation is a duty of fruitfulness for two young and healthy persons who unite before God. The only reasons which can take priority over this duty are those of a supernatural or, one might say, of a mystical order.

It nevertheless remains true that the sexual instinct and the function it activates cannot be placed in the absolute forefront of all conjugal considerations. Both the instinct and the function must be integrated harmoniously in the comprehensive plan of married life, related to the common desire of the mates to prolong themselves in the child, as well as to participate in perpetuating and extending the species. Instinct and function in sexual matters rank as a specific privilege, and must be so placed in the comprehensive synthesis of the couple's life. Sexual union must assume for them the character of a token, a guide mark, a summit in their life in common, a life so close to being oneness that creation of a new living person is foreseeable and within range of its realization. However, let it be said again: sex as a function cannot possibly be dissociated from the generative power.

In this harmonious synthesis of all personal elements, an integration which represents the whole life of the couple, it is quite evident that sex, though it has a quality of supreme intensity, constitutes no more than a rather short and secondary moment in the live-long day. Life in common stretches day after day into areas of activity usually far removed from anything directly relating to sex, and if the search for unity were given up or allowed to become haphazard in all these other areas, it would be useless to look for truth and worth-while union on the sexual plane. Moreover, even if unity were achieved exclusively in sex—a unity which the least pessimistic observer could describe as a simple synchronizing of enjoyment—it would amount to bitter illusion. The mutual and true giving of self goes on all through the days, all through the minutest details of life together; it does not just happen to occur in the fleeting moment of the sexual act. The gift of self is more exacting in its demands and more difficult to achieve when thus set against the background of daily humdrum existence. It requires on the part of each member of the marital team a constant and methodically deliberate effort to drive oneself beyond one's laggard self; a straining to give for the sake of unity and true balance, really everything one has, not just each individual's sexual potentialities.

The sexual behavior of a married couple, therefore, fits into the synthesis of their general behavior; and this, in turn, can hardly be conceived—at least in a Christian perspective—as anything but the corporate disciplining, training and education of *all* the power of their instinct, of *all* their impulsive dynamisms, of all things, in brief, over which the mind has not as yet achieved sufficient control. Love, in the most spiritual sense of the word, is alone capable of wrenching free these two persons from their congenital selfishness and of setting them on this course of corporate and mutual education. And no instinct can be allowed to be taken out of the curriculum, not the sex instinct any more than the others. Man's ultimate destiny demands that he aim for the highest possible mastery through mind and spirit over the ill-defined and unpremeditated forces of his being or, in other words, that he achieve maximum disentanglement from the tricky snares of mere sensory pleasure and, with greater reason, rank carnality. In wedlock, release of this kind is effected by joint effort, and it is quite normal that the sexual instinct should in this regard be of common concern. Conjugal chastity shall not then primarily consist in *avoiding sin,* but rather in moving together toward a commonly achieved balance and poise which will be an emancipation from instinctive compulsions. Thus set free, man will have clearer insight into the post-temporal world of the resurrection in which, as St. Paul says, the flesh even as to its most hidden impulses will be wholly and sovereignly penetrated with the light of the spirit.

In concrete terms, the ideal couple would be the one in which both spouses had reached such a degree of common balance that in the face of the necessity, for example, of practicing continence over rather long periods both husband and wife would not find it at all difficult to forego intercourse, *precisely on account of love and its demands.* I am thinking here of a couple whose story I was privileged to know: a new birth was out of the question for many long months to come, but the husband as he held his wife in tender embrace, spontaneously and in apparent unawareness of the tremendous implication of his words, said: "I love you too much, even too much to desire you." Apart from their spiritual and religious significance, such words revealed the presence in both persons of a singularly well-balanced condition of emotions and instincts.

Berdyaev's profound observation in his book, *The Destiny of Man,* is in line with this couple's true-to-life intuition: "Genuine love is the most powerful means of rising above sexual lust, the source of downfall and enslavement."

Obviously, for the sake of conforming with an integral view of marriage, sexual union will have to be invested with certain characteristics imparted to it by the actual life experience of the partners. Though it is commonly said that the question for them is to avoid bogging down in mere search for sensual enjoyment, it is definitely not a question of denying this pleasure, or of considering it evil, or of rejecting it. The real point is that delight of the flesh must serve as a prop for something else, and is not to be sought exclusively for its own sake. Doing so would constitute at least a venial fault, according to the teaching of Pope Innocent XI in 1679, in his condemnation of laxism.

Ideally, sexual intercourse should be viewed graciously, and not under precept, by each partner as a fulfillment of the other partner's well-being for the good of their community. The joy of their union and even its delight should above all consist for one partner in the rebound of the joy and delight experienced by the other, through the complete oneness of the couple. This, it should not be forgotten, must always be in mutual exchange, as the most effective way of checking the human tendency toward self-centeredness.

Moreover, to square with ideal psychological normalcy, sexual intercourse should be viewed only as tied in with the joint procreative powers of the couple. The woman is able readily enough to take this view, but the man must also adopt it, though in slightly different psychological focus and adjustment.

RECAPITULATION

This then is the ideal integral concept of sexuality in married life which the Church and which Revelation and tradition invite us to consider as our goal and exemplar. It is out of the question for the Church to accept any devaluation whatever of a synthesis which gives to the most natural aspirations of love their ultimate crowning and perfection from above, while at the same time it sets aside as fundamental inadequacies all deliberate defaults or transgressions.

Love means the total mutual gift of self; the acceptance of the necessity of a corporate asceticism; the joint training of the sexual instinct and its orientation toward goals that transcend its own quality; the refusal to dissociate sex from its reproductive ends; the curbing in each mate of selfish reflexes even in carnal union. Such are the essential points of the Church's moral and ideal directive teaching on marriage as related to humanity's ultimate destiny: the world of the resurrection.

PRACTICAL RESULTS OF THE INTEGRAL VIEWPOINT

Short of self-contradiction the Church is bound to mark as a fault any infringement of her magnificent ideal. A couple that consents, in common judgment of values worth seeking, to such infringement is fatally in error, and perhaps in sin, if consent is clear, deliberate, and given in full freedom of mind and with full knowledge of the facts.

In another connection, since the sexual function is directly related to love and the generating of life, it must not be undervalued. For sex indeed commits man to participate in the most mysterious and greatest dynamism in the whole universe, and it is essential in the highest degree that his participation be flooded to a maximum with the light of conscience and spirit. Moreover, the force of natural attraction and of creative fusion in two persons of complementary sex is appropriated by the sacrament in the act of their mutual consent officially entered into before the Church. In this perspective conjugal love becomes in the proper sense a mystery, that is to say, a reality by which not only divine power but also the grace of eternal salvation will be actuated here on earth. When husband and wife do their utmost to conform with the ideal described by the Church, their harvest is a flowering of eternal values. This is nothing like a mystery in the psychological sense, much less a kind of taboo or setting apart of persons from which something magic is expected to result. It is a religious reality even before it is a moral one, for it is a rite of nature with a biological and emotional significance of natural proportions; but the grace of the sacrament broadens its significance until somehow it concerns even God Himself.

In concluding this chapter, it ought to be noted that we have dwelt on only the *objective* aspect of the question of conjugal morality. In other words, it was a presentation of the *Law,* of the aggregate of norms required by such a concept of sex and marriage as had received its pointing-up through touches of Revelation and Christian tradition.

But it was all theoretic, general, and hence impersonal. What about the *subjective* aspect of the matter, the real condition of people both individually and as couples as they face this ideal pattern of behavior? The ideal is powerfully supported by the natural laws of the universe and by the word of God, enough to elicit firm belief from anyone whose eyes are lighted by faith.

NOTES

[1] Luke 20:27-36; Mark 12:18-25; Matthew 22:23-29.

IV

ON BEING RESPONSIBLE
IN CITIZENSHIP

INTRODUCTION

"The war in Vietnam is immoral and unnecessary. I refuse to go."

"To allow de facto segregation in housing, employment, and education to continue is intolerable. Only crisis-packed situations which dramatize injustice will bring about the necessary changes. We must have more demonstrations."

"To refuse to serve one's country in time of war is the height of irresponsibility. Conscience is the refuge of the coward."

"Obedience to the laws of our country is the first requisite of responsible citizenship. We have legal provision for changing laws we do not like or cannot agree with. Protests and demonstrations are not included."

Statements like these are heard every day. The fact that the actions and remarks of the New Left and the American Legion, or SNCC and John Birchers, polarize the issues in an apparently irreconcilable fashion does not obscure the basic dilemma of our time: What does it mean to be a responsible citizen today? What is a responsible position toward constituted authority?

Obviously in traditional societies or more stable times such questions occurred very rarely in acute form. One's own conception of his responsibility to the larger society happily coincided for the most part with society's understanding of it. Public authority has always involved the right to impose obligations upon its people, obligations which went hand in hand with their rights. But however close these two definitions of responsibility may have been, Christians have been chary about allowing the state to define altogether the dimensions of their public responsibility. From earliest times they have insisted upon distinguishing between the *expression* of authority embodied in the state, and the *source* of that authority deriving from God. And generally they have claimed the right to appeal directly to the source of authority when conscience conflicted with certain demands of the state for obedience. Thus while Christians have honored obedience to the law as obedience to God, they have refused to identify the authority of the state with the authority of God. Further, while the state was the sole possessor of coercion, if it was forced to rely heavily upon threats and punishment, that was seen as an indication that its authority had seriously declined. By insisting that the authority of the state is real and yet derived, they have implicitly protected their right to evaluate the justice of certain actions and policies.

The state does not exist in and for itself; it exists for the good of all its people and derives its legitimacy from their consent. This common good, as the encyclical *Pacem in Terris* suggests, requires a careful balance between co-ordinating and protecting the rights of its citizens on the one hand, and promoting or enlarging these rights on the other. And it is in light of an increasing recognition of what that common goal should be that civic responsibility is being framed today. For example, in a time of social change when the wealth of a nation is constantly expanding through technology, it appears increasingly difficult to justify denying whole segments of the population a fuller life by semipermanent exclusion from a share in that wealth.

However, the attempt to move toward greater justice and equity in the realization of the common good introduces tension between the protection of existing rights on the one hand and the expansion of the rights of those less generously included on the other. Justice has always meant a fair share, but the understanding of what constitutes that share is itself the issue in question. *Pacem in Terris* declares that unless effective action is taken by those in power, especially with regard to economic and political matters, inequalities among citizens tend to become more pronounced and confirmed. To refuse to act would lay the state open to the charge that it represents the interests of some more than others, thereby seriously eroding its moral authority.

The question as to what one's responsibility to constituted authority is cannot be separated from the purpose for which that authority exists, namely the good of all. A signal example of how existing laws may stand in contradiction to the stated aims of the government was dramatically silhouetted in the early days of the civil rights struggle. Once the Supreme Court had struck down the "separate but equal" provision upon which legalized segregation had rested, there remained hundreds of laws, especially in the South, which upheld and enforced separation of the races in public facilities. Many people decided that civic responsibility lay not in continued obedience to such laws, even though they still continued on the books, but rather in open violation of them. It was hoped that by means of such dramatic gestures their injustices and illegality might be revealed. The purpose of such intentional disobedience was not to flout the law, but to uphold the declared law of the land and bring subordinate laws into conformity with it.

But a still more aggressive kind of responsibility appears to be gaining acceptance in our time. Where in the past the authority of government was accepted by the people unless and until there was rank oppression or flagrant injustice, it appears that today people are exercising in a conscious way their right to moral evaluation, if not of government itself, at least of many of its acts and policies. This new attitude has been accompanied by increased awareness of how conditions shape life, and a desire in turn to attempt to fashion those conditions to provide for larger fulfillment of life. When that knowledge and awareness is coupled with resources considered adequate to deal with the situation, moral pressure for change mounts. Martin Luther King's "Letter from Birmingham Jail" is now an historic index of such pressure. In the letter, framed in response to an appeal from a number of white clergymen of three faiths, Dr. King rejects their plea for patience and appeals to the need for creative protest as a necessary condition to bring about social change. From his standpoint, these clergymen had voiced an opinion common to most Americans, that of preferring a "negative peace" as the absence of tension to a "positive peace" signifying the presence of justice. For Dr. King and his followers, the situation had reached a point where there could be no further delay, where there was clearly "no alternative" to direct nonviolent action.

Distinguishing between two kinds of law, "just and unjust," Dr. King asserted that he spoke out of essential respect for law. In so doing, he was claiming the right to pass moral judgment on the degree to which positive law corresponded to the *purpose* of government. But he was doing more than evaluating existing laws and structures; he was also claiming that conscientious responsibility required him to demand that unjust conditions themselves be changed. To remain quiet, to assume that obedience to the stated laws constituted responsible citizenship, would be tacitly to condone the perpetuation of injustice. Civic responsibility lay in creating situations so "crisis-packed" that the way to negotiation in a community would be opened, eventually leading to a "positive peace" with justice. Responsible citizenship, then, is not so much a matter of reflecting without evaluation the existing laws and social patterns of the land— like a thermometer—as in seeking to change them according to more inclusive standards of justice—like a thermostat.

Using the analogy of Dr. King, how does a society determine at what degree the setting shall be? Or, to change the figure, does responsible citizenship include the obligation to see that the setting is more representative of the good of all? Dr. King is not only concerned to express the anger and aspirations of the Negro in American society, but to educate the American conscience to the point where it will not only consent to but will actively pursue the goal of full participation by all members of the society. That is to say, he is championing a concept of responsible citizenship in which a majority of the people accept as a part of their duty the continuing movement toward greater social justice.

As long as the civil rights struggle sought to realize the supreme law of the land, the thermostat had been set, as it were, officially and legally, and the task was to bring all other laws into correspondence with it. But as the struggle moved beyond these legal skirmishes to issues of social—as well as legal—justice, the norm itself was an issue. Thus to the extent that a majority of the people reject Dr. King's enriched definition of responsibility a serious rift in the common end of society emerges. Appeals to moral suasion would appear to have reached their limit, at least for the time being. The alternative, for many who feel their rights are at stake, is the threat of if not the resort to violence. What is one's civic responsibility under these circumstances? Some would claim that a willingness to condone, if not justify, violence constitutes an admission that appeal to moral authority—to the rightness of one's acts—has given way to bare contention between the have's and the have-nots. They conclude that there is a more basic responsibility after all, that of upholding the essential authority of the state even though one may actively protest its actions and legal expressions.

But the problem of justice is not so easily subordinated to social order. Once we move beyond the rather elementary differentiation of just and unjust laws, by what criteria do we determine the concept of the just itself? On this point the encyclical makes some pertinent comments, outlining certain broad goals which give substance to the more formal concept of equality. Responsibility as a citizen entails not only minding one's own business within the limits of the law, but also embodying a concern—a sense of responsibility—for those whom tradition, custom, and often law itself have effectively disenfranchised. Dr. King might term this active, as opposed to passive, responsibility. Further, only by means of such active responsibility can credentials of trust be reestablished which can overcome the alienation among many who have lost both faith and hope in the possibility of becoming full participant members in our society. Thus responsibility in relation to authority is seen to include the exercise of our rights of citizens to make the government more responsive to the needs and rights of all.

Such creative protest—the effort to make government more expressive of the moral authority it represents—depends upon an aroused moral conscience among its citizens. This may or may not obtain. But the question of civic responsibility in relation to war cannot be avoided by most young men. The inevitability of the draft poses this problem in a uniquely concrete way. Again, traditionally, young men have for the most part accepted without question the idea that their duty in time of war consisted simply in fighting for their country. More than at other times, war demands unquestioned obedience, an obedience reflected in the strict discipline imposed in military service. To be sure, there have always been some who voiced an objection to war on principle, who put obedience to a divinely burdened conscience above obedience to the state. Their position could be said to rest upon what Max Weber, in the selection included in this section, calls an ethic of "ultimate ends." By that he means that for some, war is so horrendous that they cannot bring themselves to participate in it, that killing is absolutely forbidden and therefore they cannot bear arms. While such a position is taken in relation to a commandment, the divine law, prohibiting the taking of life, it is not an instance of mere "legalism" as some would suggest. Obedience to that command is not based upon a slavish devotion to the law, but springs from a deeply felt conviction that the purpose for which the law was framed, namely, the protection of life, stands above all values and cannot be compromised. Obedience to the commandment is really secondary to the value the commandment affirms and upholds: human life. A conscientious objector cannot calculate the consequences pro and con of taking life; all killing violates the boundary beyond which human calculation comes to naught. In such cases responsibility to the state on the state's terms has been superseded by obedience to God. And all war, regardless of cause or aim, is rejected in principle.

The Vietnam war, however, has posed the question of responsible participation in war in a unique way. For the first time in living memory, young men are balking at serving in the armed forces. There is a more critical mood concerning the war itself, as to whether it is in fact "necessary" and therefore justified, with attendant moral questions about the way it is being waged and for what ends. Many who would not embrace outright pacifism as a moral posture toward all war have adopted the stance of "selective conscientious objection," claiming that only such protest can alert the nation to the moral culpability entailed in waging this particular war. What we see, really, is an extension of the same mood and attitude which is evidenced concerning social justice, viz., an unwillingness to take government authority on its own terms and a claim of the right to evaluate policy and program as to its genuine legitimacy.

For instance, the Vietnam war has not appeared to many to be the only possible response to a "clear and present danger" which confronted the nation. To the contrary, it has given evidence of being a highly calculated response in light of a particular reading of world power and intentions. In the minds of many, two insistent questions remain. One, the interpretation of the world situation could be faulty, or else so rigid as to set in motion policies that become self-generating rather than being responses to the reality; two, the calculation of consequences and costs of involvement proved tragically wrong. In other words, the costs of the war mounted without clear evidence of either ceiling or solution. If the war was undertaken in view of a calculation of probable consequences and not out of inescapable necessity, it becomes difficult to keep free citizens from assessing the consequences themselves and making their own judgments about its effectiveness and rightness.

Under such circumstances, what is my responsibility as a young man of draft age? What kind of duty is incumbent upon me as a moral person in a society waging this kind of war? Do I have any obligation to speak out on the injustice of a "business as usual" attitude on the part of the majority of the people, while the burden of sacrifice falls upon a relative few? Is it responsible to accept college deferment and thus escape the draft altogether while less fortunate fellow citizens who could not get into college or could not afford to go are quickly conscripted?

In the selection included from Karl Barth's *Church Dogmatics,* he has some pertinent things to say about what he terms "revolutionary loyalty" to the state. He suggests that any consideration of responsibility to the state in time of war should rest on a moral position which could be recommended as the position the state itself should take. To refuse to fight, for Barth, must be based on the wrongness of the war itself, a moral wrongness which must be witnessed to at all costs. But such a witness defeats its own purpose if it accepts immunity from the consequences of war. This would appear to raise questions about an attitude which accepts scholastic deferment as simply a means of avoiding the ambiguity and nastiness of a guerrilla war, but which is unwilling to take a stand one way or another regarding the rightness of the war itself.

Yet another kind of protest is heard about the war, that of the inordinate cost to the economy at the expense of further social equality here at home. This kind of evaluation is based upon an assessment of the total resources of the society, and the alternative uses to which the costs of the war could be put. All of this is to say that as government assumes greater initiative in modifying social and economic conditions, or in providing a basis for their modification by private initiative, the responsibility of citizens actively to participate in determining ends to be pursued is correspondingly greater. There appears to be a growing sense that while those who bear delegated responsibility must in the final analysis make the decisions which affect us all, a citizen's responsibility does not end with passive acquiescence but must also include active concern and participation.

In a sense, then, modern democratic citizenship entails a "vocation to politics" in the broadest sense of the term. The kinds of considerations which Max Weber points to in his essay are seen as appropriate not just for the few who aspire to office, but for all who would exercise their existing responsibility as citizens. Weber sees three elements involved in political responsibility: passion, a concern for consequences, and distance. He defines passion—or as we might say, commitment to some overriding value or purpose—as that end in the service of which consequences are evaluated. Pursuit of a value, or simple reliance upon a principle without regard to the practical implications, is possible only for one who feels no sense of responsibility for others. Because political responsibility is above all else concerned with choice among conflicting values and interest, it will result in a cost which must be borne by others and not just oneself. That is why responsibility, as distinct from obedience, must consider what actions mean for others.

Distance, or detachment, is also a constituent element of political responsibility because of the constant distortion personal feeling introduces into one's judgment. It is the attempt to consider objectively what consequences will flow from a given course of action. It is the subordination of the self to the common good in the determination of one's responsibility. Weber would not agree that such subordination of the self is contrary to self-realization; in pursuit of the good of all undertaken with passion and an eye for consequences, he would see political responsibility as the height of personal fulfillment.

Does Weber offer some clues toward a contemporary understanding of what it means to be responsible in modern society? Is it feasible to assume the model of a vocation to politics as appropriate for responsible citizenship? It would appear that in a time when the dynamics of society and the accompanying obligations of its citizens are so great, responsible decisions may best be understood as the effort to maintain some equilibrium among the three elements Weber emphasizes. The readings which follow are offered to help illumine the situation in which we are called to be responsible to authority and for each other.

Martin Luther King, Jr.

LETTER FROM BIRMINGHAM JAIL*

April 16, 1963

MY DEAR FELLOW CLERGYMEN:

While confined here in the Birmingham city jail, I came across your recent statement calling my present activities "unwise and untimely." Seldom do I pause to answer criticism of my work and ideas. If I sought to answer all the criticisms that cross my desk, my secretaries would have little time for anything other than such correspondence in the course of the day, and I would have no time for constructive work. But since I feel that you are men of genuine good will and that your criticisms are sincerely set forth, I want to try to answer your statement in what I hope will be patient and reasonable terms.

I think I should indicate why I am here in Birmingham, since

* From MARTIN LUTHER KING, JR., *Why We Can't Wait* (New York: Harper & Row, 1963). pp. 77-100. Copyright © 1963 by Martin Luther King, Jr. Reprinted by permission of Harper & Row, Publishers. Dr. King is the well-known civil rights leader and Protestant clergyman.

AUTHOR'S NOTE: This response to a published statement by eight fellow clergymen from Alabama (Bishop C. C. J. Carpenter, Bishop Joseph A. Durick, Rabbi Hilton L. Grafman, Bishop Paul Hardin, Bishop Nolan B. Harmon, the Reverend George M. Murray, the Reverend Edward V. Ramage and the Reverend Earl Stallings) was composed under somewhat constricting circumstances. Begun on the margins of the newspaper in which the statement appeared while I was in jail, the letter was continued on scraps of writing paper supplied by a friendly Negro trusty, and concluded on a pad my attorneys were eventually permitted to leave me. Although the text remains in substance unaltered, I have indulged in the author's prerogative of polishing it for publication.

you have been influenced by the view which argues against "outsiders coming in." I have the honor of serving as president of the Southern Christian Leadership Conference, an organization operating in every southern state, with headquarters in Atlanta, Georgia. We have some eighty-five affiliated organizations across the South, and one of them is the Alabama Christian Movement for Human Rights. Frequently we share staff, educational and financial resources with our affiliates. Several months ago the affiliate here in Birmingham asked us to be on call to engage in a nonviolent direct-action program if such were deemed necessary. We readily consented, and when the hour came we lived up to our promise. So I, along with several members of my staff, am here because I was invited here. I am here because I have organizational ties here.

But more basically, I am in Birmingham because injustice is here. Just as the prophets of the eighth century B.C. left their villages and carried their "thus saith the Lord" far beyond the boundaries of their home towns, and just as the Apostle Paul left his village of Tarsus and carried the gospel of Jesus Christ to the far corners of the Greco-Roman world, so am I compelled to carry the gospel of freedom beyond my own home town. Like Paul, I must constantly respond to the Macedonian call for aid.

Moreover, I am cognizant of the interrelatedness of all communities and states. I cannot sit idly by in Atlanta and not be concerned about what happens in Birmingham. Injustice anywhere is a threat to justice everywhere. We are caught in an inescapable network of mutuality, tied in a single garment of destiny. Whatever affects one directly, affects all indirectly. Never again can we afford to live with the narrow, provincial "outside agitator" idea. Anyone who lives inside the United States can never be considered an outsider anywhere within its bounds.

You deplore the demonstrations taking place in Birmingham. But your statement, I am sorry to say, fails to express a similar concern for the conditions that brought about the demonstrations. I am sure that none of you would want to rest content with the superficial kind of social analysis that deals merely with effects and does not grapple with underlying causes. It is unfortunate that demonstrations are taking place in Birmingham, but it is even more unfortunate that the city's white power structure left the Negro community with no alternative.

In any nonviolent campaign there are four basic steps: collection of the facts to determine whether injustices exist; negotiation; self-purification; and direct action. We have gone through all these steps in Birmingham. There can be no gainsaying the fact that racial injustice engulfs this community. Birmingham is probably the most thoroughly segregated city in the United States. Its ugly record of brutality is widely known. Negroes have experienced grossly unjust treatment in the courts. There have been more unsolved bombings of Negro homes and churches in Birmingham than in any other city in the nation. These are the hard, brutal facts of the case. On the basis of these conditions, Negro leaders sought to negotiate with the city fathers. But the latter consistently refused to engage in good-faith negotiation.

Then, last September, came the opportunity to talk with leaders of Birmingham's economic community. In the course of the negotiations, certain promises were made by the merchants—for example, to remove the stores' humiliating racial signs. On the basis of these promises, the Reverend Fred Shuttlesworth and the leaders of the Alabama Christian Movement for Human Rights agreed to a moratorium on all demonstrations. As the weeks and months went by, we realized that we were the victims of a broken promise. A few signs, briefly removed, returned; the others remained.

As in so many past experiences, our hopes had been blasted, and the shadow of deep disappointment settled upon us. We had no alternative except to prepare for direct action, whereby we would present our very bodies as a means of laying our case before the conscience of the local and the national community. Mindful of the difficulties involved, we decided to undertake a process of self-purification. We began a series of workshops on nonviolence, and we repeatedly asked ourselves: "Are you able to accept blows without retaliating?" "Are you able to endure the ordeal of jail?" We decided to schedule our direct-action program for the Easter season, realizing that except for Christmas, this is the main shopping period of the year. Knowing that a strong economic-withdrawal program would be the by-product of direct action, we felt that this would be the best time to bring pressure to bear on the merchants for the needed change.

Then it occurred to us that Birmingham's mayoral election was coming up in March, and we speedily decided to postpone action until after election day. When we discovered that the Commissioner of Public Safety, Eugene "Bull" Connor, had piled up enough votes to be in the run-off, we decided again to postpone action until the day after the run-off so that the demonstrations could not be used to cloud the issues. Like many others, we waited to see Mr. Connor defeated, and to this end we endured postponement after postponement. Having aided in this community need, we felt that our direct-action program could be delayed no longer.

You may well ask: "Why direct action? Why sit-ins, marches and so forth? Isn't negotiation a better path?" You are quite right in calling for negotiation. Indeed, this is the very purpose of direct action. Nonviolent direct action seeks to create such a crisis and foster such a tension that a community which has constantly refused to negotiate is forced to confront the issue. It seeks so to dramatize the issue that it can no longer be ignored. My citing the creation of tension as part of the work of the nonviolent-resister may sound rather shocking. But, I must confess that I am not afraid of the word "tension." I have earnestly opposed violent tension, but there is a type of constructive, nonviolent tension which is necessary for growth. Just as Socrates felt that it was necessary to create a tension in the mind so that individuals could rise from the bondage of myths and half-truths to the unfettered realm of creative analysis and objective appraisal, so must we see the need for nonviolent gadflies to create the kind of tension in society that will help men rise from the dark depths of prejudice and racism to the majestic heights of understanding and brotherhood.

The purpose of our direct-action program is to create a situation so crisis-packed that it will inevitably open the door to negotiation. I therefore concur with you in your call for negotiation. Too long has our beloved Southland been bogged down in a tragic effort to live in monologue rather than dialogue.

One of the basic points in your statement is that the action that I and my associates have taken in Birmingham is untimely. Some have asked: "Why didn't you give the new city administration time to act?" The only answer that I can give to this query is that the new Birmingham administration must be prodded about as much as the outgoing one, before it will act. We are sadly mistaken if we feel that the election of Albert Boutwell as mayor will bring the millennium to Birmingham. While Mr. Boutwell is a much more gentle person than Mr. Connor, they are both segregationists, dedicated to maintenance of the status quo. I have hope that Mr. Boutwell will be reasonable enough to see the futility of massive resistance to desegregation. But he will not see this without pressure from devotees of civil rights. My friends, I must say to you that we have not made a single gain in civil rights without determined legal and nonviolent pressure. Lamentably, it is an historical fact that privileged groups seldom give up their privileges voluntarily. Individuals may see the moral light and voluntarily give up their unjust posture; but, as Reinhold Niebuhr has reminded us, groups tend to be more immoral than individuals.

We know through painful experience that freedom is never voluntarily given by the oppressor; it must be demanded by the oppressed. Frankly, I have yet to engage in a direct-action campaign that was "well timed" in the view of those who have not suffered unduly from the disease of segregation. For years now I have heard the word "Wait!" It rings in the ear of every Negro with piercing familiarity. This "Wait" has almost always meant "Never." We must come to see, with one of our distinguished jurists, that "justice too long delayed is justice denied."

We have waited for more than 340 years for our consti-tutional and God-given rights. The nations of Asia and Africa are moving with jetlike speed toward gaining political independence, but we still creep at horse-and-buggy pace toward gaining a cup of coffee at a lunch counter. Perhaps it is easy for those who have never felt the stinging darts of segregation to say, "Wait." But when you have seen vicious mobs lynch your mothers and fathers at will and drown your sisters and brothers at whim; when you have seen hate-filled policemen curse, kick and even kill your black brothers and sisters; when you see the vast majority of your twenty million Negro brothers smothering in an airtight cage of poverty in the midst of an affluent society; when you suddenly find your tongue twisted and your speech stammering as you seek to explain to your six-year-old daughter why she can't go to the public amusement park that has just been advertised on television, and see tears welling up in her eyes when she is told that Funtown is closed to colored children, and see ominous clouds of inferiority beginning to form in her little mental sky, and see her beginning to distort her personality by developing an unconscious bitterness toward white people; when you have to concoct an answer for a five-year-old son who is asking: "Daddy, why do white people treat colored people so mean?"; when you take a cross-country drive and find it necessary to sleep night after night in the uncomfortable corners of your automobile because no motel will accept you; when you are humiliated day in and day out by nagging signs reading "white" and "colored"; when your first name becomes "nigger," and your middle name becomes "boy" (however old you are) and your last name becomes "John," and your wife and mother are never given the respected title "Mrs."; when you are harried by day and haunted by night by the fact that you are a Negro, living constantly at tiptoe stance, never quite knowing what to expect next, and are plagued with inner fears and outer resentments; when you are forever fighting a degenerating sense of "nobodiness"—then you will understand why we find it difficult to wait. There comes a time when the cup of endurance runs over, and men are no longer willing to be plunged into the abyss of despair. I hope, sirs, you can understand our legitimate and unavoidable impatience.

You express a great deal of anxiety over our willingness to

break laws. This is certainly a legitimate concern. Since we so diligently urge people to obey the Supreme Court's decision of 1954 outlawing segregation in the public schools, at first glance it may seem rather paradoxical for us consciously to break laws. One may well ask: "How can you advocate breaking some laws and obeying others?" The answer lies in the fact that there are two types of laws: just and unjust. I would be the first to advocate obeying just laws. One has not only a legal but a moral responsibility to disobey unjust laws. I would agree with St. Augustine that "an unjust law is no law at all."

Now, what is the difference between the two? How does one determine whether a law is just or unjust? A just law is a man-made code that squares with the moral law or the law of God. An unjust law is a code that is out of harmony with the moral law. To put it in the terms of St. Thomas Aquinas: An unjust law is a human law that is not rooted in eternal law and natural law. Any law that uplifts human personality is just. Any law that degrades human personality is unjust. All segregation statutes are unjust because segregation distorts the soul and damages the personality. It gives the segregator a false sense of superiority and the segregated a false sense of inferiority. Segregation, to use the terminology of the Jewish philosopher Martin Buber, substitutes an "I-it" relationship for an "I-thou" relationship and ends up relegating persons to the status of things. Hence segregation is not only politically, economically and sociologically unsound, it is morally wrong and sinful. Paul Tillich has said that sin is separation. Is not segregation an existential expression of man's tragic separation, his awful estrangement, his terrible sinfulness? Thus it is that I can urge men to obey the 1945 decision of the Supreme Court, for it is morally right; and I can urge them to disobey segregation ordinances, for they are morally wrong.

Let us consider a more concrete example of just and unjust laws. An unjust law is a code that a numerical or power majority group compels a minority group to obey but does not make binding on itself. This is *difference* made legal. By the same token, a just law is a code that a majority compels a minority to follow and that it is willing to follow itself. This is *sameness* made legal.

Let me give another explanation. A law is unjust if it is inflicted on a minority, that, as a result of being denied the right to vote, had no part in enacting or devising the law. Who can say that the legislature of Alabama which set up the state's segregation laws was democratically elected? Throughout Alabama all sorts of devious methods are used to prevent Negroes from becoming registered voters, and there are some counties in which, even though Negroes constitute a majority of the population, not a single Negro is registered. Can any law enacted under such circumstances be considered democratically structured?

Sometimes a law is just on its face and unjust in its application. For instance, I have been arrested on a charge of parading without a permit. Now, there is nothing wrong in having an ordinance which requires a permit for a parade. But such an ordinance becomes unjust when it is used to maintain segregation and to deny citizens the First-Amendment privilege of peaceful assembly and protest.

I hope you are able to see the distinction I am trying to point out. In no sense do I advocate evading or defying the law, as would the rabid segregationist. That would lead to anarchy. One who breaks an unjust law that conscience tells him is unjust, and who willingly accepts the penalty of imprisonment in order to arouse the conscience of the community over its injustice, is in reality expressing the highest respect for law.

Of course, there is nothing new about this kind of civil disobedience. It was evidenced sublimely in the refusal of Nebuchadnezzar, on the ground that a higher moral law was at stake. It was practiced superbly by the early Christians, who were willing to face hungry lions and the excruciating pain of chopping blocks rather than submit to certain unjust laws of the Roman Empire. To a degree, academic freedom is a reality today because Socrates practiced civil disobedience. In our own nation, the Boston Tea Party represented a massive act of civil disobedience.

We should never forget that everything Adolf Hitler did in Germany was "legal" and everything the Hungarian freedom fighters did in Hungary was "illegal." It was "illegal" to aid and comfort a Jew in Hitler's Germany. Even so, I am sure that, had I lived in Germany at the time, I would have aided and comforted my Jewish brothers. If today I lived in a Communist country where certain principles dear to the Christian faith are suppressed, I would openly advocate disobeying that country's antireligious laws.

I must make two honest confessions to you, my Christian and Jewish brothers. First, I must confess that over the past few years I have been gravely disappointed with the white moderate. I have almost reached the regrettable conclusion that the Negro's great stumbling block in his stride toward freedom is not the White Citizen's Councilor or the Ku Klux Klanner, but the white moderate, who is more devoted to "order" than to justice; who prefers a negative peace which is the absence of tension to a positive peace which is the presence of justice; who constantly says: "I agree with you in the goal you seek, but I cannot agree with your methods of direct action"; who paternalistically believes he can set the timetable for another man's freedom; who lives by a mythical concept of time and who constantly advises the Negro to wait for a "more convenient season." Shallow understanding from people of good will is more frustrating than absolute misunderstanding from people of ill will. Lukewarm acceptance is much more bewildering than outright rejection.

I had hoped that the white moderate would understand that law and order exist for the purpose of establishing justice and that when they fail in this purpose they become the dangerously structured dams that block the flow of social progress. I had hoped that the white moderate would understand that the present tension in the South is a necessary phase of the transition from an obnoxious negative peace, in which the Negro passively accepted his unjust plight, to a substantive and positive peace, in which all men will respect the dignity and worth of human personality. Actually, we who engage in nonviolent direct action are not the creators of tension. We merely bring to the surface the hidden tension that is already alive. We bring it out in the open, where it can be seen and dealt with. Like a boil that can never be cured so long as it is covered up but must be opened with all its ugliness to the natural medicines of air and light, injustice must be exposed, with all the tension its exposure creates, to the light of human conscience and the air of national opinion before it can be cured.

In your statement you assert that our actions, even though peaceful, must be condemned because they precipitate violence. But is this a logical assertion? Isn't this like condemning a robbed man because his possession of money precipitated the evil act of robbery? Isn't this like condemning Socrates because his unswerving commitment to truth and his philosophical inquiries precipitated the act by the misguided populace in which they made him drink hemlock? Isn't this like condemning Jesus because his unique God-consciousness and never-ceasing devotion to God's will precipitated the evil act of crucifixion? We must come to see that, as the federal courts have consistently affirmed, it is wrong to urge an individual to cease his efforts to gain his basic constitutional rights because the quest may precipitate violence. Society must protect the robbed and punish the robber.

I had also hoped that the white moderate would reject the myth concerning time in relation to the struggle for freedom. I have just received a letter from a white brother in Texas. He writes: "All Christians know that the colored people will receive equal rights eventually, but it is possible that you are in too great a religious hurry. It has taken Christianity almost two thousand years to accomplish what it has. The teachings of Christ take time to come to earth." Such an attitude stems from a tragic misconception of time, from the strangely irrational notion that there is something in the very flow of time that will inevitably cure all ills. Actually, time itself is neutral; it can be used either destructively or constructively. More and more I feel that the people of ill will have used time much more effectively than have the people of good will. We will have to repent in this generation not merely for the hateful words and actions of the bad people but for the appalling silence of the good people. Human progress never rolls in on wheels of inevitability; it comes through the tireless efforts of men willing to be co-workers with God, and without this hard work, time itself becomes an ally of the forces of social stagnation. We must use time creatively, in the knowledge that the time is always ripe to do right. Now is the time to make real the promise of democracy and transform our pending national elegy into a creative psalm of brotherhood. Now is the time to lift our national policy from the quicksand of racial unjustice to the solid rock of human dignity.

You speak of our activity in Birmingham as extreme. At first I was rather disappointed that fellow clergymen would see my nonviolent efforts as those of an extremist. I began thinking about the fact that I stand in the middle of two opposing forces in the Negro community. One is a force of complacency, made up in part of Negroes who, as a result of long years of oppression, are so drained of self-respect and a sense of "somebodiness" that they have adjusted to segregation; and in part of a few middle-class Negroes who, because of a degree of academic and economic security and because in some ways they profit by segregation, have become insensitive to the problems of the masses. The other force is one of bitterness and hatred, and it comes perilously close to advocating violence. It is expressed in the various black nationalist groups that are springing up across the nation, the largest and best-known being Elijah Muhammad's Muslim movement. Nourished by the Negro's frustration over the continued existence of racial discrimination, this movement is made up of people who have lost faith in America, who have absolutely repudiated Christianity, and who have concluded that the white man is an incorrigible "devil."

I have tried to stand between these two forces, saying that we need emulate neither the "do-nothingism" of the complacent nor the hatred and despair of the black nationalist. For there is the more excellent way of love and nonviolent protest. I am grateful to God that, through the influence of the Negro church, the way of nonviolence became an integral part of our struggle.

If this philosophy had not emerged, by now many streets of the South would, I am convinced, be flowing with blood. And I am further convinced that if our white brothers dismiss as "rabble-rousers" and "outside agitators" those of us who employ nonviolent direct action, and if they refuse to support our nonviolent efforts, millions of Negroes will, out of frustration and despair, seek solace and security in black-nationalist ideologies—a development that would inevitably lead to a frightening racial nightmare.

Oppressed people cannot remain oppressed forever. The yearning for freedom eventually manifests itself, and that is what has happened to the American Negro. Something within has reminded him of his birthright of freedom, and something without has reminded him that it can be gained. Consciously or unconsciously, he has been caught up by the *Zeitgeist,* and with his black brothers of Africa and his brown and yellow brothers of Asia, South America and the Caribbean, the United States Negro is moving with a sense of great urgency toward the promised land of racial justice. If one recognizes this vital urge that has engulfed the Negro community, one should readily understand why public demonstrations are taking place. The Negro has many pent-up resentments and latent frustrations, and he must release them. So let him march; let him make prayer pilgrimages to the city hall; let him go on freedom rides—and try to understand why he must do so. If his repressed emotions are not released in nonviolent ways, they will seek expression through violence; this is not a threat but a fact of history. So I have not said to my people: "Get rid of your discontent." Rather, I have tried to say that this normal and healthy discontent can be channeled into the creative outlet of nonviolent direct action. And now this approach is being termed extremist.

But though I was initially disappointed at being categorized as an extremist, as I continued to think about the matter I gradually gained a measure of satisfaction from the label. Was not Jesus an extremist for love: "Love your enemies, bless them that curse you, do good to them that hate you, and pray for them which despitefully use you, and persecute you." Was not Amos an extremist for justice: "Let justice roll down like waters and righteousness like an ever-flowing stream." Was not Paul an extremist for the Christian gospel: "I bear in my body the marks of the Lord Jesus." Was not Martin Luther an extremist: "Here I stand; I cannot do otherwise, so help me God." And John Bunyan: "I will stay in jail to the end of my days before I make a butchery of my conscience." And Abraham Lincoln: "This nation cannot survive half slave and half free." And Thomas Jefferson: "We hold these truths to be self-evident, that all men are created equal. . . . " So the question is not whether we will be extremists, but what kind of extremists we will be. Will we be extremists for hate or for love? Will we be extremists for the preservation of injustice or for the extension of justice? In that dramatic scene on Calvary's hill three men were crucified. We must never forget that all three were crucified for the same crime—the crime of extremism. Two were extremists for immorality, and thus fell below their environment. The other, Jesus Christ, was an extremist for love, truth and goodness, and thereby rose above his environment. Perhaps the South, the nation and the world are in dire need of creative extremists.

I had hoped that the white moderate would see this need. Perhaps I was too optimistic; perhaps I expected too much. I suppose I should have realized that few members of the oppressor race can understand the deep groans and passionate yearnings of the oppressed race, and still fewer have the vision to see that injustice must be rooted out by strong, persistent and determined action. I am thankful, however, that some of our white brothers in the South have grasped the meaning of this social revolution and committed themselves to it. They are still all too few in quantity, but they are big in quality. Some—such as Ralph McGill, Lillian Smith, Harry Golden, James McBride Dabbs, Ann Braden and Sarah Patton Boyle—have written about our struggle in eloquent and prophetic terms. Others have marched with us down nameless streets of the South. They have languished in filthy, roach-infested jails, suffering the abuse and brutality of policemen who view them as "dirty nigger lovers." Unlike so many of their moderate brothers and sisters, they have recognized the urgency of the moment and sensed the need for powerful "action" antidotes to combat the disease of segregation.

Let me take note of my other major disappointment. I have been so greatly disappointed with the white church and its leadership. Of course, there are some notable exceptions. I am not unmindful of the fact that each of you has taken some significant stands on this issue. I commend you, Reverend Stallings, for your Christian stand on this past Sunday, in welcoming Negroes to your worship service on a nonsegregated basis. I commend the Catholic leaders of this state for integrating Spring Hill College several years ago.

But despite these notable exceptions, I must honestly reiterate that I have been disappointed with the church. I do not say this as one of those negative critics who can always find something wrong with the church. I say this as a minister of the gospel, who loves the church; who was nurtured in its bosom; who has been sustained by its spiritual blessings and who will remain true to it as long as the cord of life shall lengthen.

When I was suddenly catapulted into the leadership of the bus protest in Montgomery, Alabama, a few years ago, I felt we would be supported by the white church. I felt that the white ministers, priests and rabbis of the South would be among our strongest allies. Instead, some have been outright opponents, refusing to understand the freedom movement and misrepresenting its leaders; all too many others have been more cautious than courageous and have remained silent behind the anesthetizing security of stained-glass windows.

In spite of my shattered dreams, I came to Birmingham with the hope that the white religious leadership of this community would see the justice of our cause and, with deep moral concern, would serve as the channel through which our just grievances could reach the power structure. I had hoped that each of you would understand. But again I have been disappointed.

I have heard numerous southern religious leaders admonish their worshipers to comply with a desegregation decision because it is the law, but I have longed to hear white ministers declare: "Follow this decree because integration is morally right and because the Negro is your brother." In the midst of blatant injustices inflicted upon the Negro, I have watched white churchmen stand on the sideline and mouth pious irrelevancies and sanctimonious trivialities. In the midst of a mighty struggle to rid our nation of racial and economic injustice, I have heard many ministers say: "Those are social issues, with which the gospel has no real concern." And I have watched many churches commit themselves to a completely otherworldly religion which makes a strange, un-Biblical distinction between body and soul, between the sacred and the secular.

I have traveled the length and breadth of Alabama, Mississippi and all the other southern states. On sweltering summer days and crisp autumn mornings I have looked at the South's beautiful churches with their lofty spires pointing heavenward. I have beheld the impressive outlines of her massive religious-education buildings. Over and over I have found myself asking: "What kind of people worship here? Who is their God? Where were their voices when the lips of Governor Barnett dripped with words of interposition and nullification? Where were they when Governor Wallace gave a clarion call for defiance and hatred? Where were their voices of support when bruised and weary Negro men and women decided to rise from the dark dungeons of complacency to the bright hills of creative protest?"

Yes, these questions are still in my mind. In deep disappointment I have wept over the laxity of the church. But be assured that my tears have been tears of love. There can be no deep disappointment where there is not deep love. Yes, I love the church. How could I do otherwise? I am in the rather unique position of being the son, the grandson and the great-grandson of preachers. Yes, I see the church as the body of Christ. But, oh! How we have blemished and scarred that body through social neglect and through fear of being nonconformists.

There was a time when the church was very powerful—in the time when the early Christians rejoiced at being deemed worthy to suffer for what they believed. In those days the church was not merely a thermometer that recorded the ideas and principles of popular opinion; it was a thermostat that transformed the mores of society. Whenever the early Christians entered a town, the people in power became disturbed and immediately sought to convict the Christians for being "disturbers of the peace" and "outside agitators." But the Christians pressed on, in the conviction that they were "a colony of heaven," called to obey God rather than man. Small in number, they were big in commitment. They were too God-intoxicated to be "astronomically intimidated." By their effort and example they brought an end to such ancient evils as infanticide and gladiatorial contests.

Things are different now. So often the contemporary church is a weak, ineffectual voice with an uncertain sound. So often it is an archdefender of the status quo. Far from being disturbed by the presence of the church, the power structure of the average community is consoled by the church's silent—and often even vocal—sanction of things as they are.

But the judgment of God is upon the church as never before. If today's church does not recapture the sacrificial spirit of the early church, it will lose its authenticity, forfeit the loyalty of millions, and be dismissed as an irrelevant social club with no meaning for the twentieth century. Every day I meet young people whose disappointment with the church has turned into outright disgust.

Perhaps I have once again been too optimistic. Is organized religion too inextricably bound to the status quo to save our nation and the world? Perhaps I must turn my faith to the inner spiritual church, the church within the church, as the true *ekklesia* and the hope of the world. But again I am thankful to God that some noble souls from the ranks of organized religion have broken loose from the paralyzing chains of conformity and joined us as active partners in the struggle for freedom. They have left their secure congregations and walked the streets of Albany, Georgia, with us. They have gone down the highways of the South on tortuous rides for freedom. Yes, they have gone to jail with us. Some have been dismissed from their churches, have lost the support of their bishops and fellow ministers. But they have acted in the faith that right defeated is stronger than evil triumphant. Their witness has been the spiritual salt that has preserved the true meaning of the gospel in these troubled times. They have carved a tunnel of hope through the dark mountain of disappointment.

I hope the church as a whole will meet the challenge of this decisive hour. But even if the church does not come to the aid of justice, I have no despair about the future. I have no fear about the outcome of our struggle in Birmingham, even if our motives are at present misunderstood. We will reach the goal of freedom in Birmingham and all over the nation, because the goal of America is freedom. Abused and scorned though we may be, our destiny is tied up with America's destiny. Before the pilgrims landed at Plymouth, we were here. Before the pen of Jefferson etched the majestic words of the Declaration of Independence across the pages of history, we were here. For more than two centuries our forebears labored in this country without wages; they made cotton king; they built the homes of their masters while suffering gross injustice and shameful humiliation—and yet out of a bottomless vitality they continued to thrive and develop. If the inexpressible cruelties of slavery could not stop us, the opposition we now face will surely fail. We will win our freedom because the sacred heritage of our nation and the eternal will of God are embodied in our echoing demands.

Before closing I feel impelled to mention one other point in your statement that has troubled me profoundly. You warmly commended the Birmingham police force for keeping "order" and "preventing violence." I doubt that you would have so warmly commended the police force if you had seen its dogs sinking their teeth into unarmed, nonviolent Negroes. I doubt that you would so quickly commend the policemen if you were to observe their ugly and inhumane treatment of Negroes here in the city jail; if you were to watch them push and curse old Negro women and young Negro girls; if you were to see them slap and kick old Negro men and young boys; if you were to observe them, as they did on two occasions, refuse to give us food because we wanted to sing our grace together. I cannot join you in your praise of the Birmingham police department.

It is true that the police have exercised a degree of discipline in handling the demonstrators. In this sense they have conducted themselves rather "nonviolently" in public. But for what purpose? To preserve the evil system of segregation. Over the past few years I have consistently preached that nonviolence demands that the means we use must be as pure as the ends we seek. I have tried to make clear that it is wrong to use immoral means to attain moral ends. But now I must affirm that it is just as wrong, or perhaps even more so, to use moral means to preserve immoral ends. Perhaps Mr. Conner and his policemen have been rather nonviolent in public, as was Chief Pritchett in Albany, Georgia, but they have used the moral means of nonviolence to maintain the immoral end of racial injustice. As T. S. Eliot has said: "The last temptation is the greatest treason: To do the right deed for the wrong reason."

I wish you had commended the Negro sit-inners and demonstrators of Birmingham for their sublime courage, their willingness to suffer and their amazing discipline in the midst of great provocation. One day the South will recognize its real heroes. They will be the James Merediths, with the noble sense of purpose that enables them to face jeering and hostile mobs, and with the agonizing loneliness that characterizes the life of the pioneer. They will be old, oppressed, battered Negro women, symbolized in a seventy-two-year old woman in Montgomery, Alabama, who rose up with a sense of dignity and with her people decided not to ride segregated buses, and who responded with ungrammatical profundity to one who inquired about her weariness: "My feets is tired, but my soul is at rest." They will be the young high school and college students, the young ministers of the gospel and a host of their elders, courageously and nonviolently sitting in at lunch counters and willingly going to jail for conscience's sake. One day the South will know that when these disinherited children of God sat down at lunch counters, they were in reality standing up for what is best in the American dream and for the most sacred values in our Judaeo-Christian heritage, thereby bringing our nation back to those great wells of democracy which were dug deep by the founding fathers in their formulation of the Constitution and the Declaration of Independence.

Never before have I written so long a letter. I'm afraid it is much too long to take your precious time. I can assure you that it would have been much shorter if I had been writing from a comfortable desk, but what else can one do when he is alone in a narrow jail cell, other than write long letters, think long thoughts and pray long prayers?

If I have said anything in this letter that overstates the truth and indicates an unreasonable impatience, I beg you to forgive me. If I have said anything that understates the truth and indicates my having a patience that allows me to settle for anything less than brotherhood, I beg God to forgive me.

I hope this letter finds you strong in the faith. I also hope that circumstances will soon make it possible for me to meet each of you, not as an integrationist or a civil-rights leader but as a fellow clergyman and a Christian brother. Let us all hope that the dark clouds of racial prejudice will soon pass away and the deep fog of misunderstanding will be lifted from our fear-drenched communities, and in some not too distant tomorrow the radiant stars of love and brotherhood will shine over our great nation with all their scintillating beauty.

Yours for the cause of Peace and Brotherhood,

MARTIN LUTHER KING, JR.

Karl Barth

THE PROTECTION OF LIFE*
(Conscientious Objection)

In this connexion we may conclude with a consideration of the specific problems of conscription and conscientious objection.

The pacifist demand for the abolition of conscription (cf. G. J. Heering, *Der Sündentall des Christentums,* pp. 252 f.) is shortsighted. For conscription has the salutary effect of bringing home the question of war. War is an affair of the state and therefore of the totality of its subjects, not of a minority or majority of volunteers or militarists. All citizens share responsibility for it both in peace and war. They thus share the burden of this responsibility, and must themselves face the question whether it is right or wrong. This fact is given due expression and brought right home by conscription, whereas it is glossed over in every other type of military constitution. To make military service once again something for mercenary or volunteer armies would be to absolve the individual from direct responsibility for war and to leave both war itself and the resultant "moral odium," as Heering calls it, to others. In other words, non-participation becomes a matter of particular prudence and virtue in one case, and participation of particular stupidity and wickedness in the other. If anything is calculated to perpetuate war, it is this Pharisaic attitude. Conscription, however, has the

* From KARL BARTH, *Church Dogmatics,* Vol. III (Edinburgh: T & T Clark, 1961), Part 4, pp. 466-70. Used by permission. Barth is the contemporary Swiss Protestant theologian.

invaluable advantage of confronting both the prudent and the stupid, both the peace-loving and less peace-loving, with the problem of the belligerent state as their own personal problem, and conversely of compelling them to express their own personal attitude to war in their responsibility as citizens of the state instead of treating it merely as a matter of private opinion. If the state makes participation in war obligatory upon all, the individual must face the question whether as a citizen he can approve and co-operate in war, i.e., every war as such, or whether as a citizen he must resist and evade it. The abolition of conscription would take the edge off this decision for those not personally affected. It would make it merely political rather than both political and personal. This could not possibly contribute to the serious discussion or solution of the problem of war. Pacifists, therefore, should be the very last to call for the abolition of conscription.

The dignity of an absolute divine command cannot, of course, be ascribed to military service. Although the state must claim it from the individual as a compulsory duty, and although its fulfillment is urgently prompted in the first instance by the relation of the individual to the state, it can finally be understood only as a question which is put to him and which no one can answer but himself. The state is not God, nor can it command as He does. No compulsory duty which it imposes on the individual, nor urgency with which it presses for its fulfilment, can alter the fact that the attitude of the individual to all its decisions and measures, and therefore to this too, is limited and defined by his relationship to God, so that, although as a citizen he is committed to what is thought right and therefore resolved by the government or the majority, he is not bound by it finally or absolutely. Hence it cannot be denied that in virtue of his relationship to God the individual may sometimes find himself compelled, even with a full sense of his loyalty as a citizen, to contradict and oppose what is thought right and resolved by the government or the majority. He will be aware of the exceptional character of this action. Such insubordination cannot be ventured too easily or frequently. He will also be aware of the risk entailed. He cannot but realise that by offering resistance he renders himself liable to prosecution. He cannot deny to the government or the majority the right to take legal and constitutional proceedings against him. He must not be surprised or aggrieved if he has to bear the consequences of his resistance. He must be content in obedience to God to accept his responsibility as a citizen in this particular way. The contradiction and resistance to compulsory military service can indeed take the form of the actual refusal of individuals to submit to conscription as legally and constitutionally imposed by the government or the majority, and therefore of their refusal to participate directly either in war itself or preparation for it. Such refusal means that these individuals think they must give a negative answer to the question posed by conscription, even though it is put to them in the form of a compulsory duty calling urgently for fulfillment.

Two formal presuppositions are essential if such refusal of military service by one or more individuals is to be accepted as imperative and therefore legitimate. The first is that the objector must accomplish his act of insubordination in the unity of his individual and personal existence with his existence as a citizen. There can be no question of calming his private conscience by binding his civic conscience. His relationship to God will not absolve him from his obligation to the state; it will simply pose it in a specific way, which may perhaps be this way. Quite apart from less worthy motives, it cannot be merely a matter of satisfying his own personal abhorrence of violence and bloodshed, of keeping his own hands clean. His refusal of military service can have nothing whatever to do with even the noblest desertion of the state, and certainly not with anarchy. He must be convinced and assured that by his opposition he stands and acts for the political community as willed and ordained by God, not denying the state but affirming it in contrast to the government, the majority, the existing law and constitution. His refusal of military service must have the meaning and character of an appeal from the badly informed state of the present to the better informed state of the future. Therefore, notwithstanding all appearances to the contrary, it must be intended and executed as an act of loyalty to the state.

Second, the man who objects to military service must be prepared to accept without murmur or complaint the consequences of the insubordinate form of his national loyalty, the hostility of the government or majority to which he may be exposed, and the penalty of his violation of the existing law and constitution. He cannot demand that the state which in his view is badly informed should treat him as though it were already what he hopes it will be, namely, the better informed state of tomorrow. He cannot ask, therefore, for considerate exceptions in the administration of valid decrees, or even for protective laws of exemption, in the case of those likeminded with himself. He should certainly not try to be drafted to the medical or pioneer corps instead of the infantry. He should not ask for the impossible, claiming on the one hand to act as a prospective martyr, and on the other to be spared from martyrdom after all, or at least to have it made easier for him. He must act honestly and consistently as a revolutionary, prepared to pay the price of his action, content to know that he has on his side both God and the better informed state of the future, hoping to bear an effective witness to it today, but ready at least to suffer what *rebus sic stantibus* his insubordination must now entail. If these two presuppositions are not present, there can be no question of true conscientious objection, i.e., of the objection which is commanded and therefore legitimate.

There is also a material error in conscientious objection, however, if it rests on an absolute refusal of war, i.e., on the absolutism of radical pacifism. In such a case, it is no less rebellion against the command of God than an affirmation of war and participation in it on the basis of radical militarism, i.e., of the superstition of the inevitability of war, of the view that it is an element in the divine world order and an essential constituent of the state. If we are genuinely ready to obey the command of God, we cannot go so far either to the right or to the left as to maintain such absolute ethical tenets and modes of action in loyalty to Him. On the contrary, we shall have to take account of the limitation of even the best of human views, principles, and attitudes. In the national loyalty which is always required, conscientious objection is possible only if it is relative and not absolute, and therefore if it is not tainted by the idea that the state is utterly forbidden in any circumstances either to wage war or to prepare for it. Exercised with political responsibility, it must include the readiness of the conscientious objector in other circumstances and in face of other demands to renounce the insubordination which is commanded in certain concrete conditions, and therefore to do always what he is required to do in a given case. He must never allow his conscientious objection to infringe upon either the freedom of the commanding God or his own freedom, i.e., the freedom of his civic conscience. He must fulfill it as a free person, and as one who wills to remain free, in this twofold sense. Anti-militarism on principle logically leads to an illegitimate type of conscientious objection.

On the other hand, conscientious objection may well be necessary and legitimate in a situation in which one or more persons cannot fail to see that the cause for which the state is arming or waging war is concretely an evil one, that the war in which they are asked to participate is one of the many unjust and irresponsible wars which are not risked out of genuine emergency but planned and embarked upon deliberately. It is not to be expected that in such a situation this recognition will be a general one, or that it will take a specific form among the people at large. It may often be current as an obscure premonition on the part of many, and official propaganda will naturally do all it can to prevent it breaking through. But in such a situation it will certainly abtrude upon certain individuals in such a definite form that in spite of all official propaganda they cannot conceal the fact, but are taught by the divine command, that they must protest against this war not only in thought and word but also by conscientious objection. This does not mean that they will be released from their responsibility to the state. It means that they will have to discharge this responsibility in such a way that they refuse to fulfil the duty of military service, not in principle, but in relation to the concrete military action now demanded, believing that in so doing they desire the very best for the state, ready to suffer for the fact that what they desire differs from what is desired by the government or the majority, and therefore at peace with God and also in the deepest sense with their own conscience. The fact that in a concrete political situation individuals may have to act like this, and therefore to refuse military service, according to the command of God, is a possibility for which provision can hardly be made in political law but which Christian ethics certainly cannot deny as such. It is thus strange that even Schleiermacher (*Chr. Sitte*, p. 284) should dare to make the statement: "To exclude oneself from participation in war, if one does not consider it to be just, is rebellion." This is surely wrong as a general proposition. An individual may hold an erroneous opinion as to whether a war is just. And the man who in answering this question thinks that he should act on his objection must realise that he may be mistaken, that he may not really have the command of God on his side at all, and that he thus runs the risk of being a rebel. Nevertheless this does not alter the fact that the question of responsibility for war and warlike preparation must always be heard and answered by individuals. Each has to consider whether the state and therefore he himself is really acting responsibly in a given issue. It is at this point, in relation to a concrete war, that there is a place for the personal responsibility and decision of the individual in a practical form. The government or majority in any state has to reckon with the fact that individuals cannot spare themselves but have necessarily to put the personal question of responsibility for the specific war at issue, and that it may happen that they will have to return a negative answer to the question even in practice. It would be a great gain for peace if all governments or majorities in all states knew that they had actually to take this into account.

It is, of course, self-evident that individuals cannot be left to deal with this question alone. Here if anywhere the Church, or at any rate enlightened and commissioned men within it, should be at hand and on the watch to give to the individual in changing political situations guidance and direction which are not legalistic, but evangelical, plain and unequivocal, concerning the understanding and keeping of the command of God which is really at issue. How can the Church be neutral or silent in so important and perilous a matter? How can it override the individual conscience by what it says, as is constantly maintained? For far too long the Church has failed to consider the individual conscience and made military obedience a universal duty—and this in the name of God. It is hard to see why, instead of this unhelpful standardisation, it should not first and foremost make it clear that each must decide from case to case whether the obedience demanded in the name of God does really coincide with military service. Why should the two coincide? We have seen, of course, that there are a few wars which are necessary, demanded and responsible, and where this is the case the Church should be the first to say so and faithfully to champion the view that military service applies to all and must be rendered by all. But nowhere is it written that always and in all circumstances the Church must take this line. If its eyes are open, and the command of God rings in its ears, it might sometimes have to take the opposite view. From what we may hope will be its higher vantage point, it might sometimes see things in a way which is very different from that which the government or the majority think to be right. In the light of the divine command it might find itself called to express this different outlook and to seek to establish its validity. And since it ought to be able to do this with a broader vision and greater wisdom than any solitary individual, its duty is to bring its consolation, admonition and encouragement to the aid of the free conscience of the individual. In so doing, it might have to accept the odium of unreliability in the eyes of the government or majority. In certain cases, it might have to be prepared to face threats or suffering, bearing for its part the total risk of this kind of revolutionary loyalty. But there have been prophets willing to take this risk before, and where does the Church learn that it is absolved from facing the same risk? Can it really be surprised, in the light of its origin and task, if it is sometimes asked to bear a dangerous witness and to be treated accordingly? Is this price really too high if the result is a penetration into the general consciousness that for all its weakness the Church is at least a retarding factor in regard to war, a genuinely unreliable element upon whose co-operation it is impossible to count unconditionally, since it may at any time be found in opposition? The state which is at war or preparing for it, if it knows that the Church will follow its own law and understanding, sometimes voting for military service but sometimes voting against it, will then find in the Church both its necessary frontier and yet also its deepest basis and surest support. And when can it be more salutary for the state to have to reckon with this frontier than when it is a matter of its *ultima ratio,* and therefore of the question whether it will show itself to be representative of the divine order or become a mass murderer in perversion of this order?

Pope John XXIII

RELATIONS BETWEEN INDIVIDUALS AND THE PUBLIC AUTHORITIES WITHIN A SINGLE STATE*

NECESSITY AND DIVINE ORIGIN OF AUTHORITY

46. Human society can be neither well-ordered nor prosperous unless it has some people invested with legitimate authority to preserve its institutions and to devote themselves as far as is necessary to work and care for the good of all. These however derive their authority from God, as St. Paul teaches in the words, "There exists no authority except from God."[1] These words of St. Paul are explained thus by St. John Chrysostom: "What are you saying? Is every ruler appointed by God? I do not say that," he replies, "for I am not dealing now with individual rulers, but with authority itself. What I say, that it is the divine wisdom and not mere chance, that has ordained that there should be government, that some should command and others obey."[2] Moreover, since God made men social by nature, and since no society "can hold together unless some one be over all, directing all to strive earnestly for the common good, every civilized community must have a ruling authority,

*From *Pacem in Terris: Encyclical Letter of His Holiness Pope John XXIII, Peace on Earth,* William J. Gibbons, S.J., ed. (New York: Paulist Newman Press, 1963), pp. 19-30. The late Pope John XXIII, inaugurator of a policy of *aggiornamento,* expresses in this encyclical his concern for peace with justice. Used by permission of Paulist Newman Press.

and this authority, no less than society itself, has its source in nature, and has, consequently, God for its author.[3]

47. But authority is not to be thought of as a force lacking all control. Indeed, since it has the power to command according to right reason, authority must derive its obligatory force from the moral order, which in turn has God for its first source and final end. Wherefore Our Predecessor of happy memory, Pius XII, said:

That same absolute order of beings and their ends which presents man as an autonomous person, that is, as the subject of inviolable duties and rights, and as at once the basis of society and the purpose for which it exists, also includes the State as a necessary society invested with the authority without which it could not come into being or live. . . . And since this absolute order, as we learn from sound reason and especially from the Christian faith, can have no origin save in a personal God who is our Creator, it follows that the dignity of the State's authority is due to its sharing to some extent in the authority of God Himself.[4]

48. Hence, where authority uses as its only or its chief means either threats and fear of punishment or promises of rewards, it cannot effectively move men to promote the common good of all. Even if it did so move them, this would be altogether opposed to their dignity as men, endowed with reason and free will. As authority is chiefly concerned with moral force, it follows that civil authority must appeal primarily to the conscience of individual citizens, that is, to each one's duty to collaborate readily for the common good of all. Since by nature all men are equal in human dignity, it follows that no one may be coerced to perform interior acts. That is in the power of God alone, who sees and judges the hidden designs of men's hearts.

49. Those therefore who have authority in the State may oblige men in conscience only if their authority is intrinsically related with the authority of God and shares in it.[5]

50. By this principle the dignity of the citizens is protected. When, in fact, men obey their rulers, it is not at all as men that

they obey them, but through their obedience it is God, the
provident Creator of all things, whom they reverence, since He
has decreed that men's dealings with one another should be
regulated by an order which He Himself has established. Moreover, in showing this due reverence to God, men not only do not
debase themselves but rather perfect and ennoble themselves.
For "to serve God is to rule."[6]

51. Since the right to command is required by the moral
order and has its source in God, it follows that, if civil authorities legislate for or allow anything that is contrary to that order
and therefore contrary to the will of God, neither the laws made
nor the authorizations granted can be binding on the con-
sciences of the citizens, since "we must obey God rather than
men."[7] Otherwise, authority breaks down completely and results in shameful abuse. As St. Thomas Aquinas teaches:
"Human law has the true nature of law only insofar as it corresponds to right reason, and therefore is derived from the eternal
law. Insofar as it falls short of right reason, a law is said to be a
wicked law; and so, lacking the true nature of law, it is rather a
kind of violence."[8]

52. It must not be concluded, however, because authority
comes from God, that therefore men have no right to choose
those who are to rule the State, to decide the form of government, and to determine both the way in which authority is to be
exercised and its limits. It is thus clear that the doctrine which
we have set forth is fully consonant with any truly democratic
regime.[9]

ATTAINMENT OF THE COMMON GOOD IS THE PURPOSE OF THE PUBLIC AUTHORITY

53. Inasmuch as individual men and intermediate groups are
obliged to make their specific contributions to the common welfare, it especially follows that they should bring their own interests into harmony with the needs of the community. They
should direct their goods and services towards goals which the
civil authorities prescribe, in accord with the norms of justice,

in due form, and within the limits of their competence. Manifestly, those who possess civil authority must make their prescriptions not only by acts properly accomplished, but also by acts which clearly pertain to the welfare of the community or else can lead to the same.

54. Indeed since the whole reason for the existence of civil authorities is the realization of the common good it is clearly necessary that, in pursuing this objective, they should respect its essential elements, and at the same time conform their laws to the needs of a given historical situation.[10]

ESSENTIALS OF THE COMMON GOOD

55. Assuredly, the ethnic characteristics of the various human groups are to be respected as constituent elements of the common good,[11] but these values and characteristics by no means exhaust the content of the common good. For the common good is intimately bound up with human nature. It can never exist fully and completely unless, its intimate nature and realization being what they are, the human person is taken into account.[12]

56. In the second place, the very nature of the common good requires that all members of the political community be entitled to share in it, although in different ways according to each one's tasks, merits and circumstances. For this reason, every civil authority must take pains to promote the common good of all, without preference for any single citizen or civic group. As Our Predecessor of immortal memory, Leo XIII, has said: "The civil power must not serve the advantage of any one individual, or of some few persons, inasmuch as it was established for the common good of all."[13] Considerations of justice and equity, however, can at times demand that those involved in civil government give more attention to the less fortunate members of the community, since they are less able to defend their rights and to assert their legitimate claims.[14]

57. In this context, We judge that attention should be called to the fact that the common good touches the whole man, the needs both of his body and of his soul. Hence it follows that the

civil authorities must undertake to effect the common good by ways and means that are proper to them; that is, while respecting the hierarchy of values, they should promote simultaneously both the material and the spiritual welfare of the citizens.[15]

58. These principles are definitely implied in what was stated in Our Encyclical, *Mater et Magistra,* where We emphasized that the common good of all "embraces the sum total of those conditions of social living whereby men are enabled to achieve their own integral perfection more fully and more easily."[16]

59. Men, however, composed as they are of bodies and immortal souls, can never in this mortal life succeed in satisfying all their needs or in attaining perfect happiness. Therefore all efforts made to promote the common good, far from endangering the eternal salvation of men, ought rather to serve to promote it.[17]

RESPONSIBILITIES OF THE PUBLIC AUTHORITY, AND RIGHTS AND DUTIES OF INDIVIDUALS

60. It is agreed that in our time the common good is chiefly guaranteed when personal rights and duties are maintained. The chief concern of civil authorities must therefore be to ensure that these rights are acknowledged, respected, co-ordinated with other rights, defended and promoted, so that in this way each one may more easily carry out his duties. For "to safeguard the inviolable rights of the human person, and to facilitate the fulfillment of his duties, should be the essential office of every public authority."[18]

61. This means that, if any government does not acknowledge the rights of man or violates them, it not only fails in its duty, but its orders completely lack juridical force.[19]

RECONCILIATION AND PROTECTION OF RIGHTS AND DUTIES OF INDIVIDUALS

62. One of the fundamental duties of civil authorities, therefore, is to co-ordinate social relations in such fashion that the exercise of one man's rights does not threaten others in the

exercise of their own rights nor hinder them in the fulfillment of their duties. Finally, the rights of all should be effectively safeguarded and, if they have been violated, completely restored.[20]

DUTY OF PROMOTING THE RIGHTS OF INDIVIDUALS

63. It is also demanded by the common good that civil authorities should make earnest efforts to bring about a situation in which individual citizens can easily exercise their rights and fulfill their duties as well. For experience has taught us that, unless these authorities take suitable action with regard to economic, political and cultural matters, inequalities between the citizens tend to become more and more widespread, especially in the modern world, and as a result, a man's rights and duties in some way lack effectiveness.

64. It is therefore necessary that the administration give wholehearted and careful attention to the social as well as to the economic progress of the citizens, and to the development, in keeping with the development of the productive system, of such essential services as the building of roads, transportation, communications, water supply, housing, public health, facilitation of the practice of religion, and recreational facilities. It is necessary also that governments make efforts to see that insurance systems are made available to the citizens, so that, in case of misfortune or increased family responsibilities, no person will be without the necessary means to maintain a decent way of living. The government should make similarly effective efforts to see that those who are able to work can find employment in keeping with their aptitudes, and that each worker receives a wage in keeping with the laws of justice and equity. It should be equally the concern of civil authorities to ensure that workers be allowed their proper responsibility in the work undertaken in industrial organization, and to facilitate the establishment of intermediate groups which will make social life richer and more effective. Finally, it should be possible for all the citizens to share in their country's cultural advantages in an opportune manner and degree.

HARMONIZING THE TWO FORMS OF INTERVENTION
BY PUBLIC AUTHORITY

65. The common good requires that civil authorities maintain a careful balance between co-ordinating and protecting the rights of the citizens, on the one hand, and promoting them, on the other. It should not happen that certain individuals or social groups derive special advantage from the fact that their rights have received preferential protection. Nor should it happen that governments in seeking to protect these rights, become obstacles to their full expression and free use. "Nevertheless, it remains true that precautionary activities of public authorities in the economic field, although widespread and penetrating, should be such that they not only avoid restricting the freedom of private citizens, but also increase it, so long as the basic rights of each individual person are preserved inviolate."[21]

66. The same principle should inspire the various steps which governments take in order to make it possible for the citizens more easily to exercise their rights and fulfill their duties in every sector of social life.

STRUCTURE AND OPERATION
OF THE PUBLIC AUTHORITY

67. It is impossible to determine, once and for all, what is the most suitable form of government, or how civil authorities can most effectively fulfill their respective functions, i.e., the legislative, judicial and executive functions of the State.

68. In determining the Structure and operation of government which a state is to have, great weight has to be given to the historical background and circumstances of the individual peoples, circumstances which will vary at different times and in different places. We consider, however, that it is in keeping with the innate demands of human nature that the State should take a form which embodies the threefold division of powers corresponding to the three principal functions of public authority. In that type of State, not only the official functions of government

but also the mutual relations between citizens and public officials are set down according to law. This in itself affords protection to the citizens both in the enjoyment of their rights and in
the fulfillment of their duties.

69. If, however, this juridical and political structure is to
produce the advantages which may be expected of it, public
officials must strive to meet the problems that arise in a way
that conforms both to the complexities of the situation and the
proper exercise of their function. This requires that, in constantly changing conditions, legislators never forget the norms
of morality, or constitutional provisions, or the objective requirements of the common good. Moreover, executive authorities must co-ordinate the activities of society with discretion,
with a full knowledge of the law and after a careful consideration of circumstances, and the courts must administer justice
impartially and without being influenced by favoritism or pressure. The good order of society also demands that individual
citizens and intermediate organizations should be effectively
protected by law whenever they have rights to be exercised or
obligations to be fulfilled. This protection should be granted to
citizens both in their dealings with each other and in their relations with government agencies.[22]

LAW AND CONSCIENCE

70. It is unquestionable that a legal structure in conformity
with the moral order and corresponding to the level of development of the political community is of great advantage to
achievement of the common good.

71. And yet, social life in the modern world is so varied,
complex and dynamic that even a juridical structure which has
been prudently and thoughtfully established is always inadequate for the needs of society.

72. It is also true that the relations of the citizens with each
other, of citizens and intermediate groups with public authorities, and finally of the public authorities with one another, are
often so complex and so sensitive that they cannot be regulated

by inflexible legal provisions. Such a situation therefore demands that the civil authorities have clear ideas about the nature and extent of their official duties if they wish to maintain the existing juridical structure in its basic elements and principles, and at the same time meet the exigencies of social life, adapting their legislation to the changing social scene and solving new problems. They must be men of great equilibrium and integrity, competent and courageous enough to see at once what the situation requires and to take necessary action quickly and effectively.[23]

CITIZENS' PARTICIPATION IN PUBLIC LIFE

73. It is in keeping with their dignity as persons that human beings should take an active part in government, although the manner in which they share in it will depend on the level of development of the political community to which they belong.

74. Men will find new and extensive advantages in the fact that they are allowed to participate in government. In this situation, those who administer the government come into frequent contact with the citizens, and it is thus easier for them to learn what is really needed for the common good. The fact too that ministers of government hold office only for a limited time keeps them from growing stale and allows for their replacement in accordance with the demands of social progress.[24]

CHARACTERISTICS OF THE PRESENT DAY

75. Accordingly, it follows that in our day, where there is question of organizing political communities juridically, it is required first of all that there be written in concise and limpid phraseology, a charter of fundamental human rights, and that this be inserted in the basic law of the State.

76. Secondly, it is required that the Constitution of each political community be formulated in proper legal terminology, and that there be defined therein the manner in which the State

authorities are to be designated, how their mutual relations are to be regulated, what are to be their spheres of competence, and finally, the forms and systems they are obliged to follow in the performance of their office.

77. Finally, it is required that the relations between the government and the citizens be set forth in detail in terms of rights and duties, and that it be distinctly decreed that a major task of the government is that of recognizing, respecting, reconciling, protecting and promoting the rights and duties of citizens.

78. It is of course impossible to accept the theory which professes to find the original and unique source of civic rights and duties, of the binding force of the Constitution, and of a government's right to command, in the mere will of human beings, individually or collectively.[25]

79. The desires to which We have referred, however, do clearly show that the men of our time have become increasingly conscious of their dignity as human persons. This awareness prompts them to claim a share in the public administration of their country, while it also accounts for the demand that their own inalienable and inviolable rights be protected by law. Nor is this sufficient; for men also demand that public officials be chosen in conformity with constitutional procedures, and that they perform their specific functions within the limits of law.

NOTES

[1] Romans 13, 1-6.

[2] *In Epist. ad Rom. c. 13, vv. 1-2,* homil. XXIII: PG. 60, 615.

[3] Leo XIII's Encyclical Letter *Immortale Dei, Acta Leonis XIII,* V (1885), p. 120.

[4] Cf. Pius XII's *Radio Broadcast.* Christmas Eve, 1944, A.A.S., XXXVII (1945), p. 15.

[5] Cf. Leo XIII's Encyclical Letter *Diuturnum illud, Acta Leonis XIII,* II (1881), p. 274.

[6] Cf. *Ibid.,* p. 278; and Leo XIII's Encyclical Letter *Immortale Dei, Acta Leonis XIII,* V (1885), p. 130.

[7] Acts 5, 29.

[8] *Summa Theol.,* Ia-IIae, q. 93, a. 3 ad 2; cf. Pius XII's *Radio*

Broadcast, Christmas Eve, 1944, A.A.S., XXXVII (1945), pp. 5-23.

⁹ Cf. Leo XIII's Encyclical Letter *Diuturnum illud, Acta Leonis XIII,* II (1881), pp. 271-72; and Pius XII's *Radio Broadcast,* Christmas Eve, 1944, A.A.S., XXXVII (1945), pp. 5-23.

¹⁰ Cf. Pius XII's *Radio Broadcast,* Christmas Eve, 1942, A.A.S., XXXV (1943), p. 13; and Leo XIII's Encyclical Letter *Immortale Dei, Acta Leonis XIII,* V (1885), p. 120.

¹¹ Cf. Pius XII's Encyclical Letter *Summi Pontificatus,* A.A.S., XXXI (1939), pp. 412-53.

¹² Cf. Pius XI's Encyclical Letter *Mit brennender Sorge,* A.A.S., XXIX (1937), p. 159; and Encyclical Letter *Divini Redemptoris,* A.A.S., XXIX (1937), pp. 65-106.

¹³ Encyclical Letter *Immortale Dei, Acta Leonis XIII,* V (1885), p. 121.

¹⁴ Cf. Leo XIII's Encyclical Letter *Rerum novarum, Acta Leonis XIII,* XI (1891), pp. 133-34.

¹⁵ Cf. Pius XII's Encyclical Letter *Summi Pontificatus,* A.A.S., XXXI (1939), p. 433.

¹⁶ A.A.S., LIII (1961), p. 19.

¹⁷ Cf. Pius XI's Encyclical Letter *Quadragesimo anno,* A.A.S., XXIII (1931) p. 215.

¹⁸ Cf. Pius XII's *Radio Broadcast* on the Feast of Pentecost, June 1, 1941, A.A.S., XXXIII (1941), p. 200.

¹⁹ Cf. Pius XI's Encyclical Letter *Mit brennender Sorge,* A.A.S., XXIX (1937), p. 159; and Encyclical Letter *Divini Redemptoris,* A.A.S., XXIX (1937), p. 79; and Pius XII's *Radio Broadcast,* Christmas Eve, 1942, A.A.S., XXXV (1943), pp. 9-24.

²⁰ Cf. Pius XI's Encyclical Letter *Divini Redemptoris,* A.A.S., XXIX (1937), p. 81; and Pius XII's *Radio Broadcast,* Christmas Eve, 1942, A.A.S., XXXV (1943), pp. 9-24.

²¹ John XXIII's Encyclical Letter *Mater et Magistra,* A.A.S., LIII (1961), p. 415.

²² Cf. Pius XII's *Radio Broadcast,* Christmas Eve, 1942, A.A.S., XXXV (1943), p. 21.

²³ Cf. Pius XII's *Radio Broadcast,* Christmas Eve, 1944, A.A.S., XXXVII (1945), pp. 15-16.

²⁴ Cf. Pius XII's *Radio Broadcast,* Christmas Eve, 1942, A.A.S., XXXV (1943), p. 12.

²⁵ Cf. Leo XIII's Apostolic Letter *Annum ingressi, Acta Leonis XIII,* XXII (1902-1903), pp. 52-80.

Max Weber

POLITICS AS A VOCATION*

One can say that three pre-eminent qualities are decisive for the
politician: passion, a feeling of responsibility, and a sense of
proportion.

This means passion in the sense of *matter-of-factness*, of
passionate devotion to a "cause," to the god or demon who is
its overlord. It is not passion in the sense of that inner bearing
which my late friend, Georg Simmel, used to designate as "sterile excitation," and which was peculiar especially to a certain
type of Russian intellectual (by no means all of them!). It is an
excitation that plays so great a part with our intellectuals in this
carnival we decorate with the proud name of "revolution." It
is a "romanticism of the intellectually interesting," running into
emptiness devoid of all feeling of objective responsibility.

To be sure, mere passion, however genuinely felt, is not
enough. It does not make a politician, unless passion as devotion to a "cause" also makes responsibility to this cause the
guiding star of action. And for this, a sense of proportion is
needed. This is the decisive psychological quality of the politician; his ability to let realities work upon him with inner concentration and calmness. Hence his *distance* to things and men.
"Lack of distance" *per se* is one of the deadly sins of every
politician. It is one of those qualities the breeding of which will

* From *Max Weber: Essays in Sociology*, H. H. Gerth and C. Wright
Mills, trans., ed., and intro. (New York: Oxford University Press, 1958)
pp. 115-28. Used by permission. MAX WEBER (1864-1920), German
Sociologist, is best known for his work *The Protestant Ethic and the
Spirit of Capitalism*.

condemn the progeny of our intellectuals to political incapacity. For the problem is simply how can warm passion and a cool sense of proportion be forged together in one and the same soul? Politics is made with the head, not with other parts of the body or soul. And yet devotion to politics, if it is not to be frivolous intellectual play but rather genuinely human conduct, can be born and nourished from passion alone. However, that firm taming of the soul, which distinguishes the passionate politician and differentiates him from the "sterily excited" and mere political dilettante, is possible only through habituation to detachment in every sense of the word. The "strength" of a political "personality" means, in the first place, the possession of these qualities of passion, responsibility, and proportion.

Therefore, daily and hourly, the politician inwardly has to overcome a quite trivial and all-too-human enemy: a quite vulgar vanity, the deadly enemy of all matter-of-fact devotion to a cause, and of all distance, in this case, of distance towards one's self.

Vanity is a very widespread quality and perhaps nobody is entirely free from it. In academic and scholarly circles, vanity is a sort of occupational disease, but precisely with the scholar, vanity—however disagreeably it may express itself—is relatively harmless; in the sense that as a rule it does not disturb scientific enterprise. With the politician the case is quite different. He works with the striving for power as an unavoidable means. Therefore, "power instinct," as is usually said, belongs indeed to his normal qualities. The sin against the lofty spirit of his vocation, however, begins where this striving for power ceases to be *objective* and becomes purely personal self-intoxication, instead of exclusively entering the service of "the cause." For ultimately there are only two kinds of deadly sins in the field of politics: lack of objectivity and—often but not always identical with it—irresponsibility. Vanity, the need personally to stand in the foreground as clearly as possible, strongly tempts the politician to commit one or both of these sins. This is more truly the case as the demagogue is compelled to count upon "effect." He therefore is constantly in danger of becoming an actor as well as taking lightly the responsibility for the outcome of his actions and of being concerned merely with the "impression" he makes. His lack of objectivity tempts him to strive for the glamorous semblance of power rather than for actual power. His irresponsibility, however, suggests that he enjoys power merely for power's sake without a substantive purpose. Although, or rather just because, power is the unavoidable means, and striving for power is one of the driving forces of all politics, there is no more harmful distortion of political force than the parvenu-like braggart with power, and the vain self-reflection in the feeling of power, and in general every worship of power *per se*. The mere "power politician" may get strong effects, but actually his work leads nowhere and is senseless. (Among us, too, an ardently promoted cult seeks to glorify him.) In this, the critics of "power politics" are absolutely right. From the sudden inner collapse of typical representatives of this mentality, we can see what inner weakness and impotence hides behind this boastful but entirely empty gesture. It is a product of a shoddy and superficially blasé attitude towards the meaning of human conduct; and it has no relation whatsoever to the knowledge of tragedy with which all action, but especially political action, is truly interwoven.

The final result of political action often, no, even regularly, stands in completely inadequate and often even paradoxical relation to its original meaning. This is fundamental to all history, a point not to be proved in detail here. But because of this fact, the serving of a cause must not be absent if action is to have inner strength. Exactly what the cause, in the service of which the politician strives for power and uses power, looks like is a matter of faith. The politician may be sustained by a strong belief in "progress"—no matter in which sense—or he may coolly reject this kind of belief. He may claim to stand in the service of an "idea" or, rejecting this in principle, he may want to serve external ends of everyday life. However, some kind of faith must always exist. Otherwise, it is absolutely true that the curse of the creature's worthlessness overshadows even the externally strongest political successes.

With the statement above we are already engaged in discussing the last problem that concerns us tonight: the *ethos* of politics as a "cause." What calling can politics fulfil quite independently of its goals within the total ethical economy of human conduct—which is, so to speak, the ethical locus where politics is at home? Here, to be sure, ultimate *Weltanschauungen* clash, world views among which in the end one has to make a choice. Let us resolutely tackle this problem, which recently has been opened again, in my view in a very wrong way.

But first, let us free ourselves from a quite trivial falsification: namely, that ethics may first appear in a morally highly compromised role. Let us consider examples. Rarely will you find that a man whose love turns from one woman to another feels no need to legitimate this before himself by saying: she was not worthy of my love, or, she has disappointed me, or whatever other like "reasons" exist. This is an attitude that, with a profound lack of chivalry, adds a fancied "legitimacy" to the plain fact that he no longer loves her and that the woman has to bear it. By virtue of this "legitimation," the man claims a right for himself and besides causing the misfortune seeks to put her in the wrong. The successful amatory competitor proceeds exactly in the same way: namely, the opponent must be less worthy, otherwise he would not have lost out. It is no different, of course, if after a victorious war the victor in undignified self-righteousness claims, "I have won because I was right." Or, if somebody under the frightfulness of war collapses psychologically, and instead of simply saying it was just too much, he feels the need of legitimizing his war weariness to himself by substituting the feeling, "I could not bear it because I had to fight for a morally bad cause." And likewise with the defeated in war. Instead of searching like old women for the "guilty one" after the war—in a situation in which the structure of society produced the war—everyone with a manly and controlled attitude would tell the enemy, "We lost the war. You have won it. That is now all over. Now let us discuss what conclusions must be drawn according to the *objective* interests that came into play and what is the main thing in view of the responsibility towards the *future* which above all burdens the victor." Anything else is undignified and will become a boomerang. A nation forgives if its interests have been damaged, but no nation forgives if its honor has been offended, especially by a bigoted self-righteousness. Every new document that comes to light after decades revives the undignified lamentations, the hatred and scorn, instead of allowing the war at its end to be buried, at least morally. This is possible only through objectivity and chivalry and above all only through dignity. But never is it possible through an "ethic," which in truth signifies a lack of dignity on both sides. Instead of being concerned about what the politician is interested in, the future and the responsibility towards the future, this ethic is concerned about politically sterile questions of past guilt, which are not to be settled politically. To act in this way is politically guilty, if such guilt exists at all. And it overlooks the unavoidable falsification of the whole problem, through very material interests: namely, the victor's interest in the greatest possible moral and material gain; the hopes of the defeated to trade in advantages through confessions of guilt. If anything is "vulgar," then, this is, and it is the result of this fashion of exploiting "ethics" as a means of "being in the right."

Now then, what relations do ethics and politics really have? Have the two nothing whatever to do with one another, as has occasionally been said? Or, is the reverse true: that the ethic of political conduct is identical with that of any other conduct? Occasionally an exclusive choice has been believed to exist between the two propositions—either the one or the other proposition must be correct. But is it true that any ethic of the world could establish commandments of identical content for erotic, business, familial, and official relations; for the relations to one's wife, to the greengrocer, the son, the competitor, the friend, the defendant? Should it really matter so little for the ethical demands on politics that politics operates with very special means, namely, power backed up by *violence*? Do we not see that the Bolshevik and the Spartacist ideologists bring about exactly the same results as any militaristic dictator just because they use this political means? In what but the persons of the

power-holders and their dilettantism does the rule of the workers' and soldiers' councils differ from the rule of any power-
holder of the old regime? In what way does the polemic of most
representatives of the presumably new ethic differ from that of
the opponents which they criticized, or the ethic of any other
demagogues? In their noble intention, people will say. Good!
But it is the means about which we speak here, and the adver-
saries, in complete subjective sincerity, claim, in the very same
way, that their ultimate intentions are of lofty character. "All
they that take the sword shall perish with the sword" and fighting is everywhere fighting. Hence, the ethic of the Sermon on
the Mount.

By the Sermon on the Mount, we mean the absolute ethic of
the gospel, which is a more serious matter than those who are
fond of quoting these commandments today believe. This ethic
is no joking matter. The same holds for this ethic as has been
said of causality in science: it is not a cab, which one can have
stopped at one's pleasure; it is all or nothing. This is precisely
the meaning of the gospel, if trivialities are not to result. Hence,
for instance, it was said of the wealthy young man, "He went
away sorrowful: for he had great possessions." The evangelist
commandment, however, is unconditional and unambiguous:
give what thou hast—absolutely everything. The politician will
say that this is a socially senseless imposition as long as it is not
carried out everywhere. Thus the politician upholds taxation,
confiscatory taxation, outright confiscation; in a word, compulsion and regulation for all. The ethical commandment, however,
is not at all concerned about that, and this unconcern is its
essence. Or, take the example, "turn the other cheek": This
command is unconditional and does not question the source of
the other's authority to strike. Except for a saint it is an ethic of
indignity. This is it: one must be saintly in everything; at least
in intention, one must live like Jesus, the apostles, St. Francis,
and their like. *Then* this ethic makes sense and expresses a kind
of dignity; otherwise it does not. For if it is said, in line with the
acosmic ethic of love, "Resist not him that is evil with force,"
for the politician the reverse proposition holds, "Thou *shalt*

resist evil by force," or else you are responsible for the evil winning out. He who wishes to follow the ethic of the gospel should abstain from strikes, for strikes mean compulsion; he may join the company unions. Above all things, he should not talk of "revolution." After all, the ethic of the gospel does not wish to teach that civil war is the only legitimate war. The pacifist who follows the gospel will refuse to bear arms or will throw them down; in Germany this was the recommended ethical duty to end the war and therewith all wars. The politician would say the only sure means to discredit the war for all foreseeable time would have been a *status quo* peace. Then the nations would have questioned, what was this war for? And then the war would have been argued *ad absurdum,* which is now impossible. For the victors, at least for part of them, the war will have been politically profitable. And the responsibility for this rests on behavior that made all resistance impossible for us. Now, as a result of the ethics of absolutism, when the period of exhaustion will have passed, *the peace will be discredited, not the war*.

Finally, let us consider the duty of truthfulness. For the absolute ethic it holds unconditionally. Hence the conclusion was reached to publish all documents, especially those placing blame on one's own country. On the basis of these one-sided publications the confessions of guilt followed—and they were one-sided, unconditional, and without regard to consequences. The politician will find that as a result truth will not be furthered but certainly obscured through abuse and unleashing of passion; only an all-round methodical investigation by non-partisans could bear fruit; any other procedure may have consequences for a nation that cannot be remedied for decades. But the absolute ethic just does not *ask* for "consequences." That is the decisive point.

We must be clear about the fact that all ethically oriented conduct may be guided by one of two fundamentally differing and irreconcilably opposed maxims: conduct can be oriented to an "ethic of ultimate ends" or to an "ethic of responsibility." This is not to say that an ethic of responsibility is identical with

unprincipled opportunism. Naturally nobody says that. However, there is an abysmal contrast between conduct that follows
the maxim of an ethic of ultimate ends—that is, in religious
terms, "The Christian does rightly and leaves the results with
the Lord"—and conduct that follows the maxim of an ethic of
responsibility, in which case one has to give an account of the
foreseeable results of one's action.

You may demonstrate to a convinced syndicalist, believing in
an ethic of ultimate ends, that his action will result in increasing
the opportunities of reaction, in increasing the oppression of his
class, and obstructing its ascent—and you will not make the
slightest impression upon him. If an action of good intent leads
to bad results, then, in the actor's eyes, not he but the world, or
the stupidity of other men, or God's will who made them thus,
is responsible for the evil. However a man who believes in an
ethic of responsibility takes account of precisely the average
deficiencies of people; as Fichte has correctly said, he does not
even have the right to presuppose their goodness and perfection.
He does not feel in a position to burden others with the results
of his own actions so far as he was able to foresee them; he will
say: these results are ascribed to my action. The believer in an
ethic of ultimate ends feels "responsible" only for seeing to it
that the flame of pure intentions is not quenched: for example,
the flame of protesting against the injustice of the social order.
To rekindle the flame ever anew is the purpose of his quite
irrational deeds, judged in view of their possible success. They
are acts that can and shall have only exemplary value.

But even herewith the problem is not yet exhausted. No
ethics in the world can dodge the fact that in numerous instances the attainment of "good" ends is bound to the fact that
one must be willing to pay the price of using morally dubious
means or at least dangerous ones—and facing the possibility or
even the probability of evil ramifications. From no ethics in the
world can it be concluded when and to what extent the ethically
good purpose "justifies" the ethically dangerous means and
ramifications.

The decisive means for politics is violence. You may see the extent of the tension between means and ends, when viewed ethically, from the following: as is generally known, even during the war the revolutionary socialists (Zimmerwald faction) professed a principle that one might strikingly formulate: "If we face the choice either of some more years of war and then revolution, or peace now and no revolution, we choose—some more years of war!" Upon the further question: "What can this revolution bring about?" every scientifically trained socialist would have had the answer: One cannot speak of a transition to an economy that in our sense could be called socialist; a bourgeois economy will re-emerge, merely stripped of the feudal elements and the dynastic vestiges. For this very modest result, they are willing to face "some more years of war." One may well say that even with a very robust socialist conviction one might reject a purpose that demands such means. With Bolshevism and Spartacism, and, in general, with any kind of revolutionary socialism, it is precisely the same thing. It is of course utterly ridiculous if the power politicians of the old regime are morally denounced for their use of the same means, however justified the rejection of their *aims* may be.

The ethic of ultimate ends apparently must go to pieces on the problem of the justification of means by ends. As a matter of fact, logically it has only the possibility of rejecting all action that employs morally dangerous means—in theory! In the world of realities, as a rule, we encounter the ever-renewed experience that the adherent of an ethic of ultimate ends suddenly turns into a chiliastic prophet. Those, for example, who have just preached "love against violence" now call for the use of force for the *last* violent deed, which would then lead to a state of affairs in which *all* violence is annihilated. In the same manner, our officers told the soldiers before every offensive: "This will be the last one; this one will bring victory and therewith peace." The proponent of an ethic of absolute ends cannot stand up under the ethical irrationality of the world. He is a cosmic-ethical "rationalist." Those of you who know Dostoievski will remember the scene of the "Grand Inquisitor," where the problem is poignantly unfolded. If one makes any concessions at all to the principle that the end justifies the means, it is not possible to bring an ethic of ultimate ends and an ethic of responsibility under one roof or to decree ethically which end should justify which means.

My colleague, Mr. F. W. Förster, whom personally I highly esteem for his undoubted sincerity, but whom I reject unreservedly as a politician, believes it is possible to get around this difficulty by the simple thesis: "from good comes only good; but from evil only evil follows." In that case this whole complex of questions would not exist. But it is rather astonishing that such a thesis could come to light two thousand five hundred years after the Upanishads. Not only the whole course of world history, but every frank examination of everyday experience points to the very opposite. The development of religions all over the world is determined by the fact that the opposite is true. The age-old problem of theodicy consists of the very question of how it is that a power which is said to be at once omnipotent and kind could have created such an irrational world of undeserved suffering, unpunished injustice, and hopeless stupidity. Either this power is not omnipotent or not kind, or, entirely different principles of compensation and reward govern our life—principles we may not interpret metaphysically, or even principles that forever escape our comprehension.

This problem—the experience of the irrationality of the world—has been the driving force of all religious evolution. The Indian doctrine of karma, Persian dualism, the doctrine of original sin, predestination and the *deus absconditus,* all these have grown out of this experience. Also the early Christians knew full well the world is governed by demons and that he who lets himself in for politics, that is, for power and force as means, contrasts with diabolical powers and for his action it is *not* true that good can follow only from good and evil only from evil, but that often the opposite is true. Anyone who fails to see this is, indeed, a political infant.

We are placed into various life-spheres, each of which is governed by different laws. Religious ethics have settled with this fact in different ways. Hellenic polytheism made sacrifices to

Aphrodite and Hera alike, to Dionysus and to Apollo, and knew these gods were frequently in conflict with one another. The Hindu order of life made each of the different occupations an object of a specific ethical code, a Dharma, and forever segregated one from the other as castes, thereby placing them into a fixed hierarchy of rank. For the man born into it, there was no escape from it, lest he be twice-born in another life. The occupations were thus placed at varying distances from the highest religious goods of salvation. In this way, the caste order allowed for the possibility of fashioning the Dharma of each single caste, from those of the ascetics and Brahmins to those of the rogues and harlots, in accordance with the immanent and autonomous laws of their respective occupations. War and politics were also included. You will find war integrated into the totality of life-spheres in the *Bhagavad-Gita,* in the conversation between Krishna and Arduna. "Do what must be done," i.e. do that which, according to the Dharma of the warrior caste and its rules, is obligatory and which, according to the purpose of the war, is objectively necessary. Hinduism believes that such conduct does not damage religious salvation, but, rather, promotes it. When he faced the hero's death, the Indian warrior was always sure of Indra's heaven, just as was the Teuton warrior of Valhalla. The Indian hero would have despised Nirvana just as much as the Teuton would have sneered at the Christian paradise with its angels' choirs. This specialization of ethics allowed for the Indian ethic's quite unbroken treatment of politics by following politics' own laws and even radically enhancing this royal art.

A really radical "Machiavellianism," in the popular sense of this word, is classically represented in Indian literature, in the *Kautaliya Arthasastra* (long before Christ, allegedly dating from Chandragupta's time). In contrast with this document Machiavelli's *Principe* is harmless. As is known in Catholic ethics—to which otherwise Professor Förster stands close—the *consilia evangelica* are a special ethic for those endowed with the charisma of a holy life. There stands the monk who must not shed blood or strive for gain, and beside him stand the pious knight and the burgher, who are allowed to do so, the one to shed blood, the other to pursue gain. The gradation of ethics and its organic integration into the doctrine of salvation is less consistent than in India. According to the presuppositions of Christian faith, this could and had to be the case. The wickedness of the world stemming from original sin allowed with relative ease the integration of violence into ethics as a disciplinary means against sin and against the heretics who endangered the soul. However, the demands of the Sermon on the Mount, an acosmic ethic of ultimate ends, implied a natural law of absolute imperatives based upon religion. These absolute imperatives retained their revolutionizing force and they came upon the scene with elemental vigor during almost all periods of social upheaval. They produced especially the radical pacifist sects, one of which in Pennsylvania experimented in establishing a polity that renounced violence towards the outside. This experiment took a tragic course, inasmuch as with the outbreak of the War of Independence the Quakers could not stand up arms-in-hand for their ideals, which were those of the war.

Normally, Protestantism, however, absolutely legitimated the state as a divine institution and hence violence as a means. Protestantism, especially, legitimated the authoritarian state. Luther relieved the individual of the ethical responsibility for war and transferred it to the authorities. To obey the authorities in matters other than those of faith could never constitute guilt. Calvinism in turn knew principled violence as a means of defending the faith; thus Calvinism knew the crusade, which was for Islam an element of life from the beginning. One sees that it is by no means a modern disbelief born from the hero worship of the Renaissance which poses the problem of political ethics. All religions have wrestled with it, with highly differing success, and after what has been said it could not be otherwise. It is the specific means of legitimate violence as such in the hand of human associations which determines the peculiarity of all ethical problems of politics.

Whosoever contracts with violent means for whatever ends—and every politician does—is exposed to its specific consequences. This holds especially for the crusader, religious and revolutionary alike. Let us confidently take the present as an example. He who wants to establish absolute justice on earth by force requires a following, a human "machine." He must hold out the necessary internal and external premiums, heavenly or worldly reward, to this "machine" or else the machine will not function. Under the conditions of the modern class struggle, the internal premiums consist of the satisfying of hatred and the craving for revenge; above all, resentment and the need for pseudo-ethical self-righteousness: the opponents must be slandered and accused of heresy. The external rewards are adventure, victory, booty, power, and spoils. The leader and his success are completely dependent upon the functioning of his machine and hence not on his own motives. Therefore he also depends upon whether or not the premiums can be *permanently* granted to the following, that is, to the Red Guard, the informers, the agitators, whom he needs. What he actually attains under the conditions of his work is therefore not in his hand, but is prescribed to him by the following motives, which, if viewed ethically, are predominantly base. The following can be harnessed only so long as an honest belief in his person and his cause inspires at least part of the following, probably never on earth even the majority. This belief, even when subjectively sincere, is in a very great number of cases really no more than an ethical "legitimation" of cravings for revenge, power, booty, and spoils. We shall not be deceived about this by verbiage; the materialist interpretation of history is no cab to be taken at will; it does not stop short of the promoters of revolutions. Emotional revolutionism is followed by the traditionalist routine of everyday life; the crusading leader and the faith itself fade away, or, what is even more effective, the faith becomes part of the conventional phraseology of political Philistines and banausic technicians. This development is especially rapid with struggles of faith because they are usually led or inspired by genuine leaders, that is, prophets of revolution. For here, as with every leader's machine, one of the conditions for success is the depersonalization and routinization, in short, the psychic proletarianization, in the interests of discipline. After coming to power the following of a crusader usually degenerates very easily into a quite common stratum of spoilsmen.

Whoever wants to engage in politics at all, and especially politics as a vocation, has to realize these ethical paradoxes. He must know that he is responsible for what may become of himself under the impact of these paradoxes. I repeat, he lets himself in for the diabolic forces lurking in all violence. The great *virtuosi* of acosmic love of humanity and goodness, whether stemming from Nazareth or Assisi or from Indian royal castles, have not operated with the political means of violence. Their kingdom was "not of this world" and yet they worked and still work in this world. The figures of Platon Karatajev and the saints of Dostoievski still remain their most adequate reconstructions. He who seeks the salvation of the soul, of his own and of others, should not seek it along the avenue of politics, for the quite different tasks of politics can only be solved by violence. The genius or demon of politics lives in an inner tension with the god of love, as well as with the Christian God as expressed by the church. This tension can at any time lead to an irreconcilable conflict. Men knew this even in the times of church rule. Time and again the papal interdict was placed upon Florence and at the time it meant a far more robust power for men and their salvation of soul than (to speak with Fichte) the "cool approbation" of the Kantian ethical judgment. The burghers, however, fought the church-state. And it is with reference to such situations that Machiavelli in a beautiful passage, if I am not mistaken, of the *History of Florence,* has one of his heroes praise those citizens who deemed the greatness of their native city higher than the salvation of their souls.

If one says "the future of socialism" or "international peace," instead of native city or "fatherland" (which at present may be a dubious value to some), then you face the problem as it stands now. Everything that is striven for through political action operating with violent means and following an ethic of responsibility endangers the "salvation of the soul." If, however, one chases after the ultimate good in a war of beliefs, following a pure ethic of absolute ends, then the goals may be damaged and discredited for generations, because responsibility for *consequences* is lacking, and two diabolic forces which enter the play remain unknown to the actor. These are inexorable and produce consequences for his action and even for his inner self, to which he must helplessly submit, unless he perceives them. The sentence: "The devil is old; grow old to understand him!" does not refer to age in terms of chronological years. I have never permitted myself to lose out in a discussion through a reference to a date registered on a birth certificate; but the mere fact that someone is twenty years of age and that I am over fifty is no cause for me to think that this alone is an achievement before which I am overawed. Age is not decisive; what is decisive is the trained relentlessness in viewing the realities of life, and the ability to face such realities and to measure up to them inwardly.

Surely, politics is made with the head, but it is certainly not made with the head alone. In this the proponents of an ethic of ultimate ends are right. One cannot prescribe to anyone whether he should follow an ethic of absolute ends or an ethic of responsibility, or when the one and when the other. One can say only this much: If in these times, which, in your opinion, are not times of "sterile" excitation—excitation is not, after all, genuine passion—if now suddenly the *Weltanschauungs*-politicians crop up *en masse* and pass the watchword, "The world is stupid and base, not I," "The responsibility for the consequences does not fall upon me but upon the others whom I serve and whose stupidity or baseness I shall eradicate," then I declare frankly that I would first inquire into the degree of inner poise backing this ethic of ultimate ends. I am under the impression that in nine out of ten cases I deal with windbags who do not fully realize what they take upon themselves but who intoxicate themselves with romantic sensations. From a human point of view this is not very interesting to me, nor does it move me profoundly. However, it is immensely moving when a *mature* man—no matter whether old or young in years—is aware of a responsibility for the consequences of his conduct and really feels such responsibility with heart and soul. He then acts by following an ethic of responsibility and somewhere he reaches the point where he says: "Here I stand; I can do no other." That is something genuinely human and moving. And every one of us who is not spiritually dead must realize the possibility of finding himself at some time in that position. In so far as this is true, an ethic of ultimate ends and an ethic of responsibility are not absolute contrasts but rather supplements, which only in unison constitute a genuine man—a man who *can* have the "calling for politics."

Now then, ladies and gentlemen, let us debate this matter once more ten years from now. Unfortunately, for a whole series of reasons, I fear that by then the period of reaction will have long since broken over us. It is very probable that little of what many of you, and (I candidly confess) I too, have wished and hoped for will be fulfilled; little—perhaps not exactly nothing, but what to us at least seems little. This will not crush me, but surely it is an inner burden to realize it. Then, I wish I could see what has become of those of you who now feel yourselves to be genuinely "principled" politicians and who share in the intoxication signified by this revolution. It would be nice if matters turned out in such a way that Shakespeare's Sonnet 102 should hold true:

> Our love was new, and then but in the spring,
> When I was wont to greet it with my lays;
> As Philomel in summer's front doth sing,
> And stops her pipe in growth of riper days.

But such is not the case. Not summer's bloom lies ahead of us, but rather a polar night of icy darkness and hardness, no matter which group may triumph externally now. Where there is nothing, not only the Kaiser but also the proletarian has lost his rights. When this night shall have slowly receded, who of those for whom spring apparently has bloomed so luxuriously will be alive? And what will have become of all of you by then? Will you be bitter or banausic? Will you simply and dully accept world and occupation? Or will the third and by no means the least frequent possibility be your lot: mystic flight from reality for those who are gifted for it, or—as is both frequent and unpleasant—for those who belabor themselves to follow this fashion? In every one of such cases, I shall draw the conclusion that they have not measured up to their own doings. They have not measured up to the world as it really is in its everyday routine. Objectively and actually, they have not experienced the vocation for politics in its deepest meaning, which they thought they had. They would have done better in simply cultivating plain brotherliness in personal relations. And for the rest—they should have gone soberly about their daily work.

Politics is a strong and slow boring of hard boards. It takes both passion and perspective. Certainly all historical experience confirms the truth—that man would not have attained the possible unless time and again he had reached for the impossible. But to do that a man must be a leader, and not only a leader but a hero as well, in a very sober sense of the word. And even those who are neither leaders nor heroes must arm themselves with that steadfastness of heart which can brave even the crumbling of all hopes. This is necessary right now, or else men will not be able to attain even that which is possible today. Only he has the calling for politics who is sure that he shall not crumble when the world from his point of view is too stupid or too base for what he wants to offer. Only he who in the face of all this can say "In spite of all!" has the calling for politics.